SOUND, ORDER AND SURVIVAL IN PRISON

The Rhythms and Routines of HMP Midtown

Kate Herrity

BRISTOL
UNIVERSITY
PRESS

First published in Great Britain in 2025 by

Bristol University Press
University of Bristol
1–9 Old Park Hill
Bristol
BS2 8BB
UK
t: +44 (0)117 374 6645
e: bup-info@bristol.ac.uk

Details of international sales and distribution partners are available at bristoluniversitypress.co.uk

© Bristol University Press 2025

British Library Cataloguing in Publication Data
A catalogue record for this book is available from the British Library

ISBN 978-1-5292-2945-5 hardcover
ISBN 978-1-5292-2948-6 paperback
ISBN 978-1-5292-2949-3 ePub
ISBN 978-1-5292-2950-9 ePdf

The right of Kate Herrity to be identified as author of this work has been asserted by her in accordance with the Copyright, Designs and Patents Act 1988.

All rights reserved: no part of this publication may be reproduced, stored in a retrieval system, or transmitted in any form or by any means, electronic, mechanical, photocopying, recording, or otherwise without the prior permission of Bristol University Press.

Every reasonable effort has been made to obtain permission to reproduce copyrighted material. If, however, anyone knows of an oversight, please contact the publisher.

The statements and opinions contained within this publication are solely those of the author and not of the University of Bristol or Bristol University Press. The University of Bristol and Bristol University Press disclaim responsibility for any injury to persons or property resulting from any material published in this publication.

Bristol University Press works to counter discrimination on grounds of gender, race, disability, age and sexuality.

Cover design: Hannah Gaskamp
Front cover image: Getty/Flavio Coelho

Bristol University Press' authorised representative in the European Union
is: Easy Access System Europe, Mustamäe tee 50, 10621 Tallinn, Estonia,
Email: gpsr.requests@easproject.com

An ethnography of prison, the book includes expletives
and reference to violence,
self-harm, death, distress and mental illness.

For the men and women of HMP Midtown, and, as always, for Jason.

In memory of Richard Smith. May you be united with as many of Bowie's guitars as you can handle, and the man himself.

Contents

Acknowledgements — viii

1. Just Landed — 1
2. What Are You Hearing Right Now? — 9
3. Warp and Weft — 18
4. "He's Never Even Had a Magnum!" — 26
5. Weft and Warp — 32
6. A Night Inside — 39
7. Talk to Me — 46
8. Kackerlackas — 52
9. A Kettle, a Penguin and a Word Arrow — 59
10. Emotional Contagion — 66
11. Arrhythmia — 74
12. Polyrhythmia — 81
13. Jingle Jangle — 89
14. Disentangling Power and Order — 97
15. Learning the 'Everyday Tune' — 105
16. Listening to Power — 113
17. Singing Frogs, Looping the Slam — 121
18. 'The Auld Triangle' — 129
19. The Hustle and Bustle — 136
20. Phasing — 145
21. Polyrhythmia Revisited — 153
22. Bells, Whistles, Ships and Prisons — 160
23. Shipping Out — 168

Notes — 176
References — 182
Index — 192

Acknowledgements

Many thanks to the men and women of HMP Midtown for your kindness and generosity. My heartfelt appreciation for all those who spent time with me, whether stopping to chat or giving me an interview. My life is richer for having known you. To all those men who passed by the 'sound lady' under the stairs may you go well, wherever you go. I think of you often.

My deep gratitude to King's College Cambridge and the Mellon Foundation for awarding me a Junior Research Fellowship, which has given me the time and space to get this thing written. Finally. It has been a slow and painful process and one requiring the facing of many demons. Endless love and appreciation for Jason Warr, whose support and encouragement regardless of how much I bore him is a phenomenal demonstration of patience. Thanks to Michelle McFarlane and Katherine Engler for faith and the gifs. Many thanks to my wonderful colleagues at Kings for providing me with support and encouragement, endlessly fuelling my curiosity and being such a nourishing community. A shout out to Nick Marston for impromptu trips to the Eagle, enormous help with music theory and crushing sardonic wit. I realize you would hate being shouted out to. Thanks to the University of Leicester for awarding me a studentship, which enabled me to focus on my PhD in ways which would otherwise have been impossible. Thanks to SB and AF for your support, curiosity and warmth. Thank you so very much HF, PN and RL. I did not want to oblige you to acknowledge association with this book, nor did I want to make it any clearer where Midtown is, but I will be forever grateful for your trust and accommodation. You, of course, know who you are. The project, never mind this book, would not have been possible without you. It takes courage to open your doors to the likes of me, and enormous trust to allow me to remain. I hope I have done you proud.

Thank you to my friends, colleagues and co-conspirators at the Prisons Research Centre, Institute of Criminology, Cambridge. Much gratitude to my examiners Richard Sparks and Kate Gooch. Thanks to Richard also for the ongoing interest and support. Thanks to my various supervisors, Yvonne Jewkes for supporting my studentship, Jennifer Fleetwood for endless enthusiasm, ideas and soundness, Jo Phoenix for the rigour and kind read-through before I submitted and thank you Sam King for seeing me to the end. I also owe Bristol University Press much gratitude for my endless delays and promises of delivery. It really did exist though! Thank you Rebecca, Becky and Grace for ridiculous patience (sorry), and to my reviewers for your attention and kindness. My endless gratitude to the reviewer of my typescript for your engagement and generosity.

1

Just Landed

I enter the prison through a series of concentric circles. The outer ring is largely traversed by staff and sanctioned vehicles. Mumbled conversation is carried on the wind, though it is quiet here. With the exception of the solitary gardening orderly who issues pleasant greetings to all who pass, prisoners are barely glimpsed in this outer layer, other than briefly on the way in or out through reception, or when being escorted to and from legal visits. Calm, voices across concrete, separated from life outside but metres away from the busy traffic and bustle of city life just beyond the wall.

I perch outside, breaching the convention of always 'coming/going through' and listen to the thrum of living from the ghostly figures at windows. A lively symphony of radios, tellies, voices. I hear the bang of doors below. The thump of pulsing dance escapes from the gym, its vibrations nudging my sternum. Footsteps and keys on metal stairs hugging the buildings' walls. Bass, conversation, shifting light as people move within. The sound of Whitney Houston's 'I Wanna Dance with Somebody' makes me smile. I am curious about the source of these sounds, the listeners to this music, and wonder whether I will come to know them. Chats, trading, bartering, bantering.

Through the second circle, footfall is dampened on carpet tiles. I hear the more familiar thrum of office life; jovial voices, ringing phones, tapping keyboards. Workers' movement is accompanied by the less commonplace percussion of jangling keys. Beneath me I can hear, and feel, comings and goings through clunking doors. Metal on metal below my feet as staff move through the main body of the prison. Offices are separated by plasterboard partitions which do not reach floor or ceiling, bleeding sounds of laughter, sneezes, radio. At HMP Midtown it appears privacy is scarce for all. Keys, jangle of chain, thunk as lock bites, clunk of lock, creak of gate. Lock and unlock has a rhythm. Entry is invisible from my vantage point upstairs. I begin to discern a difference in footsteps. Staff are more measured, heavier boots and stride. Admin workers have a faster pace, IMB[1] (members of the Independent Monitoring Board, walking through for monthly meeting) skipping, purposeful step. Rhythm of walk affects the jangle. Entering bit by bit, disorientating doors that lead to unexpected places, or sometimes nowhere at all.

I walk to Education and Skills, male voices drift over the concrete from the windows as I go, whistling for attention, rushed bartering, promises of burn.[2] I lurk guiltily, listening to industrious chatter. I walk back and forth unsure of my purpose or destination. I travel upstairs to seek out peace and respite from the imagined imposition of purpose on my movement, to think, in the chapel. I let myself in; I am, at least, becoming less clumsy with my unwieldy bunch of keys. I cannot see through the mix of frosted and stained glass of the grubby windows. Sounds merge, their direction unclear; planes, building works, sirens, reminders of life outside but curiously dislocated. I hear loud music, clunking of gates. More gates opening and closing all around; I'm not yet sufficiently attuned to recognize which ones or what this movement indicates about the point of the day nor the specific activity. At some point I will learn to recognize the specific gates as well as the likely reason for their opening. I will come to gauge a sense of the day from the tone of voice of various members of the community I have come to know, and in some cases greatly look forward to seeing. From the bowels of the prison I hear laughter, violins? Strains of 'Will You Still Love Me Tomorrow' echo across the way, evoking a pang of recognition of shared humanity and curiosity about whose day this is providing the soundtrack for. Everyday rhythms of bustling life from behind those doors contrast with the serene solitude of the chapel. Just the sound of my pen on paper to keep me company as the clock ticks, intrusively.

Why sound?

This is the first empirical study of sound in prison, an aural ethnography of the community of HMP Midtown,[3] which formed a PhD thesis, completed in 2019. Years before returning to education, I signed up for a rare opportunity to visit HMP Wandsworth as part of a library-training initiative. I felt the disorientating effect of lingering at the central control point, in the eye of the swirling soundscape (BSI, 2014);[4] the well-known 'central star'. Disembodied shouts, screams, laughter joined with bangs, clangs and jangles to dizzying and unnerving effect. I could hear far beyond my line of vision. The alien soundscape evoked a response that exceeded my attempts to understand it. I was frustrated at how little I could find in the literature. Prisoner accounts frequently mentioned the particularities of its sounds; why was there such infrequent mention of it elsewhere? While the quest for a satisfactory answer to this was to prove ongoing (Herrity et al, 2021),[5] the more immediate question continued to rattle my curiosity; was this significant to prison social life, and if so in what ways? The little precedent in literature was matched by a similar absence of previous uses of methodology foregrounding sound in prisons research. I had no roadmap to follow when entering the field, though I used my masters to develop and pilot a means of exploring the prison soundscape (Herrity, 2015). I spent a very limited time at two prisons while conducting research for that project; a category C prison with a capacity of around 2,100 – a relatively recent build – and a young offenders institution holding around 400, opened in the mid-19th century. A doctoral project was a challenge on a different scale.

I took my time learning the prison's geographies and the rules and rituals which shaped the days of those living and working there. It is both the 'doing' of the research, and what the Midtown community taught me about and through the soundscape that form the content of this book. I hope that it will provide an explanation of how this methodology was developed as well as how that worked in practice. This is also a journey into the world of HMP Midtown, the men and women who formed its community and the soundscape which both shaped and conveyed the meaning of its rhythms and routines.

The overarching claim is that we shape the understandings we can reach when we design our frame of exploration differently. Foregrounding sound, and the sensory more broadly, changes the way we understand the social worlds that form the focus of social science. The argument that attending more closely to the sensory brings us nearer to our actual processes of empirical understanding is elaborated elsewhere (for example, Serres, 2008). I return to these ideas in the context of their role informing the methodological frame of this project, but it is the community of HMP Midtown and the process of working with them to understand their social world more deeply that I am concerned with here. When writing the proposal, I intended that the findings, and reflections on theory and methodology, would form alternate chapters. In practice, I found it difficult to separate out these strands of what is an intrinsically iterative process. It proved disruptive to forging a coherent narrative and I grew frustrated with it, abandoning the idea. I use creative writing from fieldnotes as a means of echoing the soundscape and bridging distance between there and here. I have deliberately made Midtown and its community the focus of the book. I did not want to drown their voices with endless theoretical discussion. My thesis contains a deeper exploration of literature and I have included a link in the endnotes.[6] I did not wish to reproduce it and have rewritten much of it as a means of foregrounding the accounts and reflections of those who taught me about their relationship with the soundscape.

Stethoscope-ing (auscultation)

Auscultation is the practice of listening as a part of medical diagnosis, usually of organs such as the heart or lungs and with a stethoscope. The idea that the social body can be likened to an organism is deeply entrenched within social science (for example, Durkheim, 1893; Spencer, 1895). It follows that auditory knowledge is both a means and method of understanding social life (Cohen, 2010; Rice, 2010, 2013). Despite periodic attempts to enliven a sociology of the senses, this has remained a rather niche interest, failing to dislodge the predominance of what we can see in our interpretations of our social world (Simmel, 1907; Vannini et al, 2013). With few exceptions (for example, Chee, 2002), sound is rarely the focal point for ethnography, and has never before been the focus of enquiry for prisons ethnography. Connections between sound, the brain and behaviour are well documented in other disciplines; for example, psychology of music and biological sciences (Sloboda, 2005; Lenc et al, 2021), but we have been slow to follow.

Listening allowed me to discern the rhythms of social activity, order and its disruptions that were central to Midtown life. Particularities of the soundscape were unique to Midtown, though these also reflected the specificity of the auditory environment of prisons (shaped by hard surfaces and big, crowded spaces). Broader experience of those I spoke with consistently provided a frame of reference and useful comparison as a means of accounting for the significance of what we were hearing. The principles of attending to the auditory as a means of understanding social life is in no way limited to prison, but rather reflects the broader contention that 'rhythms shape human experience in timespace and pervade everyday life and space' (Edensor, 2010: 1). Spending time, passing time, doing time, were all fundamental to how spaces in Midtown were experienced. Understanding this was a central component of developing relationships with both community and place. As fieldwork progressed the extent of the relationship between sound and time (Toop, 2010), as well as space, became clearer. Foregrounding this aspect of social experience brought different aspects of life to the fore, which might otherwise have been relegated to the periphery. This also altered the tone of communication and enquiry.

As I sought to understand the rhythms and routines that characterized life at Midtown, many took to calling me the 'sound lady', a habit that has persisted beyond the prison walls. There was a broad refusal to use my name, either to guard against perceptions of over-familiarity, social convention or because it did not matter. A preferable alternative to 'Miss', I was happy to accept this compromise though I was slow to grasp its broader significance. Listening, a sociological as well as social art (Back, 2007), carries particular potency in a place where people so frequently feel unheard. Not only are 'listeners' specifically designated and important in a place where distress and desperation feature, but sound was a benign if leftfield subject which allowed conversations to roam across and between disparate groups and topics. Making sense of the soundscape was a collaborative endeavour in which knowledge was democratically shared and hierarchies upended. While I was not of Midtown's community, our mutual subjection to sensory intrusions lent a correspondingly common frame of reference which diminished distance. While I could leave when I chose, I was there to try to decipher a soundscape we all inhabited. At times, my own sense of time and space were similarly distorted by exposure to Midtown's swirling cacophony.

Welcome to "chaos"

HMP Midtown is a small, regency-era prison in the city centre of the community from which it draws just under two thirds of its population. An unusually small prison with a population hovering around 300[7] (one hundred more than the prison was designed to hold), Midtown is characterized by the domination of one, main wing in which most of the community live and work. Serving the courts of the town city and county, it contained a substance use treatment unit and also had a resettlement function for those approaching the end of their sentence. As with other local prisons, Midtown was subject to high rates of 'churn'[8] with an average stay of 46 days[9] (No. 1[10]). Its population comprised a complex range of needs and sentence conditions, subject to the increasingly unpredictable vagaries of recall, resettlement and uncertain sentence length (PRT, 2018).[11] Many prisoners were on a merry-go-ground of release and return with the matrices of vulnerabilities this entailed and compounded (for example, substance use, disrupted family life, unemployment, homelessness, petty crime) (MoJ, 2018). A number left and returned repeatedly during my stay, rubbing shoulders with bewildered first-timers. While ostensibly 'local', these prisoners served portions of their sentence alongside others who had been recalled, were lifers passing through or who were serving indefinite sentences of IPP[12] or HMP,[13] but who were on appeal, parole or pre-hearing hold.

The layout and population of Midtown proved ideal for the project. Sharing the same space with most of the prison meant we had the same point of reference, while the diversity of the Midtown community provided a rich pool of insight. The small size of the prison enabled me to develop good relationships. It proved easier to demonstrate my observance of security protocol in an environment where I was interacting with the same, smaller group of uniformed and managerial staff. Spending most of my time on the wing allowed me to introduce the project in a more considered and ethical way. People could listen to my conversations with others – though they were remarkably thoughtful about withdrawing when someone wished to discuss something sensitive – and I was accessible to answer questions as well as for the various other purposes to which I was increasingly put.

Midtown was unusual in size, and degree of a sense of community. Both staff and prisoners likened the prison to a "council estate" in the sense that many of its residents had grown up in the same area (Tommy, Officer Rose, Lugs). As Ket, an officer, described the prison:

'It's a community in there. Most definitely ... it's not totally separate from the outside it's just a different ... obviously it's more restricted in there than what you can do outside. But that community in there, them prisoners, yeah, they've got to do what they've got to do to live, and to earn, to hustle, to get by. Yeah, that's what it is. You talking about prisoners or you talking about staff? ... Well no, I s'pose from the hustling side of it ... yeah it's all the same, yeah, you know you stick together, you've got each other's back. You know, you try and help and support one another yeah, it's the same ... And to be quite honest I've never looked on it like that, I've always kind of separated the two.'

The size of the prison also created a particularly intense, or 'challenging' environment (HMP Midtown visitors' pamphlet). One officer's description described Midtown in contrast to other prisons:

'This place is more intense ... than most ... It's more concentrated, imagine it's like a squash ... This is undiluted, yeah tension on the wing. You go to some wings in some prisons, and you can make a pint out of a little bit, like that, and it's relaxed, it's okay, I can deal with a 14-hour shift on there, it's fine, it's not a problem. You do a morning on there, or a couple of hours in the morning, and your head's just battered just because of the noise, constant buzz, constant dum de dum de dum de dum. You know? Constant, constant, like trains going past you all the time. It's that intensity. Full on. Unless you're ready for that, you know, you're going to find it really difficult.' (Derek, Officer)

When asked to describe the soundscape, staff frequently responded by talking about the effects – "we take it with us, definitely", their coping strategies – "you learn to numb it out" or their inability to share it with those in their personal lives – "you couldn't describe it to your best mate" (No. 2).[14] Prisoners often responded with descriptions of the prison soundscape: "a jungle", "chaos", "a madhouse", "a maelstrom", "a cattle market", "controlled mayhem" (fieldnotes). Quotes are taken from interviews and fieldnotes. When not attributed to particular people the text is taken from scribbled snippets of conversations I had with people, or reflections from the time. Staff members are indicated with reference to their role, while prisoners are indicated by their absence of one.

Orientation

As I wrote them, it became increasingly clear the pages resisted the artificial imposition of a binary organization. Life at HMP Midtown was richer, more diffuse and considerably more dizzying and, I am afraid, my thinking and storytelling are far too chaotic to submit to such clarity. Instead, I have presented the story of Midtown and my time there a little more faithfully to the experience of attuning to its rhythms. I hope to take you with me. The book is loosely divided into three sections: time and space, order and power. Titles and subheadings are vague. Not to confuse or obfuscate but because this is a faithful representation of how it felt to listen as sounds and spaces slowly offered up their secrets. In 'Just Landed' I introduce Midtown, asking 'Why sound?' I reflect on method and methodology more closely in 'What Are You Hearing Right Now?' 'Warp and Weft' explores how sound lends additional nuance and dimension to temporal and spatial dimensions of prison experience, while '"He's Never Even Had a Magnum!"' considers the warping and slowing of time specifically, using music theory to make sense of prisoners' accounts of doing time. 'Weft and Warp' shifts the emphasis to prison spaces, while 'A Night Inside' considers how perceptions of space are rendered strange and unfamiliar at different points of the day, specifically as night encroaches and the prison moves into patrol state (the particular set of routines and operations which take place at night). In 'Talk to Me' I consider the nuance and difficulty of operating ethically in a place where the human impulse to nurture and heal can pose its own series of threats and problems. 'Kackerlackas', the Swedish word for cockroach, considers the various ways in which prison spaces contaminate, as well as some of the efforts to resist its stigma. 'A Kettle, a Penguin and a Word Arrow' (a 'word arrow' is a paper-based word game, similar to a basic crossword) considers some of the challenges of balancing human relationships in a space which broadly interprets these through the cynical prism of security.

In 'Emotional Contagion' I borrow from psychological theory to explore how shifting power relations are partially audible, and how the 'mood' or emotional climate can be manipulated through the soundscape. In 'Arrhythmia' I borrow from Lefebvre to consider breakdowns in order, and I borrow from Lefebvre again in 'Polyrhythmia' to consider what a good day sounds and feels like, and what this tells us about how power imposes a particular sense of time and space in prison. The symbolic potency of the prison reverberates through the soundscape and the 'Jingle Jangle' of keys, a symbolic violence upon the imprisoned body as well as of those who linger in these spaces (Bourdieu, 1992). Foregrounding sound enables a more definitive disentanglement of power and order, which eased the process of 'Learning the "Everyday Tune"'. 'Listening to Power' reflects on how the soundscape revealed various operations of power and its contestations, while 'Singing Frogs, Looping the Slam' explores the role of sound in reinforcing the power (and order) of the institution. '"The Auld Triangle"' (an Irish song) draws on wider cultural representations of the prison to consider the potency of its soundscape, and how much of the Midtown community subverted this as an expression of belonging and identity interwoven with the maintenance of order in the rhythms of daily life. 'Hustle and Bustle' examines the particularities of these rhythms and their centrality to order. In 'Phasing', I again borrow from music theory to explore the process of moving back into a predictable, orderly state. This process is often, I argue, a co-produced effort between many members of the community which indicates that an orderly state is a matter of co-governance rather than imposed by the institution and its agents, themselves members of a community. I revisit polyrhythmia, to tie these strands of time, space, power and order together before considering the broader social meaning of sound and space in the context of prison in 'Bells, Whistles, Ships and Prisons'. I conclude, in 'Shipping Out', by considering the various possibilities and problems raised by listening to countless goodbyes, including my own.

This is a book about sound in prison which is about neither prison nor sound. Aural experience formed a theoretical lens and focus of inquiry that enabled me to develop different orientations to relationships between people[15] and place, as well as to begin to understand these facets of experience in a different light. In many ways though, this is as much a story about a community of people and the time I spent with them, and an exploration of the motivations for working cooperatively (or not) in a stark environment which seemingly offers little incentive for doing so. The relationships I observed, as well as those I formed, with those at Midtown demonstrated that social order is rooted in the daily, micro interactions that characterize it rather than being motivated by an abstract perception of structural legitimacy. Legitimacy is a concept which has assumed widespread acceptance within, while drifting some distance from, its initial applications to prison studies. Listening to the social world of Midtown led to a consideration of its usefulness for understanding how rhythms and routines were broadly maintained here, despite the disparate circumstances which brought this community together. Legitimacy does not, I argue, provide an explanation for why so many actively work to keep the prison ticking over, nor the array of ways in which they encouraged others to do the same.

2

What Are You Hearing Right Now?

Stretch: Never mind research and about being in and out of prisons. Tell me what's happening in this prison right now.
Me: I can't.
Stretch: I'll tell you now, they're feeding dinner. They've got some of the high fours out and some of the high threes, and they're feeding the low threes.

Stretch was one of the first people I met at Midtown. He showed me around the wing and introduced me to others. He also helped me put up posters on the landings which I used to signal the purpose for my visit while inviting participants for the project. The men largely used these for roach[1] material (to roll cigarettes). During our interview, he told me he had been in and out of the place for the past 38 years. His familiarity with the prison made him an invaluable guide. Stretch taught me a great deal about interpreting the soundscape by generously sharing his knowledge. I draw on his reflections here as a frame for considering the process of acclimating to the sound environment as well as how sound featured in his daily life inside. I then draw upon Stretch's account of his uses of sound as a means of decentring vision from the research process and the implications of this for researcher positionality. I return to the use and meanings of sound in more depth, drawing on the theoretical framework underpinning my research, finishing with a consideration of how this framing shaped my understanding of Midtown.

While I was initially unable to answer him, Stretch's questions anchored my efforts to learn the soundscape and I would return to them repeatedly (Feld, 1984). I would come to understand the rather obvious point that there was a limit to the ways 'feeding time' was likely to be organized given the goal of maximum speed, efficiency and orderliness. For this portion of the day, it was qualitative distinctions in the soundscape rather than its broad markers that contained the most valuable information about the social climate of the community. What this exchange underscored was that there was a means of, as well as a purpose to, interpreting the soundscape. This sense-making process required familiarity with both the activities underway and the broader social context in which they took place. Only then could I decipher what I was hearing. Stretch's reflections taught me much about how I would come to understand what I was listening to, and its significance for those living and working in the community.

Various members of the community at HMP Midtown offered instruction and insight about their relationship with the soundscape, but my exchanges and interview with Stretch were particularly useful for outlining and exploring methodology. He was the first prisoner I interviewed but most of our discussions took place informally, on the wing and the first-night centre[2] where he sometimes worked.

Relegating the interview

I spoke to most people passing through these spaces and many asked my purpose. I quickly became known as the 'sound lady' and, initially, sought out positions where my vision was partially obscured (without compromising personal safety) but where I could easily be seen, both by staff – as much for security concerns and to limit any additional drain on resources or energy my presence represented – and prisoners. In *The Prisoner Society* Ben Crewe (2009) talks about feeling awkward on the wing during periods of undirected observation. In contrast, attending to the soundscape reversed the more usual relationship between periods of fieldwork spent in shared prison spaces and the interview, upending the relative weight assigned to these aspects of prison ethnography. My time listening, chatting and taking notes constituted the main source of understanding. As a consequence, I was far more relaxed about interviews and reconciled myself to the possibility some participants might not engage with my focus of interest but instead use the time as an opportunity to speak about subjects of their choice. Conversely, the relative absence of agenda increased their richness. Fieldnotes taken during these periods were points of reference in more formal discussion. Interviews provided a means of drilling down into the significance of a particular event I had struggled to comprehend, or an opportunity to have a rambling, sit-down chat with someone I had often come to know quite well. Given my broad research question I had no set agenda for those I spoke with beyond ensuring both staff and those living in the prison were represented. Aside from the prison governor (No. 1) and second in command (No. 2) I preferred to include those who approached me to express an interest in participating, at which point I would explain the practicalities and key ethical considerations, quickly learning that few would read through my carefully drafted information and consent sheets.

Prison's spartan spaces offer little opportunity for privacy and I had no wish to reinforce that sense of exposure. I missed out on the chance to interview a number because I relied on availability and readiness both of rooms and interviewees (prisoners were always interviewed on the wing while staff were interviewed off it – in either case spare, private space was hard to come by). Such is the relentless 'churn' of the local population many had moved on before I managed to secure the golden combination of mutual availability and an empty room. On the odd occasion this extended to staff.

The men used my presence as a means, first, of satisfying their curiosity and then to express interest in participation, while staff stopped to ask questions or reflect on the day. I had constructed an elaborate means for securing contact to ensure both prisoners and staff could communicate outside of other's hearing and preserve their anonymity. I negotiated for shared use of the Independent Monitoring Board (IMB) box, keeping it stocked with envelopes, as well as a temporary 'dug' or pigeonhole so that those addressed to me could be delivered ready for my daily check and collection. I advertised widely, distributing posters around the prison on the wing, in offices and the staff areas. I wrote a message to staff which was repeatedly included in the global bulletin and offered extended explanations about the project while in conversation with those who passed by, sometimes while I restocked the envelopes which, it turned out, would exclusively be used for IMB correspondence. One prisoner contacted me using this method, and this was largely about convenience because he was so busy availing himself of every opportunity to learn or engage in activities that he was often off the wing during time-out-of-cell. These elaborate strategies for anonymous communication were relegated to a purely symbolic gesture of ethical practice but offered profound instructive value; in a place where the printed word so often brings unwelcome news, word-of-mouth and face-to-face are the trusted mediums of communication. Some only spoke to me when no one else was near, others would refuse to speak to me at all unless they were performing orderly duties while the rest of the population were behind the door – one prisoner explained he did not wish to look at me because my smiling would make him respond in kind. Prison was not a place where smiles proliferated though laughter was plentiful. Still others avoided me altogether or remained indifferent or oblivious to my presence, talking around or of me rather than to me. While most of those passing through these spaces did speak with me, whether to engage in protracted, personal conversations or in momentary greeting, there were a minority of both prisoners and staff who gave me a wide berth.

Being seen talking to a known member of the community undoubtedly had an impact on vouching for me though of course the complexities of relationships and rivalries are difficult to gauge in a place where so much of what you see and hear is what you are shown. The instructive value of learning under Stretch's guidance, while moving through and reflecting on the shifting sounds in these prison spaces, was far easier to gauge. Learning in this way afforded me a practical course in navigating the prison soundscape through the ears of one who had dwelled in them for decades.

Acclimating and positioning

> 'I can tell you exactly what's going on every minute of the day just by sounds in this prison ... I can tell you when they're coming on the morning, I can tell you when they're doing the count just by footsteps, cell bells, people shouting, I can tell you exactly what's happening round the prison. It's crazy, it's mad. Because this is my domain. This is my manor.' (Stretch)

Stretch taught me about what he could hear, as well as his practices of listening. Through him I learned the importance of developing competence at decoding the sound environment for surviving and thriving in the prison community. Under his sometimes-exasperated tutelage, I learned how members of the community listened as a means of understanding developments around the prison, as well as what they were listening for as sources of information. Sound operated as a site of surveillance from above as well as beneath[3] – or 'sousveillance' (Fernback, 2012) – a facet of prison life which alerted the listener to flows of power through both people and place. These were valuable lessons in understanding the soundscape, but also in operating ethics in praxis, encouraging a sensitivity to where I posted myself and the implications of that for what I was able to hear.

There were parallels between my physical placing and developing awareness of my shifting positionality. I was sensitive to the desire of some to avoid both the penetrating gaze of others, and the intruding ear. At the same time, I was mindful of the need to remain in view of the staff to avoid giving them one more focus of concern. Other than specific and isolated instances when I sought permission to go to someone's doorway (so they could show me something they had made, or photographs of people they had told me about in conversation) I avoided going to cells. Frequent offers of hospitality sometimes made this achingly difficult. I wedged myself in corners, being mindful of where I stood under walkways to minimize the amount of unidentifiable detritus falling on my head, before settling on my spot. This also meant I was near doors for easy exit, and security alarms which I never needed to sound. My positioning gave me maximum chance to side-step trouble, or leave, preferably before being told to "fuck off" which the No. 1 did on the odd occasion. Decentring my vision heightened other senses, and with it the awareness of how I was making sense of my environment as well as how those within the environment were making sense of me.

Adjusting to the disparity between a rigorously designed research method and how this translated to the messy social reality of fieldwork was a daunting prospect as a new researcher. This represented both a steep learning curve and an opportunity to use that learning to hone and develop the project. I frequently found myself amending my interview schedule to better reflect being situated in the environment. My fieldnotes are shot through with observations and comments about prison spaces, followed by a rephrased question, as the significance struck me: 'I find the quiet of the chapel strangely comforting after the hectic symphonies of coming-and-going elsewhere in the prison – *What do you do when you want some time to yourself?*'

Listening for power

Methodologies which foreground sound have the potential to shift positionality, collapsing distance and departing from approaches which replicate social hierarchies. This is not to deny or minimize importance of sonic dimensions of research and social practices which reproduce inequality. In *The Sonic Colour Line,* Jennifer Lyn Stoever (2016) argues that race and racism are constituted and maintained through practices of listening. I anticipated that racism would emerge as a consistent thematic thread as the cultural politics of the soundscape unfolded. Contrary to my expectations, sound did not feature explicitly in accounts of exchanges prisoners identified as racist or charged with racist assumptions. It was difficult to discern as a feature of prison life in staff accounts at all, which may well be as much a reflection of my relationships with them as their experience. Neither observation discounts or denies the ubiquity of racism in prison[4] but rather reflects that accounts were interwoven with other facets of identity and social experience. Duke was one of few to explicitly refer to racist treatment, but this was related to reflections on his neurodivergence and aspects of his physical appearance which were not only, but also, about black male bodies, masculinities and their relation to perceptions of violence and risk (Warr, 2020).

> 'I've been known, once or twice, to say that they're racist innit, because how else am I supposed to see it when there's hundreds of people and they come to me, and obviously I can understand why you would see me out of all of them people, cos I'm six foot, I got a big afro and that, you get me? And I'm loud and a big presence you get me, but surely, if there's all these people running around in front of you, how do you go from all these people need to get back to their pads, to he needs to get back to his pad?'

Cams' assessment of his relationship with officers echoed this, in that he was a known "face" in neighbouring areas, identified as having "gang" involvement and looking at a considerable sentence. Respect was important for him, and he spoke of being treated with more reverence than those he identified as being "bullied" because he was, not to put too fine a point on it, built like a brick outhouse.[5] His perceptions of relative racism and the fear he engendered of pushback because he was more able to look after himself were wrapped up in racist tropes of black male bodies but also gang involvement, as well as distinctions between 'wing rats' and those higher up the prison hierarchy. Wing rats was a name given to the prison rank and file, often charged with high-risk errand running and given to moving across the wings between more elusive and powerful characters. Lamar, in contrast, repeatedly referred to worsening relations between himself and various staff members whom he identified as wrongly associating him with nefarious activities on the wing. These suspicions largely involved trouble-making and distributing drugs. He did not, to my knowledge, spend time in segregation pending outcomes of 'intelligence' – a mysterious means of isolating those thought to be involved in fomenting discontent or disruption of various sorts while concrete information might be found – and I heard nothing directly from staff. While I had encountered numerous instances of people being held in care and segregation on this basis at other prisons, I did not come across cases of this at Midtown. Lamar felt punished for his otherness, but primarily because he was not a local. In Lamars' experience racism and perceptions of unjust treatment were interwoven with complex iterations of localism and identity.

Urfan reflected at length on the treatment he had received. He bemoaned the lack of support and, consequently, respect, for religious observance. He and fellow Hindus were sometimes not unlocked for chapel ('chapel' is the place for all faith-based social activities regardless of belief system), and he felt Muslims received preferential treatment. They almost certainly did, if largely because they were so much greater in number, particularly when Ramadan approached. It took me some time to realize what the interesting-looking boxes were that a surprising number of men were receiving at evening meal in place of the standard at this time of year. Urfan's vegetarian diet, aligned with his faith, often left him subsisting on bread and potatoes and he felt this injustice particularly keenly given he identified as a hardworking, law-abiding man of good character and social standing. Wrongly accused and utterly confused about the circumstances in which he found himself, Urfan was at pains to distinguish himself from the broader prison population. His ability to navigate the unspoken complexities of prison life was undoubtedly compromised by adopting this position. His perception of injustice was interwoven with his ethnicity but also his Hinduism and caste. These were complex issues married with various aspects of identity as well as personal circumstance, sentence, offence history and – particularly prevalent – a sense of localism. They were not easily nor accurately reduced to generalized observation about differential treatment, not least because racism was interwoven with the deprivations of autonomy, a perpetual feature of the pains of imprisonment.

What are you listening to?

The complexities of sound, and how we translate this to social spaces, was indicated by the difficulty I had in explaining what I was doing there. Prisoners tended to make their own, creative explanations and offered help by banging doors or imitating tropical birdsong, neither of which was particularly well received by staff. As the community became more accustomed to my presence, people quickly took to asking how it 'sounded' today. This was a nod to my project, though sound often functioned as a synonym for 'feel' (numerous members of the community – including Jean, head of the local IMB and Claire a senior psychologist, both of whom I would pass the time of day with quite regularly – would often comment on how the day 'felt'; for example, "it feels calm today" (Jean, in fieldnotes). This alerted me to the complex meanings of 'quiet' which might otherwise serve as an alternative expression for 'calm' but which carried loaded, complex and contradictory meanings inside.[6] Literal quiet was frequently a harbinger of trouble. Violent incidents were usually preceded by a marked drop in sound, a subject I return to later. In its more figurative sense, 'quiet' was treated as akin to invoking 'The Scottish Play' in the theatre.[7] Doing so was an error that exposed my ignorance, both tempting fate and inviting trouble. The invocation of quiet was heaped with suspicion and premonitory power; a 'jinx'. While these observations indicated a concern with what I was listening *for*, they also indicated an enduring importance of outlining precisely what I was listening *to*.

Sound is a complex phenomenon, bound with social processes of meaning-making. This project uses a more nuanced and complex understanding of what constitutes sound than the merely physiological. The latter would include everything that can be heard, an unmanageably large, and sometimes mundane brief. Sound is intrinsically subjective, questioning what is noisy and to whom provides a colourful demonstration of this, rarely are tastes more divided and divisive than in questions of musical taste. Beyond questions of preference, however, are those relating to more political distinctions between high culture and low, and the demarcations of social standing these are bound up with. Sound is inextricably interwoven with social processes, and places, which construct its meaning. Scrutinizing who gets to define what constitutes 'noisy' and who has the power to escape it intimates a further political component to its interpretation and imposition (Keizer, 2012). Sound, then, is an intricate process of meaning-making, transmitting packages of information which allow us to make sense of our environments and direct social behaviour within them. A phenomenon unbounded by divisions governing other aspects of social life, it traverses space and time, straddling imagination and experience. This reading echoes the potency of the auditory imagination and its utility for exploring the meaning of space and social worlds. 'Auditory imagination' (Eliot, 1933; Kitchen, 1991) refers to the process of interpreting the meanings of what we hear. In literature this refers to feeling evoked by patterns of sound beneath text.

> What I call the 'auditory imagination' is the feeling for syllable and rhythm, penetrating far below the conscious levels of thought and feeling, invigorating every word; sinking to the most primitive and forgotten, returning to the origin and bringing something back, seeking the beginning and the end. It works through meanings, certainly, or not without meanings in the ordinary sense, and fuses the old and obliterated and the trite, the current, and the new and surprising, the most ancient and the most civilised mentality. (Eliot, 1933: 118–19)

In philosophy *auditory imagination* refers to auditory aspects of mental life, though I extend it to account for the ways in which people engage in mutual meaning-making (Ihde, 2007). Sound exists both out there, a measurable objective phenomenon, and internally, in the imagination and the world of memory and expectation. The British Standards Institute (BSI) describes the soundscape as: 'The perceptual construct of the physical phenomenon' (BSI, 2014). By defining the soundscape in this way, the BSI is making an explicit association with our subjective interactions with, and interpretations of, the acoustic environment and what can objectively be heard in any given space. This is particularly potent in prison, where the impact of the soundscape is enhanced by lack of control over exposure (Wener, 2012), and where its unique specificity is compounded by the totemic significance of the space. In the prison context, sound is implicated in processes of order; a means of remaking the social significance of prison spaces. Elvis – an older, local prisoner serving the latest in a string of sentences and with whom I often chatted – echoes this: "The first thing I noticed when I came to prison, sounded like a jungle." This definition of sound emphasizes the importance of a methodological approach which reflects the subjective complexities of interaction with the prison soundscape. This would require an ongoing process of listening and reflection, conferring with those better placed to interpret its meaning than I.

Elvis' reflections emphasized the power of the prison soundscape over those subject to it. The insights he offered about his experience and the specificity of the soundscape underscored the value of considering it as a distinct aspect of prison life. In this way the impact of prison spaces, mediated through sound, were shown to operate separately from the conditions which kept the daily routine ticking over, and of which order was comprised. Stretch's lessons about reading the soundscape reinforced this understanding, underscoring the time- and space-traversing qualities of auditory experience.

3

Warp and Weft

For Stretch, sound worked as a means of keeping abreast of social developments around the prison. 'Reading' the soundscape was a means of situating himself and others in the shifting social order, as well as physically locating events and individuals as developments unfolded. Sound lends texture to the spaces we live in and pass through, but also the times we spend within them. Inextricable connections between the way we experience time and space become more discernible when we shift sensory perception. David Toop's (2010) description of sound as the 'temporal sense' serves as a reminder of this complex relationship.

> What comes together through sound is emergent and passing time – a sense of duration, the field of memory, a fullness of space that lies beyond touch and out of sight, hidden from vision. Sound must be trusted, cannot be trusted, so has power. When sound that should be present seems to be absent, this is frightening. (Toop, 2010: xv)

Auditory experience traverses the boundaries of time just as it permeates walls, evoking memory, eliciting expectation and heralding markers of the daily routine. In Midtown, where movement and access to stimuli were constrained, sound could provide a particularly potent means of reconfiguring spatial experience, reminding prisoners of the world beyond the walls, and their time and place within it. Sound was a means of reconnecting with the outside world, prompting the memory of happier times. The function of sound as a powerful means of eliciting memory was not limited to other times and spaces but also existed within the present. Focusing on sound illuminated the different treatments space received from staff and prisoners, reflecting their relationships with the space within and beyond the prison to the wider community of Midtown.

The soundscape echoed and amplified the power of the constraints of the physical environment, carrying a force distinct from that shared between officers and prisoners, and between these actors and the prison. Time is 'the essence of sentencing and imprisonment' (Wright et al, 2017: 232). Understood as the 'basic structuring dimension of prison life', time lies at the heart of punishment and the deprivation of agency which it signifies (Sparks et al, 1996; Morin and Moran, 2015; Kotova, 2019). Everyday life at HMP Midtown was characterized by the imposition of temporally and spatially bounded routines which jarred and clashed with recollections and longing of other times and places. Time was not only associated with the substantive elements of punishment but with its normative components – the form its experience took, as well as the experiencing, or 'doing' of it.

Beyond the walls

Sound was implicated in processes of becoming part of the place. Subjection to iterations of time through the stop-go of the prison regime was interwoven with others associated with place and belonging. Sounds triggered memory of being among broader society, in the company of friends, family and familiar surrounds of 'home'. Strains of the outside soundscape permeated prison walls and personal memories, resonating with enforced separation from the world beyond. Audible aspects of daily rhythms in the present of prison, and the longed-for alternative beyond the prison walls were mutually constituted, enhancing the pains of imprisonment. Sound allows for a more nuanced understanding of how these alternative presents are interwoven with memories of times past – both outside and inside – and possible, hopeful and uncertain futures. The spatial constraints of the prison give rise to additional multiplicities of time remembered, experienced and imagined. Those spoken to slid between various dimensions of experience, demonstrating the need for awareness that the pains associated with temporal aspects of imprisonment were experienced in non-linear complexity. Much of the pain of being held at Midtown lay not only in a keen awareness of time passing, but also in memory of times past, consciousness of other, possible times as well as those of an imagined future.

Sound traverses space and time, reinforcing their mutual constitution: 'space is in its very nature temporal, and time spatial' (Parkes and Thrift, 1980). Sound was interwoven with the marking of time and the rhythms of the prison day, what Derek, a senior officer whose insights I return to later, referred to as "the everyday tune that's normal for here". Action and behaviour which deviated from, and harmonized with, the rhythms of the everyday tune combined to form the warp and weft of the fabric of daily life at HMP Midtown. Prisoners used sound to explain how they experienced time and place in ways which differed from more common depictions of 'doing time'.

Sound was bound up with elicitation of memory for those at Midtown, and they frequently spoke of particular relationships with memories of people, time and space. Space and time were not passively experienced but subject to complex processes of remaking in which people attempted to curate the soundscape, both real and imagined, as a means of shoring up a sense of self. Those I spoke with offered accounts of how place itself, its meanings and its impact vacillated over time, implicating sound in complex and shifting relationships between people and place. Listening to prisoners' accounts of their interactions with the soundscape, it appeared much of the pain of separation presented by a prison sentence derived from their experience of time in multiplicities of loss, hope and remembrance.

Certain songs

Sound prompted memory, carving out spaces for the men to remember other times and places. Duane explained: "One thing I am acutely aware of are 'normal' outside noises. I love to hear them as it reminds me that life goes on outside these walls." Activating the auditory imagination went some way to bridging the gap between the inside and beyond:

> '[It] makes you remember that there is normality going alongside you. D'you know what I mean? Because when you're in here you forget about normality ... in the city centre you're more conscious to things like that. And then you're like, it can bring you down, cos you're hearing stuff, or you miss home, or miss, or it can, like I say if I hear the football stadium roaring when they're playing, I'll be like yay go on Midtown ... It kind of brings me up d'you know?' (Lamar)

Both Duane and Lamar refer to the 'normality' of life outside, for which sound acted as a reminder, enhancing the temporal strangeness of their present circumstances. Listening to the Midtown soundscape extended a feeling of connectedness with the outside for Lamar. When I stayed late to hear the men listening to a home game, I was struck by how the cheers inside reverberated with those I could hear from the surrounding streets as I emerged from the prison. Lamar pointed out these reminders could be bittersweet depending on the memories evoked and the mood he was in. It could remind him of "miss[ing] home" which could bring him "down". Robert enjoyed the sound of planes, as it reminded him of times spent going "to the airport [to] sit and watch" them. He also spoke of hearing "a motorbike everyday going past" – this was significant for him because "I don't know if it's the same one, but I hear it every night and I always think it's my brother". Sound reconnected him with memories of former, happier times, and important relationships. Robert described himself as a 'loner' and was denied access to his children. His relationship with his brother was one of few spoken of positively. Boyd underscored the way in which sound elicited memories of times with loved ones:

'Yeah, if I'm listening to CDs, like there's certain songs, when I was with my partner and the kids all doing funny things, and that song comes on again, it reminds you of good times, when we were all doing silly things, like that, that's a good thing I suppose.'

While it was music that elicited this memory for Boyd, it evoked a wider auditory imagining of other times in the company of his loved ones. Boyd spoke of his family often, particularly his children. Those who talked about experiencing sound, time and space in these multimodal ways present a challenge to treatments of time in prison as a singular though variable and relative flow. Lamar, Duane, Robert and Boyd experienced time in the now, the past and the future in complex interwoven ways which were mediated by sound. Prison time did not dull awareness of traditional 'markers' and milestones enjoyed in freedom (O'Donnell, 2014). Rather they felt their absence, experiencing these precious moments of life at a forced remove. For them, wider relationship with the outside and an awareness of possible and real worlds existing alongside prison time, operating in alternative time signatures, created a *temporal vertigo*. For the men I spoke to at HMP Midtown, the sense of temporal vertigo derived not from a 'time–offence nexus' but rather the nexus of multiple and possible temporalities which imprisonment rendered the prisoner passive within. The imprisoned self, sat uneasily alongside the possible self in other times with family, in freedom, imposing an ontological arrhythmia between reality and possibility. Ian O'Donnell (2018) speaks about the difficulty of passing time, of disposing of it, in solitude. Comparisons between his correspondents and the inhabitants of Midtown indicate a social dimension to the management of time and its passing through a prison sentence; a relationship between space-time/sound and the social.

Thinking of the ways sound informed experience of time had the dual effect of amplifying the inextricable association between temporal and spatial experience, and their complexity. If time was simultaneously felt in multiple modalities so too was space (Lefebvre, 1991). Sound adds an additional dimension to carceral geography's depiction of liminal spaces within prison – areas between the inside and outside (Moran, 2013). Boyd recalled the value of spending time on visits and the connection of this to sound: "There's no good sound in prison, is there? A good prison is at night-time when it's quiet. Nah, the sound of your family on a visit, that's the best sound you're gonna hear in prison, isn't it."

"The best sound you're gonna hear"

It is more peaceful in visits for officers as they only have those viewing the cameras in their ear. Not for the first time I am told by a member of staff I should get a radio at some point, so I know what it is to have the distraction of two sets of sonic information (this is repeated by various members of staff and alluded to by prisoners though their observations refer to what it tells them. Staff tell me it is hard, and constant, but you get used to knowing what you need to listen to, you sort of 'drown it out'.

The prisoners are brought in first and directed to their pre-assigned seats. Partially depending on which section of the prison they are from with particular note taken of vulnerable prisoners who have a separately assigned series of places. They wait anxiously for their loved ones to arrive, some for much of the visiting time and I imagine the suppressed anxiety of concern in case they do not show. Have they been stood up or is there some emergency and will they get to hear about it or live in anxious wonder? It takes a while for people to clear the security process which they do party by party. Some are also presumably late, or need the loo before going in, or, particularly in the case of children, during the visit. There are no toilet facilities for the men, one of whom is narrowly prevented from removing his member to pee in a cup in front of his three female relatives and everyone present. There is some rustling and kerfuffle as he is warned he will be taken straight back, his visit over, if he tries this again. Unfortunately, he spends much time with his hand down his trousers which is not unusual in those who have been in and out of institutions, but which results in ripples of antsiness among others present as well as staff. I marvel at how quickly I have internalized some of the prison's values. What is a man to do if he wishes both to see his family and to relieve himself? When did the sight of genitals become so utterly distressing?

There are staff positioned at either end of the hall, and several times during the visit they call each other to check in/ease the boredom. At the end she informs me this visit has gone quickly, that the time often drags inexplicably. Saturdays are the worst day to come for the noise she tells me, far more children come at the weekend because of school. Others say Sunday is the worst as the volunteers who staff the makeshift café do not come on Sunday (they are from the local church and Sunday is a busy day elsewhere). The absence of food and drink, he says, drives the noise higher in the absence of distraction …

The noise builds to uncomfortable levels. Someone tells me they often get a terrible headache after visits. It sounds less specific to particular prison spaces, but then the more you listen (carefully standing back from individuals engaged in various, personal, intimate exchanges) the more striking is the difference. Here, the soundscape signals what is more usually absent from daily prison life. There are women and children as well as men here. Mothers, grandmothers, sisters, brothers, lovers, friends (and the odd visitor who, judging from familiarity with staff has not long since spent some time here themselves). While it could sound like any crowd – a queue for the cinema, an audience watching a street performer – the only ones unrestrainedly communicating are the children. Their frequent tears and tantrums, running, laughing, their occasional falling over, increasing boredom, fractiousness accompanied by demands for sweets or the need for the toilet seem incongruous in this most spartan of institutional spaces. Toddlers periodically throw toys about, distributed by another, weary-looking volunteer. Staff proudly show me the colouring-in pictures they've stockpiled to hand out to children when she fails to turn up. She is here today but no tea; the second day without and the officer is surprised at the lack of 'fuss' this has caused. I assume this is because of the importance of visits, until it occurs to me this conforms to complex rules of hospitality. Not being able to supply their mum with a cup of tea, or child with chocolate is likely to ratchet up ill feeling. Indisputable confirmation that their loved ones are also doing time.

There is all emotion here; the squelch of lingering kisses and hungrily snatched moments of intimacy, reaffirming romantic ties, soaked in sexual frustration, lust, loneliness, anxiety. The hiss of harsh words staccato under the breath, mindful of surveilling eyes and others sat mere inches away. One couple are clearly engaged in a row, the staff say they're watching – he's had a 'lot of issues lately'. The brother takes the kids away, there are tears, raised voices but some resolution and reassuring embraces before time is abruptly shouted. People are taken back to wings bit by bit. Some early, one cos he's 'going to piss himself'. The last ones are given some sensitive latitude and gently, individually reminded time is coming to an end. When the last ones have been taken back, all the property brought by family gone through, swapped and distributed by glove-wearing members of staff, the room feels like a club after closing when all the punters have gone home, and the lights go up. Though there is markedly less wreckage and of a different kind.

Shouting mostly absent here though there is little laughter, I notice. Less than might be heard on the wing. It feels, sounds(?) somehow strained, a touch artificial, as if there is an additional force to fronts of coping and forced cheeriness, punctuated by the inevitable emotional leakage of worries borne amid the missing of one another. Added to this is the occasional, fraught query from a family member approaching the raised platform on which the officer in charge sits. How do they send extra money through? Can they swap old ones in property for these new pants they have brought with them but left in the waiting room?

'Finish up your minutes please' an officer says, voice raised but not excessively so. The private intimacies conducted in view of others fight for supremacy with the desire to keep things hidden whether for decency, respect or out of anxiety. The weight of dignity, privacy, grief, lust, skin hunger, worry, anger, frustration hang heavy in the close soundscape. An absence of banging makes this part of the prison relatively quiet by comparison, but I find listening and observing here uncomfortably intrusive despite the men repeatedly assuring me they were fine with it (and my insistence on remaining too far away to hear the specific nature of their exchanges). The detritus left behind, all that remains of the painfully personal interactions conducted here only moments before; ghostly remnants of emotion soup. (Fieldnotes)

Absence

Sounds of children, stolen intimacies, laughter between loved ones, amplified the poignancy of their absence in the rest of the prison. Comparison between spaces and the sounds within them offered an additional source of understanding. There was, of course, deep intimacy between those forced to live at such close quarters and, frequently, both familial and quasi-familial relationships between prisoners as well as deep friendships. Lovers too, no doubt, though while the affairs of several members of staff were common knowledge throughout the prison, those between prisoners were kept secret, as far as I could tell, unsurprisingly given the rampant homophobia. Part of what characterizes the total institution is the round of life lived within it. It felt vaguely intrusive to be present when the men emerged, bleary-eyed for the first round of unlock, smelling traces of toothpaste and remnants of sleep on the air. The poignancy of what was absent enhanced this sensation. These were domestic scenes, private, personal, but absent the sounds of children reluctant to put their shoes on, hungry pets or jostling for the bathroom. Marrying Lamar's words on hearing the home team score from behind his door, or Boyd's yearning for his children, to these scenes in front of me lent their vitality a discomforting charge. Expressions of heartache and passion were made alongside performance of the most basic, human functions of peeing in cups to prolong the visit, passing illicit substances, getting a little amorous or breaking bread. My presence felt like complicity in this considerable assault on the dignity of those forced, by necessity, to conduct their business absent the privacy afforded by the usual divisions of space.

Spending time in the visitors' hall was uncomfortable but taught me a great deal about honing other senses. I found a position, awkward but respectably far away from the tables, by the stage the staff used for enhancing surveillance, though I kept enough distance that they could also hold conversations without me overhearing. I attempted to convey respect for the privacy of those on visits by pointedly averting my gaze. I was not *watching*, and in being sufficiently far away I could not hear the subject of their exchanges, but the broader tone of the room. The brusque formality of officially administered personal interactions contrasted with the sensitivity of some of the staff. A number were chattier here, and I pondered whether this reflected the more domestic tone of the room, the relatively rare opportunity to be still, the personalities of those more likely to perform these duties or, perhaps, a combination of these things. Spending time in visits revealed that *watching* appeared to be laden with particularly stark power relations in a way that *listening*, or at least doing so carefully and collaboratively, sometimes did not.

Listening to the soundscape revealed the nuance and multiplicity of temporal and spatial experience inside. For prisoners, time was experienced in multiple, jarring modalities. The carceral soundscape was frequently punctured by sensory intrusions from other times and places, both remembered and imagined. Other possible worlds, selves and circumstances were a continual source of longing and regret.

4

"He's Never Even Had a Magnum!"

Mooch made this comment while discussing how time appears to bend and warp while inside, only to flex unpredictably when rejoining the thrum of 'normal' life. He was illustrating the unimaginable length of a fellow prisoner's sentence, who had been inside so long the world had left him behind, oblivious to developments in the ice cream industry. Mooch had a compelling way of making the more abstract aspects of prison life tangible and often funny. A restless soul with itchy feet and fingers in many illicit pies, he found passing the time a challenge which preoccupied much energy, and ironically disposed of a lot of it. This was not his first sentence, though he swore it would be his last. He confided he had "one last big plan", the cliché seemingly escaping him. His pad mate Harry – a good friend and co-d (co-defendant) who was unfailingly amiable and good-natured – and he would bet on the horses through the night,[1] play cards or monopoly and affect blindness and deafness when one or other needed time to alleviate their respective frustrations. I was not convinced Harry had the better end of this arrangement, but their loyalty and companionship undoubtedly made the time go faster, and a little easier, for them both.

Occupying time was a constant preoccupation though methods and success were variable. Part of the challenge lay in the distorting effects of *doing* time. Temporality was experienced relationally. Time inside passed in dissonance with that on the outside, and between those who were moving and standing still, between those serving short terms and those whose sentence end was unclear, uncertain and thus rendered cruelly interminable. Listening to these dissonant, competing rhythms made the layered textures of time and its relation to the shifting sense of prison spaces audible.

"Pretending to press the brakes"

Prisoners reported experiencing time as strangely distorted and uneven, contrasting both within prison spaces and between inside and the outside. On the one hand, people reported feeling time passing speedily: "It does, the week flies by. If I was in another jail ppfftt" (Mooch). "It goes fast behind that door though Kate, very fast" (Lugs). At the same time, there was a sensation of time warping within the rhythms of the prison relative to the rapidity of the world whistling by outside:

> 'Cos when you're in jail, everything's slow. You get out there, and even when my sister picked me up from Bickley, and I jumped in the car, I was scared coming home. Everything's too fast ... I'm like that – putting my feet in the footwell like that, pretending to press the brakes and there's not even brakes there. Mad.' (Mooch)

Moochs' reference to a fellow prisoner having spent so much time inside that the world had adapted sufficiently to accommodate the arrival of Magnum ice creams,[2] voiced a keen awareness of the potential for the world to move on without him. Mooch was speaking of the sensation of the outside advancing at cracking speed, leaving prisoners languishing in slow motion. For Mooch, this resulted in a jarring effect when he returned to life on the out. These dissonant temporal experiences enhanced his awareness of the potential for being left behind, forgotten by time – 'cavemen in the era of speed-of-light technology' (Jewkes and Johnston, 2009). Sarah Armstrong (2018) refers to this enforced inaction as 'the cell and the corridor; imprisonment as waiting and waiting as mobile'. The prison soundscape evokes this sense of movement without progress; a dislocation from the ways in which time and space were experienced beyond the prison walls. Enforced idleness enhanced the sense of social exclusion.

Efforts to diminish a lack of power over time by increasing control over it took many forms. Many did their best to sleep as much of the time away as possible, like Will, but were often hampered by the intrusive soundscape. Others sought movement either as necessary steps to advance their sentence plan, like Lamar, or in the hopes that adjustment to new scenery would pass some time: "I want to move, it makes the time go quicker. I've been here a long time now, gets slow" (Robert). The desire to move, alongside complaints of boredom and frustration at the lack of things to do emphasized the way time and the doing of it lay at the heart of the pains of imprisonment (for example, Tommy, numerous fieldnotes). Temporal vertigo is useful for illustrating this aspect of experience: 'an overwhelming feeling of dizziness resulting from the sense that time was warping and falling away' (Wright et al, 2017: 232). Serena Wright et al (2017) were looking at the processes of coping and adaptation of long-term prisoners, specifically those convicted of murder. This term relates to their identification of an offence–sentence nexus specific to pains of this group. This concept also usefully describes how prisoners at HMP Midtown experienced time passing. Where they differed was in reporting a greater degree of dislocation in its unpredictability. The bustling hubbub of good days ticking over was contrasted against the stillness of a day behind the door. Depending on degree of immersion in the rhythm of activities, these could be experienced in conjunction with, or contrasting against, the beat of the regime. Adjusting to doing time to the extent that one went with it, while a powerful tool in the armoury of survival, was not always possible. The tide of time was not always sufficiently predictable to allow for following its patterns (Wright et al, 2017).

From temporal vertigo to temporal dissonance

Listening to time was a means of discerning how power operated. This was apparent in restrictions on how and when prisoners could spend it. Enforcing movement and stillness also worked to distort prisoners' sense of time passing. The warp and weft of time, both inside and out, had aural qualities. Sounds of dawdling and killing time, industry and activity, could emphasize the sense and sound of time passing or slowing. The imposition of constraints on movement had a corresponding impact on how time was felt as a source of dislocation. While a category-B local, Midtown was home to a diverse range of prisoners serving an array of sentences whether stuck or passing through, which lent the community a diverse character and broader array of daily rhythms. The ebb and flow of life at Midtown was a hubbub of comings, goings and staying-puts. Senses of powerlessness to affect time passing was heard and felt relationally as well as individually, deepened by existence alongside people whose conditions of incarceration differed markedly. Bobbing on the tides of time were those, like Mo, who expected to be released but despite knitted brows and collaborative, pencilled calculations between him and various officers, always seemed to be in past his expected leaving date (he nevertheless left and returned many times while I was there). Sid who was determined not to expedite his release, and therefore the amount of time he had to spend subject to the unpredictable vagaries of being on licence and at risk of the disorientating snakes and ladders of recall – administrative or otherwise – which would have him back inside. Stevie who fully expected to be greeted by police at the gate,[3] waiting to arrest him for some outstanding offence or other and send him straight back in doors, and others, such as Brian, who longed for the relative stability and community of life inside the walls, the moment they were out.

There was a contrast between the way the individual experienced time, and how time was sounded collectively; the warp and weft of time, which knitted the prison fabric together. As has been mentioned earlier in more detail, the nature of HMP Midtown meant that people came from a diverse range of places and were subject to an array of sentences. People could 'land' there by chance (such as getting 'locked out' of the prison they were destined for, or could become stuck on remand or parole hold, or because they were nearing release. Locals made up an unusually large number of the population but existed alongside others in all manner of circumstances. Many of those I spoke with most frequently were longer-term prisoners, perhaps because of a greater desire to kill time, because they were more settled or more inclined to launch in first if curiosity was piqued.[4] Those who were relatively settled existed among a rhythmic chorus of "I've just landed, sort us out?" or "You back again?!" issuing from those repeatedly returning. Robert described this: "You get the people in here though, who go out, come back, go out, come back. That's no life man." Relations between people and time were experienced in the space they shared with others, in addition to but not always in the same way as they experienced their own time. Indeterminate sentence for public protection (IPP) prisoners, or those with long sentences, could experience the impact of their sentence in particularly acute ways which were enhanced by others – "He has to change cell, his pad mate's out in ten weeks – he just got 17 years" (fieldnotes). In contrast, while Tommy felt disadvantaged by his outsider status – he was both a southerner and Traveller so only ever 'local' in the sense that fellow Travellers tended to recognize one another and form some degree of allegiance in prison spaces – he described other prisons as being much harder to inhabit both because of his case[5] and the environment. Tommy classified category A and B prisons as the "worst" he had been in: "It's quiet, it's probably the drearier thing and it's probably the scary bit about it because it's so silent. And it's a dangerous environment. It's terrible, I couldn't stand it." He preferred "these prisons cos a lot of people ain't warped, they've still got a bit of sense to them, and you get a half-sensible conversation". Doing time was easier for him among the ebb and flow of the local community, where life had more bustle, the environment was infinitely noisier and where he felt less oppressively immersed.

Excerpts from my fieldnotes in the previous chapter are taken from the time I spent in visits, early on in fieldwork. I was struck by how unlike other prison spaces they felt. Precious and fleeting time with loved ones and the presence of women and children all generated a multiplicity of tones. Anxious mothers, sisters, lovers and wives, bored or weeping children and buoyant friends (some of whom greeted the officers with a familiarity suggesting they had not long ago been on the other side of the table). Staff reported the noise as particularly wearing, though I wondered whether some of this was attached to the labour of being steeped in this emotion soup. Anna Kotova (2019) explores the broader impact on the experience of time when the temporal pains of prisoners' families are considered. The sound of these more liminal prison spaces reflected the bittersweet, social nature of time and space experienced with and through others. Accounting for 'lost' time better captures the multiplicity of ways in which it is experienced, both between and on behalf of others (Kotova, 2019).

Temporal vertigo is a useful concept for exploring how sensations of time were altered by prison. It adds nuance to explorations of how time was experienced when power over how you spend it is removed, as well as how time was meted out in an environment in which all must adhere to a central routine. Returning to the ways in which sound both echoes and mediates relationships between people and prison spaces disrupts this rather singular portrayal of time. Much of the jarring unease of a prison sentence for those I spoke with related to a temporal dissonance between their incarcerated self and other, between possible selves and worlds conveyed through memory, imagination and communications with those outside. While this could be experienced as vertiginous, much of the pain of social dislocation emerged from a dissonance between their incarcerated self and the other times and spaces occupied by their alternative selves. Conway and Limayem (2010) define this: 'the affective reaction an individual has to a salient lack of temporal congruity', but its use in music is of far longer standing and arguably more germane to capturing this experience (for example, Thomas, 1996). In music, temporal dissonance refers to 'rhythmic and metrical conflicts' (McKee, 2000: 97). The music of Robert Schumann is layered with examples of this technique (Krebs, 1999). Listening to the prison soundscape reveals the metre of prison life, its recurring patterns and accents, and it is through this process that disruptions and disharmony become more discernible. Carceral and Flaherty (2021) argue the standardized nature of prison time strips temporal experience of its diversity for prisoners, imposing a sense of narrowing, shrinking down to the here and now. In contrast, while those I spoke with cited this as a source of painful frustration, its potency was partially derived from the contrast between impositions of prison time, set against a keen awareness of times, places and people beyond their reach.

Leaving it behind

Staff interactions with time and space added clarity to prisoners' experience by offering a point of comparison and contrast. Whereas prisoners actively worked to bridge and diminish distinctions between time and space inside and out, staff actively sought to leave the inside behind them and avoid taking work home. In a community prison where many of the staff and prisoners had known one another for decades, attended the same schools, had sometimes dated members of the same family and shared the same streets, this could prove problematic. Ket was invariably cheery and jovial, greeting everyone he encountered and laughing often. His contribution to the sound environment operated as a shield from his personal concerns, strictly delineating between work and home: "No, no not at all. No one would know if I had problems at home, or if something was going on with me." Other members of staff spoke about how sound featured in processes of de-prisoning and guarding against 'spill over' (Crawley, 2004). Ket's laughter served performative purposes in displaying aspects of his identity which protected more vulnerable (if no more personal) aspects of his self. Sound was used as a membrane between social and internal worlds. Derek spoke about how working to attend to various aspects of the prison soundscape "builds all your stresses up, so it's nice sometimes just to sit back, close your eyes and listen to nothing". These distinctions in seeking either to enforce or diminish distinctions between different zones of time and space echoed disparities of power in how these groups navigated and participated in ordering temporal and spatial experience. Both were distinct from the ways the broader institution worked to impose a collective sense of order.

5

Weft and Warp

Sound is inextricably bound with spatial as well as temporal experience; a means of designating and reinforcing social meanings and functions of spaces (Hendy, 2015). We understand this when we enter a place of worship, for example, or a busy pub. There are various sensory and visual prompts too, but architectural detail is bent to the purpose of generating particular social experience and meaning (Blesser and Salter, 2009). This aspect of life was more pronounced in a space marked by the relative dearth of sensory stimuli, and limited ability to curate sensory experience. Visual peripheries are both more limited and controllable; we lack earlids with which to exclude unwanted sound (Simmel, 1903; Carpenter and McLuhan, 1960).

Listening lent an audible quality to the metrics of time passing and stagnating through different zones. Even in a space marked by its particular purpose and consequent elision of personal and private distinctions, prison spaces hummed with the social purposes assigned to them. Shifting soundscapes signposted and inflected the emotional geographies of Midtown's spaces. Its occupants asserted their identities and purposes, sometimes to the metric of the broader prison concerto, at others demonstrating opposition and resistance to its rhythms (Labelle, 2018). Attuning to the prison soundscape revealed distinctions between the tune of the wider social organism and individual agents whether working through the everyday or seeking sanctuary from the punishing sensorium.

Emotional geography

I was often encouraged to listen to different prison spaces. These frequently corresponded to areas of particular interest among the prisoners (Boyd, having landed a prestigious kitchen orderly position was most keen for me to hear how different it was there), but was also born of the recognition that: "Different places sound different" (Officer Stillman). As with time, spatial experience was bound up with power relations – nowhere more starkly illustrated than by entrance and exit rituals: for example, "Coming/Going through" and "Let me through?" The former was a ritualistic expression of intent to follow, uttered by most staff and operating as both a greeting, a sign of movement and a direction not to lock the gate. The latter was frequently expressed in growing volume and levels of agitation as a prisoner waited for someone to let them through in order that they might move around on the wing, perform work tasks and get on with their day. In these ways both emotional geography and the differentiated spaces these consisted of were bound up with power relations which lent them form and order. Carving out personal space in an environment where no one was ever far from other people, and in which all aspects of human life were conducted, presented additional contestations to order and power.

Ben Crewe et al (2014) point out that prisons are differentiated emotional spaces where different ranges of emotional expression are acceptable. They describe the variable emotional geography of prison spaces, and the 'consumptive wariness' which characterizes how they are experienced. This prompts further exploration of how this works, and why this is experienced so widely or consistently when so much of prison life is experienced from behind the door. Sound offers an explanatory mechanism for this process. As they assert, not all prison spaces are subject to the same 'feel'. I sometimes took refuge in the relative calm of the library. Officer Rose reflected, during interview, that this was a much quieter space – he speculated that perhaps this was because the "books absorbed sound". While the softer furnishings – carpet – (and books) undoubtedly contributed, as did the restricted number of men allowed at any one time, both the men and staff generally conversed and moved in gentler, softer ways in this space.[1] They could also be observed doing things – such as crosswords – together in companionable quiet. The chapel was one of the first places I paused in as I attempted to orientate myself. I let myself in when no one was around and sat, listening to disembodied sounds from around the prison. My sight was obscured by the grubby stained-glass windows, but I was also free from scrutiny. Solitude was hard to come by in such a frantic environment. The stillness, relative comfort and socially prescribed function of the place lent it a somewhat liminal air, some of which was retained even when it was packed with excited men during a music event. The education department also offered space to explore a different emotional range, though I felt unusually uncomfortable and unwelcome there so seldom visited.

Feeling the range

As Hemsworth (2016) asserts, and was demonstrated by the community at HMP Midtown, sound is a modality of emotion. Different spaces sounded different, indicating the 'feel' or range of emotions expressed within them. However, these were not passively experienced. Members of the community actively contributed to them, exerting influence over spaces and reasserting identities. Tonk explained the relief in expressing himself and carving out his own sonic space:

> 'I went gym this morning, done some chest, then I come back I was a bit RRRraaaaa Midtown. Y'know what I mean? Released, release, that's what I do, like I need music in my cell. I need music. Like, I love to just sing and let it out. You know what I mean? If I ain't got music I'll either bang my door or shout out my window or shout to other lads like.'

If prisoners were privy to a partially concealed dimension of prison life, one audible through walls and behind closed doors, they also used this as a means of enacting agency to combat the physical restrictions of the environment. Mooch, Cam, Stretch and others spoke about knowing what was going on from the vibrations through the walls. Lugs, a local who had spent many years in and out of Midtown alongside a number of friends and relatives, referred to the way he used to communicate with other prisoners by emptying the toilets and talking through the pipes. Mooch illustrated how pivotal the hidden, sonic world of prison life was for those inside:

> 'Specially if I'm listening to the TV yeah and I can't hear it, and they're all shouting. But that's what it is. That's when you hear the noise, when you're behind the door. You can hear. If people are on the landing and that, you can hear all different noises. That's what, aye. You don't hear it as much when you're out there. But when you're behind the door you can hear it.'

These reconfigurations of prison spaces were the site of contestations to the imposition of order, between prisoners as well as staff. 'Window warriors'[2] are a well-known phenomenon in prison – those who shout, and sometimes bully by shouting at windows. Window warriors were more prevalent in young offenders as Boyd explained of his time there: "Just shit. Full of idiots as well. All you hear is: 'Are ya listening?' That's all you hear all the time. That's what they shout out the window: 'Are you listening? Are you listening?'" Tommy also referred to means of imposing dominion over prison spaces in different parts of the estate:

> 'You can hear people shouting, cos it was like the young offender side, so then you got more of the idiots shouting at the window and making people sing out the windows and bullying them, and this, that and the other. Because you're thinking oh god, imagine if someone calls ya, cos you'd just have to say fuck off.'

It was bartering, borrowing and gossip about impending moves and sentences which formed the constant buzz of window-to-window communication at HMP Midtown. Shouting at windows remained a feature of the soundscape; it was not uncommon for the yard to ring out with angry abuse or threats of retribution yelled from the windows during bang up or from 'Seg'. Sound provided a means of accessing this otherwise inaccessible aspect of prison life, and the social ordering, underscored by power relations conducted within it. When interviewing the No. 1 in a cell, he articulated this in a way which echoed the space we were in:

> 'The noise in here would be terrifying. That fact that him next door might be setting fire to his cell ... I worked in young offenders ... and they still kind of haunt me, that you'd be on night duties and there'd be the window warriors shouting out the window: "I've shagged your Mum, her knickers are under my cell bed", or whatever, and this prisoner's like "oh, don't say that". Sing a song and we'll stop taking the piss out of ya. Nah, nah. "Sing a song and we'll stop taking the piss." I can't sing. "Well sing a nursery rhyme". And you're sat there thinking please don't sing, please don't sing. And then he starts singing baa baa black sheep and of course they're just ba ba ba. They're on him again and he's just – what's the point of me coming out of my cell in the morning cos I'm gonna get a kicking.'

I had heard versions of this tale before from people who had been or were in prison. Like other narratives which do the rounds among prisoners both within and between prisons it served a purpose. 'Baa baa black sheep' was a parable about the dangers of giving in to bullies and showing weakness. The endurance of this story illustrated how sound was bound up with contestations for dominance over space. Listening more closely also rendered distress more audible. "Are ya listening?" – a call for attention and remembrance as much as a demand to be heard. Stretch explained, people made "noise" because "they want to be heard". In a place of such concentrated population and diversity of needs, "If you're not being heard, you're getting left behind, ain't ya?"

Asking the men about sound allowed me to understand some of the more hidden parts of the prison social world and the complicated nature of power and social standing among them. Violence was common but performed many functions depending on whether it was perpetrated where it could be seen and heard or concealed from prying eyes and ears. Stretch explained his perception of its necessity:

> 'There's a saying in life, and if you remember this you'll always do well: "Some people can't hear, so they have to feel." And that goes for,

you're trying to talk to someone about a problem and they don't listen, so you have to beat 'em. Not hearing, feel (palm in fist). Not hearing, feel.'

There was a code which extended throughout much of the community in relation to saving face and conducting business. Getting 'mugged off' damaged standing. Disputes should be dealt with face to face: "I ain't gonna back down, but as I'm walking out, he's cracked me. Snaked me from right behind. And I think that's bang out of order. If you're gonna fight someone, fight someone. That's dirty fighting" (Lugs). The No. 1 explained:

'People don't want to be mugged off … if somebody feels aggrieved be it a member of staff or another prisoner, then they have to do something otherwise somebody else will take advantage. And that's a downward spiral … so I think there is the bravado.'

Reluctance to lose face was not restricted to prisoners. Though many disputes took place out of view and beyond hearing, as a number of the men made clear to me: "A lot of fights happen in pads. Like in cells. And staff don't even know about it. Staff'll probably see 'em later on with a black eye and like 'What have you done?' 'Oh banged it, that's all'" (Tonk). Lugs told me: "Whatever I do, I do behind my door." On another occasion he was telling me about something that had happened and explained: "Me and Ghet' was going in the toilet to chat to someone cos they don't … there's cameras. So if we do owt we have to go in the toilet or a cell to say 'Yo, rarara'." Davey similarly spoke of having respect for someone who came to his cell to handle a dispute "like men". At HMP Midtown a significant portion of these disputes were conducted out of sight, but when they happened where others could see, this had an instrumental purpose. Jack told me:

'But me, I've always had to fight because I've always been happy to fight, cos I'm not letting someone see me back down from one prisoner, and then next prisoner comes. So I'd rather just put him out, give him a combo, bang him out and then that's it. Go round the prison, that's it.'

Despite his bravado, or perhaps partially because of it, Jack was in the Vulnerable Prisoner Unit. I did not enquire why, and somewhat unusually the reasons for this remained opaque though the officer often in charge told me he did not like him and did not think he belonged there. Associations between sound, space and contestations of power revealed additional depths of prison life – aspects of prison society largely conducted out of sight. When speaking of a particularly loud prisoner, the No. 2 referred to the "big swinging dick" on the wing and his perceived need to play music louder than anyone else to demonstrate supremacy. Sound then, was implicated in masculine performance and the search for respect (Toch, 1997; Bourgois, 2002). This jostling for order also provided a means to assert influence over space. Sound and rhythm were used to breach, alter and remake prison boundaries (Russell and Carlton, 2018).

Sanctuary

Contributing to the soundscape and its punctuations with performative masculinity was avoided by some. Urfan, described by Cam as a "pad rat" (someone who retreats to their cell and is reluctant to participate in social life), explained his retreat from social spaces: "Just when we want the peace, open my reading books, start reading. That's it. Nothing. They are banging anything. I don't want involved. Stay inside and do with the reading. That's it." The difficulty of carving out personal space in an environment which offered little respite from the intrusive soundscape was keenly felt: "Behind your door, you turn your telly up, but you can always hear the keys" (Si). Stretch explained how this could impact on boundaries of the self:

'EEEEeeeeeeeeeeeeeee. All through the night, all through the day. That's all you hear. You know when you're having …? I've got a thing now, like I never gave myself any time I just went with the flow. But now I take two hours out of the day. An hour out the morning, an hour out the afternoon, or the evening for myself. Give myself a bit of time. An all you can hear is, it's quiet, your padmate's asleep, ah it's heaven … EEEEEEeeeeeee EEEeeee. What the fuck you ringing your bell for at 3 or 4 o'clock in the morning? You should be asleep. Unless you're like me and you don't sleep a lot.'

The noise of other people, as well as the prison, was unavoidable. For Natty, the intrusion of sound upon his sense of self was a proxy for his difficulty coping: "I don't listen to music anymore. I don't watch TV. Just silence and I hear everything going on around me." Natty had served many years over tariff on an indeterminate sentence for public protection (IPP). This was repeatedly alluded to by others and was the subject of a shared sense of injustice. The problems he came in with (unstable living arrangements, profound mental health and substance use issues) were not getting any better inside. Retreating from the bustle of the prison was a necessity for some, whether to counter episodes of distress or as a strategy of survival: "I just wanna go behind my door. What's gonna happen to me when I get out?" For Stretch, the need for sanctuary was episodic but profound:

'Some weeks it gets horrendous you know, I have blackouts, panic attacks, I don't know what's happening. I sweat from head to toe, have to run to the shower, the shower's like my saviour cos I used to be able to bolt myself in the shower and no one could get to me. I used to put things behind the door and wash the dirt off me.'

Stretch had been abused as a child and had a particularly complex and intimate relationship with the prison and its soundscape. His need for sanctuary echoed the difficulty of finding personal space in an environment where other people were inescapable.

Sound was bound up with the remaking and re-ordering of space to assert and to retain identity within the intrusive prison environment. Unpicking associations between sound, space and sense of self adds definition to the operation of agency within the constraints of the prison environment, as well as extending the field of enquiry behind the door. Sound was implicated in efforts to assert strength and maintain respect in prison spaces. It also amplified struggle and vulnerability. Recognition of others' difficulties was a feature of conversation when asking about sound and space. This added nuance to accounts of masculinity and identity in prison which frequently fail to capture the depth and prevalence of mutual support between many of these men (Maguire, 2016, 2021). Sound prompted individuals to seek sanctuary as a means of preserving self. In this context, the soundscape was a means of charting internal emotional geography, and expressing vulnerability in an environment where avoidance of being mugged off was a perpetual concern.

6

A Night Inside

Passing time was a major preoccupation at Midtown. The conditions and constraints of prison lent the hours a warped and distorted quality, fluctuating between extended periods of nothing at all and short, clipped intervals of frantic activity. While much of prison life is conducted out of view, and beyond my personal line of sight, I could hear and feel much of the activity on the wing. Once the evening meal had been collected and all returned to their cells for the night, this was reversed. Coming on to the wing after bang-up, I felt a return to those early days of listening around the periphery and wondering about the mysterious occupants within. Then I wandered around the outer perimeter making sense of what I was hearing from the outside, now I would largely be locked inside, on the wing. As night took hold and the prison moved towards patrol state, time and space took on an unfamiliar quality, stretching into dark and shadowed corners, defying its usual dimensions.

I made tentative enquiries about the possibility of spending the night with the full expectation I would be refused. As far as I knew there was no precedent in England and Wales. While I knew this would deepen my understanding of the place and its routines, I did not imagine my motives would be clear to those for whom this was a mundane aspect of working life. I was surprised when my tentative enquiries about doing so were greeted positively, and a sympathetic commanding officer sought out so that I might shadow her. Prior to beginning fieldwork, I had spent a year volunteering with the IMB[1] at another prison. I was taken aback when informed by our chair that we would need to make arrangements with the No. 1 in order to conduct unannounced night visits. At the time I interpreted this as a case of blind institutionalization, accepted as a means of saving everyone bother regardless of the potential cost – particularly to those in Care and Segregation. I still do, though my cynicism is now nuanced by an understanding of how these impediments come to be. While officers carry keys at night, they do not 'break the pouch'[2] unless faced with dire emergency. Night patrol – the state of, and set of routines occurring in, the night – has its own rules and rituals of accessibility. What follows is a passage from my notes relating to that time. I then discuss how this informed my understanding of time and space, and what this meant for various actors, particularly Brian, who I introduce later.

Night falls

Afterwards, I told the men I had been there a few nights previously. I had not wanted to tell them beforehand for fear of causing disruption. I did not want to create any expectation of conversation while they were locked up. I did not know I would be able to fulfil it and, anticipating some objection to my presence, I was reluctant to lend any justification to protests about my being there. I aimed to be as unobtrusive as possible. Afterwards, Tommy asked how I found it. I told him, as I told others, that I had felt profoundly lonely in their absence. I missed their company in the oppressive quiet, and while there was plenty to keep me occupied, I nevertheless felt the weight of it. "You should have come and talked to me through the door, I would have kept you company", he chided. I did not tell him I had spent much time wandering the landings, both revelling in the rare opportunity to do so freely and regretting the circumstances that allowed such latitude.

> I paused briefly at each door, looking at the photos of those in each cell,[3] taking comfort from their familiarity. I did not dwell at doorways beyond this, aware of the potential for intrusion of privacy – I took care not to eavesdrop, remembering my time in visits and the difficulty of balancing a sense of the collective soundscape while taking care to turn a deaf ear to the personal. I caught the sense of shifting moods within as I walked by different cells. The relative quiet, save loud music and periodic shouting, was punctuated by occasional banter with a popular officer, laughing at an inmate's incongruous choice of 'Hungry Eyes' played loudly, on repeat; 'What the fuck are you listening to? Turn that shit off!' I perch awkwardly on stairs as the staff dwindle to those lumbered with the night shift, enjoying someone's music while unsure of its source. I'm teased about this by an officer: 'I wouldn't sit there if I were you, the cockroaches swarm out of there. Well, maybe not that step.' There is an unmistakeable edge to his words. This place is not designed for comfort. Every decision to sit represents a social breach and one I would not make on the wing, while the residents ran, slid, ambled, strode and limped up and down the stairs; their status indicated by their footwear, altering the sound of shoe soles on the iron steps. No such variation in the regulation footwear of the staff, nor the rhythm of their gait; driven with morning purpose, sluggishly

reluctant after lunch. Now reduced to a few, the relative absence of tapping shoes and jangling keys are immediately locatable.

I had been at Midtown since February. Now at the tail end of a sticky August, I had grown accustomed to the familiar din of the men, animated greetings from the landings, conducting shady business in corners. Following security training I had been permitted to carry keys, the vulnerability imposed by their absence, jarred with every jangle-free step though this also enhanced my ability to move around undetected. I was unused to being reliant on staff to let me on and off the wing, which added to the strange sense of dislocation. The presence of those I had spent hours in the company of reduced to strains of TVs, music, flushing loos, coughing, conversation; sonic samples across empty spaces. The floor echoes with the recent activity conducted across it as volumes are lowered, taking their cue from the dimming lights.

I accompany the officer in command around the grounds as security routines are observed at every lock in the place. Night amplifies our steps on concrete and metal, expanding the small site to one of uncertain corners and indistinct perimeters. Dwindling, more spartan sounds come from within the cells as night deepens, escaping across uninhabited grounds. I'm conscious of our chatter, not wishing to disturb the occasional, fleeting shadows glimpsed through barred windows. The prison at night is strangely altered, unfamiliar. We stop by the Drug Treatment Unit and check in on the officer keeping watch. She is an older lady, wearing comfy slippers from home and watching the television with a cuppa. I am struck by the strange incongruity of this cosy domestic scene, while metres away men I have yet to meet are locked in for the night.

The most explicit objection to my presence came from the nurse who I had not encountered previously. Unlike many who felt the need to couch their discomfort in more socially acceptable ways, he asked 'Who are you?' in bristling tones. He did not seem satisfied by my answer, though limited himself to a few noises in response to my explanation. I was apologetic for startling him in the near-dark from my position on the stairway. He has come to attend to an incident I assume is at least moderately serious. I cannot tell if his irritation is born of surprise at finding me on the stairs, annoyance at having been called over or concern for whomever he is tending to. I try to reassure him; perhaps he is discomforted by the thought of being scrutinized where he has so little control over the outcome? Decisions about hospital care are not his to make, but the commanding officer. How strange this is, that security can matter more than life. Or some lives. At least, the life of this individual and his need for care is being balanced against the likelihood of his accepting it and the potential for additional incidents the small number of remaining staff would make it impossible to attend to.[4] The immense gravity of this decision feels weightier in the dark.

Purposeful, clustered feet on metal stairs, synchronized jangling pierce the slow routine of night patrol. 'Miss, miss' a prisoner calls to me; 'has someone died?' 'Miss?' I answer no but tell him I'll speak to him in the day and move rapidly along. I marvel at his ability to recognize my steps. Only later, when I ask him, does he tell me he could see through the crack in his door. A prisoner has hurt himself, bleeding profusely. He is moved to a neighbouring cell where he continues to harm himself. 'You might as well see it all if this is what you're here for', the teasing officer, inviting me to join from my position on the stairs. Staff retch as the smell of blood, warmed by the summer heat, reaches their noses. He refuses care and remains conscious. Not taking him to hospital will mean additional anxiety for the familiar ritual of the morning count.

To much relief he accepts a sugary cup of tea, a breakfast pack having been sought out and fetched to replace some fluids. He settles, and our footsteps withdraw from their clustering around his cell. Customary routines are resumed. Rounds are taken, notices posted under doors. Solitary boots on metal walkways, the flash of a torch. As the darkness deepens, sound retreats. Conversations drift into sleep, the occasional snore rumbles under the door. TVs are turned off. Music peters out. Time slows, stretching into indistinct corners as I find places to perch, listening as the constant electrical thrum becomes more perceptible. In the early hours of the morning a quiet calm descends, at least in these dark and empty spaces. I feel a solidarity with remaining signs of wakefulness; the stereos lowered out of respect for sleeping neighbours, the almost-company of televisions.

I resume walking around the corners of the prison, wandering downstairs into the vulnerable prisoner wing I note how much louder what I assume is the generator is from close to. There are growing numbers of cockroaches, their scuttling audible in the absence of human bustle. Back on the twos the mice are more plentiful, squeaking away, their tiny paws scratching on the lino. Now I understand the keenness of the men to sacrifice prison-issue sweaters to the service of mouse-guards, rolling them up to wedge against the cracks of doors. At some point I find myself wearying and sit down in the office on the mains to make some notes. Despite the glaring light and unsavoury creatures, I somehow manage to fall asleep on the desk. I wake, disorientated, listening to the prison begin to rouse from slumber. I am relieved I cannot leave the wing until after the count has been concluded and feel an almost palpable holding of breath as cells are checked and numbers recorded. As the new day breaks, all have made it through.[5]

In the dark

I witnessed legion efforts to stem the number of vermin and their access to personal spaces. Traps littered the walkways, and on one occasion my arrival coincided with the departure of an exterminator. He produced a brace of rat carcasses from a bag and held them aloft for the perusal of the gate staff. Their van was a frequent presence in the car park too, but I saw little first-hand evidence until I spent the night. As the volume diminished, men settling into evening rhythms of sleeping, watching telly, chatting or listening to the radio, other components of the soundscape became audible. The thrum of cell alarms (and the rhythmic lack of urgency which characterized response to them) assumed a steady note in a soundscape now dominated by rubber soles on metal walkways, the jangle of keys and, later, the squeak and scuttle of mice and 'roaches. Unable to see in the dark, I found my hearing sensitized to compensate as the lights dimmed.

Night-time altered perceptions of the contours of the prison landscape, re-shaping its emotional geography (Crewe et al, 2014). Correspondingly, time stretched out interminably and I missed the chaotic company of the men. I felt lonely. Listening to the prison at night-time illustrated the shifting complexity of the relationship between sound, the social and space/time in ways which dramatically altered the environment. Cedric had palpable mental health issues, most recently indicated by his sporting a ripped sweater arm on his head. This made it tricky to communicate meaningfully. He had managed to break his hatch and cell bell, and called out to me, beseeching me to summon staff on his behalf. They warned me he was given to spitting, but very possibly not in my direction – "I think he has mental health issues, but I'm no expert" said the officer in response to my expressing concern. This was a common refrain among staff both here and elsewhere. In the night, when the symphony of activity and frustration abated, the distress of those faring poorly was amplified. Seamus, an older prisoner in the Veeps (the Vulnerable Prisoners' Unit),[6] described how being placed near the 'Seg'[7] (short for Care and Segregation) could prove wearing:

> 'Banging, crying, screaming keeps us awake – they can't do their bang-up you see. They should leave the doors open and they'd be okay, it's all those hours locked up by themselves, they can't take it, does their head in, then none of us sleep. Keeps us awake all night. Big problem.'

As space and time beyond the door warped and contorted, many of those behind it felt the walls closing in. A number of the men encouraged me to hear it for myself, just as staff urged me to borrow a radio:

> 'You want to be here about one in the morning. People going mad. I've only been here three days but every night people banging, screaming. I guess people get frustrated. Kept awake every night so far.' (James)

Despite the evident strain of these persistent disruptions to peace, these troubled souls often received considerable accommodation and understanding from their sleep-deprived neighbours. In an environment offering little respite from the noise, smell and general intrusion of other humans' presence, it was the relative scarcity of anger and violence in response to these kinds of provocation that proved most striking to me. Behaviour which might be expected to prompt brutal retaliation[8] was more often greeted with bemused good humour and indulgence: "Yeah, right above me. It was hard work that. I don't know how he kept doing it. He must've just slept through the day, but he used to bang through the day as well!" (Davey). If the prison-to-prison exchange rate – reception staff would often try to bargain swaps for less amiable inhabitants at nearby prisons – proved unfavourable, persistent offenders might be moved between wings in larger prisons to give neighbours some respite. This was difficult in a prison of Midtown's size.

Brian

I was at pains to discuss my presence that night with Brian, unsure if he would remember given his blood loss, and uneasy about what I had witnessed. He was well known to staff, though I did not observe relationships with other prisoners. He posed a challenge for Diane in Resettlement because he had little family to anchor accommodation placements, and it was necessary to work around court orders forbidding him from various town centres. When on the out, and perilously close to the town he was forbidden to enter, it was his custom to drop by the gatehouse and chat to whomever was on.[9] Several officers told me they had tended to him as he suffered the effects of too much mamba (a synthetic cannabinoid) on the streets outside, donating bits of their packed lunch to rouse him, to the bemused indifference of onlookers. A frequent self-harmer, it was general belief that sooner or later his luck would run out. After a particularly long and intense conversation with him, I mentioned to an officer that he seemed to be in distress. He responded: "Him? Oh, he's a waste of oxygen." I saw this same officer, sitting down on the step with him following our brusque exchange. He took a considerable amount of time talking with him, disrupting lock-up to do so. The disjunct between what he said and did, suggested his dismissive words were as much a coping mechanism. One day, it was likely the count would come too late.

Brian's temporal and spatial experience was dominated by his relationship to the prison and those who worked there. For him, Midtown was a source of comfort and support, an anchor in a fast-shifting world where he struggled to gain a foothold. My engagements with him typified the strange, discomforting intimacies of prison life. Trying to look away as he showed me his self-inflicted wounds and scars amounted to a denial of what he wished to show and share. In this strange place where public and private are as perpetually difficult to navigate as proximity and distance, there was profound power in staying to listen.

7

Talk to Me

A while before spending the night, I learned that remaining into the evening without pre-negotiation was a step too far. I had failed to appreciate the significance of staying across shifts and routines, or of the specific cut-off point in the night, after which external parts of the prison are closed down and personal possessions locked in – the night patrol. I was saved from exhausting goodwill by running into a senior, security officer with whom I had established some familiarity. She immediately understood the reason for my wanting to be there, both at that point of day and the occasion. My presence was undoubtedly perceived as a nuisance but proved moderately useful in allowing officers to attend to the evening routine when the needs of one prisoner threatened to derail it.

I was there to hear the men, listening to a much-anticipated football game. I was holding out for a goal for the home team, and the celebratory banging I had been advised would be sure to follow. Stevie had been cutting himself and, given how unpredictably he was given to spiral, was allowed to remain out of cell after everyone else had been locked away. We talked as he waited for medical attention. What looked to me like a need for rather basic, but important first aid, appeared to have been designated the responsibility of someone else, or at least something that might be tended to in the fullness of time. His challenge to bear witness without flinching imposed a strange intimacy. Stevie taught me much about the complexities and contradictions of ethics in praxis as well as the absence of clarity which characterized decisions about the 'right' thing to do. These discomforting exchanges were as instructive as they were challenging, typifying the development of my relationship to people and place as I strove for deeper understanding.

"I can't"

It is a prisoner who informs staff that Stevie has cut himself: 'He's pouring blood. It's all over his cell floor. Someone needs to go see him.' He informs several members of staff, talking to everyone and no one in particular, catching my eye. His own arms are criss-crossed with self-inflicted cuts. Shallow but plentiful. We discuss this at another point, comparing scars and patterned welts on limbs offered up for scrutiny. Puckered scar tissue reopened. 'Why?' asks an officer. 'I don't know, I feel strange' he says. He makes his wound talk to me, squeezing his separated flesh together to form oozing lips. 'Hello' he says in a high-pitched voice, laughing, whether at my discomfort or his own macabre delight I cannot tell. I chide him, telling him to remove his grubby, blood-coated fingers from the undressed wound. When he is moved to the observation cell, his hand appears between glass and wall, waving, calling me for attention. I realize I cannot respond to it. I tell him 'I can't'. 'Come talk to me' he asks me. 'I can't.'[1]

As he settled a little, Stevie amused himself by playing me 'tunes' with suggestive lyrics at a suitably anti-social volume. The commanding officer came round at frequent intervals to check on him and I was reassured to hear his paternal, Scottish tones: 'Ah, so you're settling down now, that's a good lad.' The next evening, several veeps, venturing up from the bowels of the prison to collect their dinner in orderly lines, complained bitterly about the awful music issuing from above the previous night. I said nothing. (Fieldnotes)

I instinctively felt it would be dangerously inappropriate to follow Stevie's hand and resisted the compulsion to do so. I wanted to sink to the grubby floor and settle in for the night, figuring that if I was there to talk to him it might calm him a little and induce rest, sleep even. I wanted to keep him company, to reassure myself he was still breathing, just as I wanted to get him to running water and dress that wound. On closer, less forgiving scrutiny though, it was unclear to me whether I sought to give comfort or receive it by retaining proximity to him. Not for the first time I was confronted with the limits of my role as well as my capabilities. I was trained in rudimentary first aid, but not mental health support. I was a researcher, not a nurse, and there was every possibility I might do more harm than good in failing to recognize the boundaries signified by these distinctions. Later in the week, Lugs told me Stevie was in a bad way and asked if I intended to visit his cell. I explained I could not and resolved to stay away from the prison for a few days, holding my breath.

Intimacy and ethics

Resisting the urge to respond to Stevie as my initial impulse directed was informative, if uncomfortable. He was as charming as he was vulnerable. He often spoke to me multiple times a day despite frequent admonishment from others ("I said listen, you got to stop talking to that lady like you do

... she's here to do a report and that like, and learn something for herself, I said, and all she's got is you bantering in her earhole every time you see her. But he's had an horrendous childhood" [Stretch]). Topics and styles of conversation varied hugely. It was most usually Stevie who offered imitations of tropical bird song or banging as light relief. He would stop to test me with inappropriate observations he had formulated on the fly; "I don't hound girls, I pound them, innit", to talk about grieving for his best friend or loss of his children (he was not permitted access and the mother of one of his children had stopped bringing her to see him). A local, he had served several sentences both at Midtown and elsewhere in his 27 years, though he could pass for a decade younger. He elicited concern, indulgence and exasperation from various quarters of the Midtown community who understood and accommodated his complex array of needs. As was the case the night he was moved to the observation cell, he had begun spiralling without any discernible pattern or precursor which elicited additional care and concern. Imperfect as this environment was for protecting such vulnerabilities, it was nevertheless true that here he was known, understood and cared for albeit in ways I struggled to work within. I had spent a fair amount of time in prisons by this point but navigating relationships was no less challenging for that (Jackson, 2021). Offering a hug or tending to injuries was not an option in a place where touch was all but forbidden. I was there to learn and observe rather than participate, but there are no clear demarcations in the messiness of human interaction and those that do exist, stubbornly refuse to stay put.

Some argue there is no 'backstage' in the total institution (Goffman, 1959, 1961). That the elision of public and private strip the prisoner of out-of-sight spaces to curate others' impressions of them. These episodes emphasized the importance of honouring their existence. Private spaces were as contorted as broader temporal and spatial experience, warped by deprivations of imprisonment, but more precious for their fluid fragility (Sykes, 1958). The potential for physical intrusion was matched by a need to exercise care to tread lightly around private, internal worlds. Enquiring about sound amplified the auditory imagination, making the inner worlds of those at Midtown more discernible (Ihde, 2007). Scrutinizing the fragile membrane separating distinct spheres of social life inside heightened awareness of how much experience was characterized by similar permeability of the barriers between where Midtown inhabitants were and where they wanted to be. Misrepresentations of Goffman's 'total institution', as relating to insurmountable walls between inside and out, risk distorting understanding of a considerable source of pain for those longing for lives and loves just beyond the wall. Alongside the constant flow of people and media between the walls, imagination, if not physical proximity, kept objects of yearning tantalizingly close, but just out of reach.

Clashes between ethics imposed by the institution and my personal code were not always reconcilable. Explaining why I could not alleviate Lugs' itchy back, he called upon passing people to contribute to the conversation. A nurse walked by, he asked: "Is it true we can't touch in here?" "Yes, she confirmed. In training we're taught about the healing power of touch, but in here we can't." He asked an officer the same question: "No, you're not allowed" he said gruffly "but I can" before creepily running his fingers down my arm (fieldnotes). Power flowed both relationally and sensorially in directions so complex and multifarious it was dizzying to unpick and precarious to navigate. I was at once confronted with competing ethical demands on interpersonal, institutional and gendered fronts.

Davey, who was battling his own demons of vulnerability and self-harm as well as broader violence, expressed irritation about others discussing their scars with me: "I told him he shouldn't do that to you, Miss." He was dismissive of behaviour he saw as often characterized by a bid for attention and therefore manipulative:

'They only do it for the sympathy. What they'll find is people will start self-harming if they've got no tobacco or maybe if they're stressed, which is understandable, but mainly if they haven't got something and they want something, they'll do it for attention.'

My own assessment was that if attention was sought that badly, there were clearly other issues at play, warranting care and support it was beyond the prisons' ability to provide. Davey's explanation brought additional insight about distinctions between the way some prisoners and staff viewed these flows of power, and my position in their streams. The officer tending to Brian had wanted me to "see it all" to ensure I understood. Prisoners often wanted to limit my exposure, warning me to avoid unpleasantness or chiding one another – as Davey did upon seeing someone showing me their self-harm scars. Being the willing emotional mark often paid richly in terms of the understanding it extended me, an observation which accompanied keen awareness there was power in bearing witness; in being willing, and prepared, to look and listen. Listening on open terms also extended power to those whose voices were amplified by their hearing, just as there is power in refusing to (Mathieson, 2005). Exercising this sensitivity could be a fraught balance. On one occasion I was abandoned in the newly created special unit for those who found it difficult on the regular wing. A means of easing pressure on care and segregation as well as better catering for the diverse range of needs of the Midtown population. I fell into conversation with Terry (aka Bulldog), who had not long ago lost his daughter. The nature of his offence had complicated applications for compassionate release to attend her funeral, so he told me. Admiring her photographs while expressing sympathy for this monumental loss, I was somewhat startled when these were rapidly substituted for an extensive collection of pictures of women's feet. Stood at the entrance to his cell I found it difficult to effect a speedy exit from a conversation that had swerved from grief to foot fetish in the disorientating blink of an eye.

Locked in

After a time, I asked the No. 1 if he might be prepared to participate in an interview. I very much wanted to do this in a cell and was concerned he would refuse me. Rather than being a crass, tokenistic gesture the thought was to listen to how the prison sounded from within a pad. My idea was that this might function as a method of sound elicitation, prompting reflections from the No. 1's perspective. I was keen to assess their meeting points and deviations with those he presided over. When the time came, he expressed reluctance to be seen being locked away in a cell with me on the main wing. He reasoned it might prove disruptive. I am sure it would have done, though I had not intended for us to be seen (nor had I thought about the consequences of being heard). I had, again, failed to account for the complications of navigating around the regime. A recently vacated cell was found on the First-Night Centre as an alternative. Here we would only be observed by a handful of men, too shell-shocked from their recent arrival, and too few to cause much of a stir.

He was angry at the state the cell had been left in, expressing dismay that it had not been cleaned prior to the arrival of the next unfortunate occupant. I wondered if perhaps our commandeering it had prevented the usual routine being accomplished. He proceeded with a kind of filth-inventory as I took stock of the vague traces of those who had spent time here before us. Etched names and 'tags', the odd message, crumbs of tobacco and unidentifiable detritus. The absence of any sense of home left by whoever had last, however briefly, lived here somehow made the walls feel closer. I was so absorbed in these thoughts it took me a moment to register the ridiculous smallness of this barely room. The No. 1 was a particularly large man that made jointly inhabiting this space almost comically intimate. We were kindly furnished with cups of coffee, brought by an officer. An unusual occurrence which both emphasized the status of my interviewee and added an additional incongruent note of domesticity. Men were often out on the First-Night Centre, attending to the various matters arising from landing; rattling from withdrawal, bartering for necessities, examining welcome packs meant to tide new arrivals over before the transfer of credit for canteen, or attending inductions. Our arrival caused more kerfuffle than anticipated as curious faces appeared in the doorway. Seeing this, an officer decided to shield us from prying eyes by locking us in and closing the hatch (a small window in the cell door, shuttered from the outside).

Being in a cell and locked into one are decidedly different experiences. I am not for one minute suggesting I have any idea what it is like to be locked in with a stranger at such close quarters for 23 hours a day. I was not expecting to be locked in at all and was taken aback by the strength of gratitude and reassurance the No. 1's presence elicited. The meagre dimensions of the cell shaped an intimate tone to our conversation, much of which I did not transcribe and will not repeat. The interview went on longer than expected. When we got up to leave, we realized we could not. He could not immediately locate the cell bell to summon attention and panic gently rose as, listening out, we could not identify the reassuring sounds of radio or keys. I began to worry. I had consumed both coffee and water during our chat and was beginning to feel the pressure. It dawned on me I might have to pee in front of him. The meagre partition between uncovered toilet and rest of the cell offered no modesty. I was all for sharing confidences but less thrilled about the prospect of sharing bodily functions. "Do you want out, want me to call an officer?" shouted Richey from next door. I can only assume he could hear the cessation of mumbled conversation and sensed a shift in the tone of our exchange, an ending perhaps? The shift in auditory perception represented by this episode reinforced what the men had told me about how sound could heighten anxiety and powerlessness, just as it could shift senses of proximity.

Rivulets and flows of power ran in complex curves and lines through interpersonal relationships and exchanges. Heightening awareness of the need to navigate these with care and attentiveness did nothing to diminish the force of emotional fallout. Stevie expected a police welcoming committee to be waiting for him at the gate when he was released.[2] Much to everyone's surprise he went on his way, but not long afterwards Lugs told me he had heard Stevie was back on "the gear". I found myself scrutinizing human bundles in doorways around town for his face. I still do this when I return, three years later. The emotional afterimage of my time at Midtown is still with me. Perhaps it is more difficult to leave behind in a place whose relationships with the surrounding community are so dense and long-standing. This emotional stain,[3] while utterly distinct from the stigma clinging to those who linger in these spaces, deepens an appreciation of the ways it stubbornly sticks.

8

Kackerlackas

The more I ventured outside of the core day, the more acute my awareness of how much time was spent holding breath, crossing fingers and hoping everyone had survived through the night. As my familiarity grew, my sense of 'the count' and the various points of the day this was conducted sharpened, a rhythm within a rhythm, and core strand of the prison routine. This altered my own perception. There was an imposition of the prison upon those touched by the residue of residing in its times and spaces that resisted attempts to contain and account for it. Power was conveyed here, not merely between people but through the grimy walls, the eerie echoes from dark corners, lingering unpleasant smells from straining pipes.

Kackerlacka is the Swedish for cockroach. Its pleasing onomatopoeia resonates with the itching unpleasantness of the creature it denotes, and prompts thinking about how sound and other sensory aspects of life convey stigma and exclusion from associations with particular spaces. As the hubbub from the men and their activities receded into darkening shadows, common spaces were reclaimed by the mice and cockroaches. Staying in the prison brought me into intimate proximity with sensory components of stigma amplified in the enforced solitude and constrictions of night-time, as well as its periodic, anguished interruptions. Occupying these times and spaces at Midtown prompted wider considerations of stigma and stain (Ievins, 2023), and how these social processes interact with the prison soundscape. Listening to the shifting sense of space, at different points of the day, made the mutually constitutive relationship between space, sound and stigma more audible. As understanding of these aspects of life grew, so too did the points of convergence in experience of stigma, and divergence in coping mechanisms between staff and prisoners.

Geographies of emotion and exclusion

Emotional geographies of prison spaces shift, not only over different zones as Crewe et al note (2014), but also at different times of day. Listening to prison spaces over a wider period of daily activity (and lack of it once the day's regime had been completed and the prison shifted to night patrol) added definition and texture to understanding how these spaces were experienced.

While times and points of the regime shaped social practices around sound and space, the complexity of these relationships was enhanced by the way different parts of the prison inflected the soundscape and the degree of stigma attached to different populations. Units in the basement of the prison were particularly fraught emotional zones. Both the Vulnerable Prisoner Unit (Veeps) and the Segregation and Care Unit (Seg) were in the dark bowels of the prison, separated by metal gates. The subterranean location of these units at Midtown reinforced perceptions of status in the prison hierarchy.[1] Those on the Veeps were often collectively referred to as 'nonces' (a slang term for person convicted of a sex offence), despite broad recognition that this was frequently not the case. In Seg, there was a more complex system of stratification loosely based around whether an individual was placed there for protection or punishment. Assignment to particular roles in the prison emphasized the significance of these personal designations, as Officer Tone reflected:

'At one point the First-Night Centre was there, where the VPU is, so it was like off the bus, through this portcullis, into reception, downstairs where there's no natural light ... I didn't even think about it until someone pointed that out to me, how does that affect a person, going into the dungeon, down into the bottom of the dungeon, drab and dreary.'

Tone merged pondering about the effects of this environment on those in his care with observations from his own experience (he had recently moved from his role in Seg, following customary rotation). His observations of the impact of spending time in such places was echoed by Stevie's description when I asked how he would describe the prison: "Just shit holes. Grotty, horrible places, not nice at all. But you do get jails that are a lot comfier. This, this is just a shit jail, but it's alright cos it's local, that's it."

While Tone did not allude to sound at this point, the closed spaces in the basement of the prison were shaped by their location in the wider prison. Sound echoed around the main body of the prison but here those sounds were distorted by their journey through ceiling and stairs, increasing the sense of enclosure. Boyd echoed this assessment: "That's enough to do anyone's head in down there, it is, does your head in. People screaming all the time and does your head in. I wouldn't mind but I just couldn't see anyone." Interrogating the soundscape of HMP Midtown and how it was experienced illustrated that the prison was comprised not of one, monolithic zone of exclusion but a series of concentric, stigmatized layers. Sykes describes the experience of imprisonment as being characterized by the stain of physical and social exclusion from 'decent' society (1958: 67). The Midtown soundscape reverberated with a complex emotional topography, assigning differing degrees of stigma depending on the extent to which the individual was able to navigate the social complexities which shaped and reflected prison spaces.

Failing to attend to personal hygiene was greeted with disapprobation by prisoners. Not maintaining personal standards was analogous to moral failing. Keeping clean in a place with limited access to soap, showers and cleaning materials required considerable effort. Washing, changing and travelling routines indicated the importance of shedding rituals for staff. Rituals that those without divisions between work and home, public and private were unable to enact. Sources of contaminative potential proliferated the prison.

> Quite apart from the impact of living within razor wire, was the potential effect of a lack of visual stimuli, in a horizon dominated by metallic greys and institutional blues. Midtown was, to my eyes, and those of the prisoners I discussed it with, irrefutably dirty, greasy to the touch. Spending the night, I was not only greeted by the impossibility of finding anywhere comfy to perch but was forced to compete for the rare suitable surface with remnants of several meals. Limp lettuce, crumbs of unknown provenance, uninviting sheens of grease. While interviewing Lugs in a fortuitously empty office on the wing, he noted the bucket of dirty grates lifted from one of the shower/toilet areas which had been deposited an inch or so behind me in an equally grimy bucket. They remained untended to, coated in an accumulation of hair, skin and assorted slime, I assume this was mixed with a variety of bodily fluids but did not investigate further. He urged me not to touch or lean back too far lest I got too close to its contents. Offices too were coated in black dust and grease. And yet, this was far cleaner than it had been, and this improvement was spoken of with pride. (Fieldnotes)

Lugs was keen to demonstrate his cleanliness,[2] not only of his person but also the spaces he moved through, and equally keen to shield me from contamination. This observation echoed distinctions between Davey and the officer alluded to in the previous chapter. Staff encouraged me to get down with them into the dirt, while prisoners repeatedly demonstrated a desire to protect me from it. These distinctions were analogous to the way different groups navigated social systems of moral contamination. These differences were shaped by identities forged through interactions with spaces, both inside and out. Staff were keen to impress the stain of their dirty work whereas prisoners often wanted to reduce my exposure to sources of pollution. My proximity to the outside was an important conduit for relaying respective positions in the matrices of moral contaminants signified and amplified by grimy surfaces and perpetual assaults on personal dignity.

"Going for a shit, Sir?"

Prison scholars have documented the ways in which the lack of distinction between backstage and front-stage zones for performing identity constitute an assault on the self. While this is open to the charge of a rather literal reading of Goffman's dramaturgical analogy, the lack of space and privacy were a continual source of discomfort. Many in prison are required to share a cell where they can spend up to 23 hours a day. In HMP Midtown, with its Victorian build, cramped conditions and single-wing design, the sensation of being, quite literally, on top of one another presented a range of challenges. Men discussed a range of associated problems from the discomfort of living with a flatulent or snoring pad mate to the indignity of shared, lidless, doorless toilets. In daily life the deprivations of privacy and dignity were keenly felt, constituting an additional arena in which disparities of power were contested and displayed. Sound enhanced the constant sense of intrusion upon privacy, emphasizing associations between sound and stigma. The nakedness of prison life was both shaped and reflected by the soundscape; there was an aural dimension to social stigma as well as strategies for its avoidance and maintenance of meagre dignities. Prisoners were, understandably, frequently more sensitive to this than staff.

At Midtown the personal was frequently subject to public discussion in a way which emphasized the lack of distinction between spheres of life. Men frequently sought my opinion or sympathy on a range of medical issues from rotten teeth to a troublesome cyst, offering up their complaint for my bewildered inspection. One prisoner reported vomiting brown fluid, and later updated me to say he was waiting for surgery following a cancer diagnosis. I noted there barely seemed to be a man over 40 not complaining of sciatica from the poor prison mattresses. On my first visit to reception, a call came over the radio from the main wing; officers were to ask a prisoner if he would like to visit the sexual health clinic. Discretely. 'The irony of this seems lost' (fieldnotes). On another occasion, on the wing, officers speculated about the usefulness of a pair of boxers, given their size; "They won't keep much in". "I think that's the point" responded the second, "good and roomy". The first explained to me a prisoner required an additional pair as he had a boil on his bum. He went on to explain the reason for getting through such high levels of toilet paper: "They masturbate a lot" (Officer McCafferty). This lack of privacy reflects Goffman's processes of mortification; protective layers of privacy and dignity are eroded by consistent, often involuntary exposure of intimate business to and with the broader community. Long-term institutionalization could be apparent from distracted habits displayed on the wing. Hands perpetually down the front of pants was a sign of someone who had spent too much of their often-young life in an environment where they might be looked upon in their most private moments. Two pairs of underpants were also a means of keeping possessions safe or transporting contraband around the prison. Quite possibly, juggling testicles was also a means of suggesting they might be 'packing' additional items. Performative masculinities in a place of continual violence had layered and complex meanings indicating both resistance to, and incorporation of, the institution into bodily presentations.

Forced proximity is bound up with processes of 'contamination' which impacted on perceptions of self for prisoners as well as staff:

> [T]he inmate undergoes mortification of the self by contaminative exposure of the physical kind, but this must be amplified: when the agency of contamination is another human being, the inmate is in addition contaminated by forced interpersonal contact and, in consequence, a forced social relationship. (Goffman, 1961: 35)

Goffman specifically talks about effects of a lack of space and separation from others on the 'inmate'. But staff too were forced into discomforting proximity with those they oversaw (as well as one another). Blurring of boundaries could extend beyond the wall. Prisoners frequently had intimate knowledge of the personal lives of officers, sometimes gleaned from what they had witnessed on the landings or while on the out; sexual relationships between officers, impending divorce, recreational drug use, alcoholism. Elisions between public and private lives, just as between inside and out, worked in multiple directions. It was often difficult to inhabit these spaces without contributing to these processes. I could avert my gaze and keep my hands to myself. I could stay out of the range of smells too, to an extent, but it was more difficult to exclude auditory components of private life. Witnessing staff washing urgently to reduce the risk of contracting scabies following the routine strip, search and change for those coming through reception, encroached on the privacy of its subject. Talking to an education officer while accompanying a prisoner to the loo, my inadequate attempts to raise my voice to cover the sound of urinating, compounded my sense of intrusiveness on the man trying to have a pee in private, though I did not ask about it for obvious reasons.

Complicated rules governing business, discretion and privacy were difficult to navigate. The prisoners, for whom such indignities were commonplace, were keenly aware of how powerful a tool this could be when turned on staff to upend the order. Officers on duty on the wing were usually required to stay there. There was a staff toilet on the wing, receiving a constant stream of traffic. While prisoners were out, trips to the loo were often accompanied by shouts of "Going for a shit Sir/Miss?" Depriving staff of privacy was a means of subjecting staff to the intrusiveness of the prison environment in a way which challenged the social ordering, a rebalancing of power which reflected the keenness with which such deprivations were felt (Shwartz, 1972).

Stain and stigma

When staying late I noted many staff used the loud hand dryers throughout the night, an instance of institutional thoughtlessness which amplified the extent to which power permeated the most mundane minutiae of prison life. This also offered a triumphant sonic counterpoint to the mocking tones that greeted their using the facilities during the day. That this might interrupt sleep and disturb peace either did not occur or was not considered important. It seems somewhat facile to suggest these complex contestations of power and shame could be partially resolved with the introduction of a towel.

The complexity of associations between sound, privacy and order at Midtown demonstrated the significance of distinctions between public and private, dirt and purity which frame social life (Douglas, 1966). Where there is dirt, Douglas asserts, there is a system (1966: 36). What might this indicate about the fragility and intricacy of systems of social order in a place characterized by the relentless futility of battling its filth, both literally and figuratively? Attending to sensorial aspects of prison life renders systems of taint and stigma palpable. Aural aspects of prison life brought definition to the murky intricacies of stigma and taint, amplifying points of shared experience as well as separation. Staff frequently failed to recognize the power bound up in their failures to observe the dignity of those in their charge. However, these inescapable aspects of prison life served to reinforce the psychological taint of their occupational culture. Prison work was dirty work (Garrihy, 2022).

The nakedness of life inside, where people shit, shower, grieve and love nose-to-nose with countless others, intruded upon the identities of those who battled to maintain the protective membrane between their inner world and that of the prison. Pickering and Rice (2017) revisit Douglas' work to explore how sound studies can enhance understanding of purity and danger, emphasizing the transgressive and disruptive qualities of sound. Exploring the prison soundscape lends greater understanding to the political and subjective nature of 'noise' and the processes determining what is 'sound out of place' as well as the differential power of those bound up in them. Maintaining distinctions between public and private realms of life posed particularly sharp challenges in the cramped and overcrowded conditions of HMP Midtown, deepening discomfort and senses of stigma in its spaces (Goffman, 1961). Prisoners often expressed outrage at the prospect of "catching AIDS" from both people and items. Being furnished with plastic crockery of unknown provenance was a particular source of anxiety, and occasional rage. More than once I was confronted with the odd tirade about this by someone understandably upset about their receipt of a hastily located grubby bowl, the only receptacle available to contain their dinner. This emphasized the importance of an under-explored aspect of Goffman's mortifications. Prisoners have little ability to curate their sensory experience, but this extends to the food they eat and air they breathe. The prison is literally taken into incarcerated bodies. There are few more profound illustrations of the futility of attempts to resist stigma than these protestations. These literal intrusions carried moral signification. Prisoners were forced to consume the danger of the place and, through these practices, made one with it.

Immersion in the soundscape at night emphasized the inhospitable, sharp, grubby edges of the prison. This was instructive for what it revealed about the relationship between internal worlds and prison spaces. Sound was a means of elucidating the relationship between these spaces and the selves of those that lived and worked within them. Those working at Midtown were afforded a greater ability to compartmentalize their temporal experience than those who could not go home. This temporal compartmentalization shaped their relationship with space and place. Repeated attempts of prisoners to communicate moral distance from the place echoed this distinction. For staff the converse manifested in their efforts to collapse it, to make me one of them by bringing me into the dirt.

9

A Kettle, a Penguin and a Word Arrow

Qualitative prisons research is characterized by emotionally intensive edgework and the continual need to demonstrate adherence to risk logics which may be at stark odds with personal ethos (Kilty and Fayter, 2023). Practices in daily prison life frequently proved irreconcilable with my own ethics. Personal ethics did not always sit comfortably alongside professional ideals. Treading lightly around rules and rituals of moral contamination, discomforting intimacies and the demands of the institution presented continual challenges which could deflect attention from other aspects of prison life. Navigating the intricacies of unspoken rules and endless regulations permeated all aspects of life inside. The complex matrices of codes and systems, both formal and informal, extended into all manner of strange and seemingly inconsequential corners of interaction. Matters of etiquette were sometimes inconsistent with more formal directions. Working out which were important, for whom, and in what circumstances was often confusing and counterintuitive.

Uncertainty about how to proceed in an array of exchanges heightened anxiety about the potential for mis-stepping – reflections both of a personal tendency and the tense atmosphere permeating much of the prison, most of the time. Preoccupation with concerns that seemed to present the potential for suspending my access could deflect focus from more routine interactions with those who lacked the power to make such decisions, and which were therefore the most important to honour. Here too, I found myself proceeding gingerly, a means of displaying thoughtfulness and respect on all sides. Examining these exchanges is useful for assessing how far institutional logics creep into the most innocent and trivial of interactions. This chapter features three illustrative examples, as well as my instinctive recognition of the need for a transparency which sometimes descended into farce. These everyday conversations about a kettle, a penguin and a word arrow explore the delicacy of navigating the intricate matrices of sanctions and expectations.

What does this indicate about up-close practice as a prison researcher and the murky lines between participant and observer?

A kettle

What you are allowed in your possession, in what quantity and in what circumstances are all a matter of rigorous regulation in prison. Such heavy emphasis on material items of any description loads them with symbolic value and meaning. In addition, *things* are subject to intense scrutiny and subscription, representing possible security breaches on many fronts. Items can signify the recipient is being 'groomed' or smuggling contraband in, or correspondence out of the prison. The grave implications of this can sometimes imbue mundane transactions with a violent charge. While undergoing security training in another prison, the group were subject to a 20-minute instruction about the importance of not sharing biscuits. These considerations ensure that navigation around discussion, possession and transaction of *things* becomes an ethically laden process. Urfan spent our entire exchange in a heightened emotional state. He had never been to prison before and engaged in an extensive cataloguing of the indignities he had experienced since being incarcerated. Chief among these hardships was the broken kettle in his cell which prevented him from making his older pad mate a cup of tea. Despite asking staff repeatedly, his kettle situation remained unresolved. He had lost his social standing alongside his freedom. He was unable to practice his faith as he wished, his vegetarianism frequently left him existing on a diet of potatoes, bread and margarine, and he expressed recurring terror at the prospect of coming out of his cell. But not being able to have a cup of tea was the final straw. In conversation with Cam, I referred to the kettle affair, thinking he would be able to point me in the direction of a functioning one. "Tell me who it is Miss, I have a spare, I'll go give him one" was his response. When I next saw Urfan, he was wearing a beautific expression. It was the first time I had seen him smile. I interfered in daily life, in a way which in many senses constituted an ethical breach and crossed my fingers there were no unseen repercussions. On the surface, this was a harmless, human gesture from one person who happened to also be a researcher, to another in need of something (Desmond, 2016). In prison though, these interactions are laden with complexity. I had meddled with the prison ecology. When all exchanges are interpreted through the lens of risk logic, little escapes being tainted by it.

A Penguin

Gifts represented another tricky area. Every effort should be made to avoid bringing anything in or out. The rules relating to any deviation from this are intricate and difficult to navigate. I spoke often with Dwane, a lifer who worked in the kitchen. He had a medical issue which had necessitated a trip to the hospital. Seeing the outside, however briefly, had made him think about life passing him by and we shared a particularly sombre reflection. Shortly afterwards he presented me with a Penguin biscuit. I was mortified and declined immediately but politely. He then gestured across the way to the kitchen where the supervisor stood, visibly nodding. Dwane had gone to some lengths to get this gift sanctioned. In an environment where people frequently receive beatings for failing to repay their tobacco debts, this Penguin represented a bit of dignity. I thanked him profusely and confessed I hadn't eaten all day. I proceeded to make a scene when exiting the gatehouse, by brandishing it at every bemused member of staff I encountered. I had permission, I assured them. It was sealed, I demonstrated. It remains unclear whether my willingness to look like a buffoon whenever I was unclear of how to proceed was a help or a hindrance. In a place where a Penguin might be construed as a grave risk, openly expressing uncertainty seemed to offer reassurance that if I did something wrong, I might at least say so.

A word arrow

One day, I found myself cornered in the library by a rather animated gentleman who was enraged about his incarceration for, as far as I could establish in the tirade, threatening his neighbour with an axe. We had various interactions about the prison, though these were mostly quite perfunctory save for discussions about his health issues. I am not sure if I ever caught his name, but he held the distinction of having offered to share his sardines with me in a manner so unfeasibly sinister they are forever associated in my mind. He was at pains to emphasize he had not been threatening this individual but had merely happened to be holding it when the latest in a string of rather heated interactions occurred. We covered a lot of ground, including a variety of health concerns and his dissatisfaction with his probation officer as I anxiously entreated him to bear in mind we were in the library. This greatly amused everyone present who seemed to enjoy my painful education (I subsequently approached the library with caution and attempted to position myself where I could make a swift exit, but it wasn't the last time I was cornered by someone who wanted to talk about all the things, very loudly). Following this, Robert invited me to join him and the librarian doing a word arrow. It was a welcome relief. Despite my rather childish competitiveness in completing the word puzzle with someone who was working on their literacy skills, we had a very calming time with occasional contributions from the odd passer-by. Library closing time was approaching so we were forced to abandon our activities. Our oasis of convivial calm was punctured by the intrusions of the prison regime, and we reluctantly returned to the wing.

The doorway of the library was a portal between timeless peace and the relentless maelstrom of life on the wing; disparate spaces separated by mere inches. Shortly afterwards Robert approached me. The librarians sometimes gave the prisoners photocopied word arrows to do in their cells over the lunch lock-up and he wished to gift me a spare which he had fetched from his cell for me, so I could do it over my own dinner. I realized immediately that taking a piece of paper from a prisoner could easily be misconstrued.

Offers of phone numbers, attempts to borrow my fieldnotes book to write them in or give me pieces of paper were commonplace. I always made it clear I would not accept them, nor would I let my notebook out of my possession. These were often merely expressions of humanity, moments of snatched hetero-sociality or teasing attempts to see how far I could be pushed. They comprised the everyday tapestry of life inside, but also represented disregard for prison rules, possibly (I never looked at these notes so I cannot say) including illicit phones. While these proliferate in prisons in various forms and technological capacities, being caught in possession of one can carry an additional two-year sentence.[1] These notes were at once harmless, since I was never going to take them and made this clear, and gravely important. I recognized the potential for misunderstanding accepting the offer of a spare word puzzle could lead to. Nevertheless, the gift represented a significant and thoughtful transaction. I wanted to honour the spirit in which it was given, so went about demonstrating there was nothing written on it to the somewhat irritated officer in charge.

In many ways these instances were not important. Detailing them illustrates the difficulty behaving ethically and honourably on all fronts can represent. In hindsight somewhat trivial, I agonized over each at the time, both worried about offending anyone and being viewed as a security risk.

Breaking silence

When applying for clearance to conduct research in prison it is necessary to demonstrate an intention to observe prison rules. These extend to limiting confidence to matters which do not infringe on said rules. My consent forms and posters reiterated the limits of any undertaking to keep information to myself: 'Intention to break the prison rules, to hurt yourself or other people will be reported.' Reminding some of the men not to put me in an awkward position was a common occurrence, and largely performative since it did little to prevent anyone from saying whatever they wished. My frequent admonishments were met with a mimicking chorus: "Is it inappropriate Miss? Everything's inappropriate!"

I was told about plans to hurt an officer and felt obliged to pass this on to security. I was told by several people at once, and did not know their names, so could not identify the source of this information. A couple of days later this officer was the subject of a potting.[2] A few weeks after that he was assaulted. Having – somewhat – successfully navigated the dilemma of 'grassing' by not revealing the source, I now felt conflicted for a different reason. Developing events had vindicated my small indiscretion and I comforted myself with the knowledge I had not been led wrong. I had found an opportunity to demonstrate my willingness to abide by the rules without sacrificing confidences or relationships. I felt sympathy for the various misfortunes that befell this officer. Only in retrospect did I appreciate my foolishness for imagining the likelihood of these events unfolding was not plainly apparent to the broader community. One of the recent, staff, intake from the nearby young offender institution (YOI) which was closing, he had failed to moderate his manner, regularly treating prisoners with disdain and, as some saw it, disrespect. He had chided me for being too polite – "You're too nice to them. Give them an inch, and they will take a mile" he warned, knowingly. I had taken note of a different warning though in truth I only missed the potting, which took place exactly where I would normally be standing, because of a hatred of early starts: "You don't know what's going to happen, everyone seems to be getting shitted up nowadays. Don't stand next to the officers" (Ned).

I discerned some cross-over between officers and prisoners in unspoken rules covering 'grassing' which indicated more nuance than is often represented in the literature. Alerting people to something you had heard was warmly received, but the giving of names and specifics less so. Various prisoners, particularly those serving longer sentences, enjoyed reasonable relationships with some officers. On occasion, this extended to the odd blind eye to possession of illicit items on the understanding peace would be kept. Like many other arrangements, these were tenuous and ad hoc. Another instance of informal processes of mutual investment in order, and the safety – as well as various other perks – which underpinned it.

Taking it, and giving it back

A prison runs on order and control. It is therefore unsurprising to be subject to occasional censure. Knowing how to respond presented its own sets of social and ethical challenges. One morning, I arrived in the midst of the second of two incidents that morning. The governor greeted me: "Now's not a good time, fuck off and try again later." I saluted and turned tail, gingerly trying my luck two hours later, keen to sense the aftermath of a disrupted day. As the heat took hold, I ventured out on to the exercise yard with the men. On the first occasion I walked around in the customary anti-clockwise fashion for the hour of exercise. On the second I spoke to a female officer on duty out there. On the third, there was an atmosphere outside. Five minutes in an officer approached me and indicated security had informed him I had to leave via his earpiece. I sheepishly scurried inside. When the men returned and asked where I had gone, I informed them I'd been told off. Several responded by saying: "It happens to us all, it was bound to happen to you eventually, your turn." Answering that I was unsure when asked what I had done seemed to validate perceptions of power as arbitrary, opaque and inconsistent. That I was subject to it too seemed to cement my position among the prison community though following orders and looking suitably embarrassed also seemed to earn me some latitude from staff.

There were other occasions when I felt it necessary to be a little less contrite. On one occasion a prisoner became verbally abusive and threatening following a case of mistaken identity – a female officer had called others in, thinking a play scuffle was a fight, the only woman in his eyeline, he assumed it was me. I automatically challenged him, angered by his display of brutish disrespect. I was embarrassed by my inappropriate response, but a member of staff immediately remarked: "Your London came out then" while laughing. Standing ground in this instance earned me a little respect. The man later approached me and apologized before shaking my hand. He shook my hand every time he passed from that point on.

I never caught his name, or at least I failed to write it down, but I enjoyed the company of the officer frequently in charge on the Veeps. We spoke often, but never as long or as in as much depth as I would have liked. I felt we might have developed good terms given another year or so. While prisoners seemed to decide whether to speak with you on a somewhat collective and speedy basis, officers only ever made these decisions individually and usually over a considerable period. Not long after I arrived, he asked how I was settling in. I expressed anxiety about opening doors without knowing exactly what lay behind them and he responded: "It doesn't matter, as long as you lock them behind you" (fieldnotes). His reassuring warmth was quite typical of our encounters. I found he answered my rather guileless candour with openness of his own. One day I had borrowed a t-shirt while on the wing. It did not leave the wing with me but potentially represented security concerns. He was not on the main wing but saw me and expressed disapproval until I explained. I had very much wanted to catch someone as I had arranged to speak with them. Mooch informed me the prison lights made my shirt see-through. I either had to leave and miss the small window of opportunity afforded by that point of the regime, risk causing disruption while unknown numbers caught wind of my ridiculous faux pas or cover up, but what with? The significance of transparency extended way beyond my foolish sartorial choices. Though, much like my shirt, practices designed to minimize risk were as much in the performance of being seen to do so. In a place where preoccupations with security are privileged over all else, you can be forgiven for not anticipating what you walk into, just as long as you lock the door behind you. During a debrief with the No. 1 he told me

I had not been the subject of a single intelligence report. I remain unsure if this was because I aroused no serious concern or was indicative of the culture of the prison. I encountered a junior officer being informed about what intelligence reports were by more senior staff, following a prisoner describing his bedroom to him (such are the hazards of local prison life) while collecting my keys. Perhaps no one inclined to do so knew how to file them.

10

Emotional Contagion

My anxiety about accidentally falling afoul of the rules echoed the tense feeling on the wing. A number of those I spoke with referred to the prison environment as "not for everyone" (No. 1). Ronald had worked at Midtown for many years. His precise function, like his location, remained unclear to me though I gathered he maintained things and he usually wore overalls. Friendly and warm, we would often talk though I never did track him down for the interview he expressed keenness to engage in. He would reappear like a benign ghost, only to disappear for long stretches – perhaps in some corner I rarely entered. He was interested in what I was doing, and I sought to explain to him. He described having taken new recruits around, only to realize they "were not cut out" for the prison. While I was at Midtown there were several occasions when people visited Midtown only to express discomfort and a desire to leave. A substance use support worker was being shown around the prison by Joanne with a view to joining her for work. Joanne was doing her customary errand running while she was on the wing and left her in my company while she did so. I asked her how she was finding the prison – she answered: "Noisy, very noisy, and claustrophobic. It's not for me, I won't be coming here." There was a feel to this place, as there is in other prisons. The soundscape rattled and banged with high emotion.

The atmosphere on the wing could change rapidly, its concentrated population and cramped corners combining to create an intense microclimate. As Tonk explained: "You get loads of different emotions in here as well, like people are happy, people are sad, people are angry, frustrated, stressed, all, everyone's different you know what I'm saying?" Other pressures could also bring to bear on the balance of the fragile social ecology. Disruptive individuals could keep much of the prison from rest or peace. The impact of external developments could be equally profound – the prison walls were perpetually permeated by forces and events rumbling on beyond its perimeters. I draw on observations from a fraught August to reflect on how sound made emotion audible. The soundscape could carry and shape 'the feel' of the day, providing an invaluable barometer for wellbeing and stability.

Trouble rumbling

August at Midtown was heavy and close. Waves of unrest had been rippling around the country, one of the most notable being at Winson Green the previous December. Various outbreaks of trouble, much bubbling under the radar, increased numbers of those being moved around the creaking system. Each series of landings from non-local populations further irked the community, jostling in their accommodation. A local young offender institution (YOI) had shut down and small waves of redeployed staff trickled in, taking up the lockers which had travelled ahead of them, lining the corridor to the staff room as an ominous harbinger of coming disruption. Midtown staff bristled at the failure of their new colleagues to seamlessly integrate into Midtown rhythms. The taut atmosphere further ratcheted up by the introduction of the tobacco ban which had been making its way around the system. Its ripples gathered momentum throughout the prison ecology. Tempers frayed, economies were unbalanced and many using the ubiquitous mamba found themselves unable to temper its effects by mixing it as they would customarily have done before the ban sent its price rocketing. These disruptions were audible, palpable. When mamba was particularly prevalent the wing would take on a more unpredictable feel, the air sharpened with the plasticky aroma of fish food. Tommy and others had spoken of stepping over the prone forms of those incapacitated by it on the landings. Now the presence of this noxious substance was evidenced not only by the smell and 'feel' of the place, but also the sight of lurching, unsure bodies – 'spice' and 'mamba' users were often referred to as 'zombies' – being chivvied back behind the door by friends and pad mates, eager to avoid a 'nicking'.

I had not met Steve before; he had not long landed and was in the midst of a run of miserable luck he had sought to numb himself from. A big, stocky man the speed with which he greyed and hit the floor shocked me. Flanked by two men adding details to his story as his speech deserted him, me retrieving his belongings from the floor as he lost his grip, they attempted to get him steady enough to move him back in cell before he was spotted. I reflected on this when speaking with Niall, a senior officer who had not long been at Midtown but was well liked by both staff and prisoners. He had a calm, thoughtful manner which was reflected in his account of seeing his first mamba attack: "I had unlocked him for breakfast. He had his back to me, and I briefly looked away. When I looked back, he'd dropped by the toilet in an instant. He was shaking so I had thought it was epilepsy. I just picked him up and held him. It was scary."

Not long afterwards I encountered a young man in the throes of a mamba attack on my way to meet friends in town. The look of terror on his face as it possessed his lurching body was haunting. Howling as if in pain, writhing on the floor as he lost control of his bladder. I accompanied a woman over the road to tend to him, attempting to keep him safe while we waited for the ambulance. Both paramedics were visibly irritated to have been called to what was for them frustratingly routine. A woman shouted from an upstairs window, did he have a bracelet? He was obviously fitting, she inaccurately concluded. Various others attempted to administer first aid, robustly dismissing my attempt to explain this was a mamba attack. They had no frame of reference, mistaking what is unmistakable once you have seen it. Mamba was coursing through the city and its prison, as it was in other towns – contagion of a different kind.

"Burn is your currency"

Tensions were ratcheting up at Midtown, providing a staccato backdrop to the interview between Duke and I. During our conversation, we are interrupted by the sound of disturbance on the wing. The staff have sounded the emergency alarm to summon additional assistance. We cannot see much from inside the office. Fridays are 'canteen' day. A fraught day for those who will not have sufficient goods delivered to pay off debts.

Duke: It's Friday though, everybody's stressed on Fridays innit.
Me: Is it worse on Friday or worse on Monday?
Duke: Friday. Especially nowadays cos they ain't got no burn.
Me: Do you feel it?
Duke: I can feel it. I don't feel it personally, but I've always had a way of sensing tensions and shit. I keep my eye on it, but I don't really feel it. For me burns nothing, like if I don't got it I don't want it but, I don't care about nothing like that. As long as I got music on blood.
Me: I don't think it's just about burn though, is it?
Duke: Nah, I don't think it is about burn, it's more about like riots innit.
Like you come jail and you get locked behind your door and it's like, Yo, I ain't got the right to sleep in a pad on my own. I ain't got a right to stay away from somebody, I ain't got the right to come out my pad at night and go to the shop and go to the garage. I ain't got the right to go pick up a draw, smoke some weed, go get a bottle, have a drink, you get me? I ain't got the right to go see my Missus, and now they're saying you don't have the right to smoke tobacco either. You don't have the right to have lighters, you don't have the right to have incense sticks, they just take stuff. It's like they're taking everything from you. Obviously to people outside, they might not think it's a big deal but when you're inside you know from

being in jail, burn is your currency right? With burn you're alright innit, but if you ain't got burn, then obviously other things start to play … cos then you got the drug heads like the mamba heads and that, they need burn for their drugs and if they ain't got that burn then they're gonna be on pipes, and they're all gonna start dropping like flies and shit.

Duke was battling his own issues at this point, and his frustration partially reflects this though his account of ratcheting tensions echoed my own feeling, as well as others I spoke with. My fieldnotes became increasingly peppered by staff and prisoners saying "Oh, I thought it had kicked off then" expressing surprise it had not, or a sense of foreboding that it was about to, as if we were stuck in a collective, perpetual count. We were all holding our breath.

'Bubbly'

Elaine Crawley (2004) describes prison as an 'emotional arena' – a space where the nature of confinement, its heightened tension and anxiety combine to create a charged atmosphere. There are terms used as shorthand for periods of volatility in prison to describe the 'mood' or emotional climate, such as 'Bubbly' and 'Spikey'. After a few visits, my fieldnotes become littered with reflections on how the day 'feels' in relation to how it sounded ('feels quiet', 'feels calm today – feels?', 'feels stable but I have no idea what I'm basing that on … No rumble underfoot?'). This was a regular topic of conversation with members of the community, during which explanations would be offered: "spice and that. They start holding it back cos they can't afford it. That's what it is more than likely. Looking at the landings now, I know it's gonna kick off" (Wes); "Cos it were canteen sheets last night. Fridays and Mondays are the worst days in the prison" (Stretch); "Yeah, you know who's gonna kick off anyway. There's something in the air, and it's all over mamba" (Robert). Sound was frequently conflated with emotion – though sometimes for my benefit – and functioned as a means of assessing the temperature on the wing. Stretch made the association explicit when he said: "If you've got no sound, you've got no feelings." As Hemsworth (2016) argues, the emotional atmosphere of a prison can be gauged by attuning to its soundscape. The Midtown community routinely practised 'feeling the range' as they came on to the wing, whether from deeper within, or outside. Officer McKie identified sources of unrest squarely with a 'disruptive' element: "You have people influencing the attitude and conduct of others, but generally it's the disruptive ones that have a disproportionate influence on the atmosphere." It was not entirely clear how he had assessed this, since calming effects would be noticeable by the absence of trouble, but his observations supported the idea that the atmosphere could be shaped and affected by actions and behaviours within the community. Staff were equally implicated in processes of generating or spreading mood. Prisoners often complained about being shouted at and disrespected by staff, but staff could also heighten one another's anxiety. One officer came back on to the wing saying to another: "I can hear you stressing", clearly picking up on his underlying tension from familiarity with the tones of his voice.

In the highly regulated and restricted social life at Midtown, sound operated as a means of emotional transference. People echoed the emotional state of others in circumstances where they could hear, but often could not see (Nakahashi and Ohtsuki, 2015). Emotions were articulated aurally – through tone of voice, or volume, shouting, banging, whooping or singing. Feelings – attempts to articulate or think about emotion – were conveyed through sound, such as with exaggerated sighs and so forth. In this way emotions could be spread around prison spaces and 'caught' as others were infected. The shifting nature of the atmosphere was particularly notable in HMP Midtown where the deputy governor noted: "The feel of the place can change like that, you're always on your toes. I'll probably never work in a place like it again, it's unique" (No. 2). The deputy governor's assessment of the emotional climate of HMP Midtown reflected its small size and composition. The soundscape carried emotion in a place where close proximity and the inescapability of others heightened potential for infection. Sound was a vector for emotional contagion; 'a multiply determined family of social, psychophysiological and behavioural phenomena' (Hatfield et al, 1994: 7–10). Put simply, sound was a means by which emotion was conveyed and felt by others.

Earworms

At Midtown, emotions could operate like infectious earworms. Different strains were more-or-less virulent and contagious depending on the source of infection and how conducive the environment was to its spreading. Davey explained how easily emotion could spread in a confined space: "Say if you wake up to people shouting in the morning. You want to wake up naturally not to people shouting so you're gonna be pissed off all day or pissed off for a bit." The 'mood' of the place could be drastically altered by individuals. Sadness might be endured in the privacy of cell, though could equally carry and lower the mood (particularly if someone had received bad news). Anger and violence were frequently expressed at a louder volume and could therefore be heard more easily, increasing others' agitation.

Hatfield et al (1994: 11) argue that 'emotional information processing is not always accessible to conversant awareness'. Attending to sound enabled articulation of this process, providing an account of how emotion is experienced, and a lexicon for the feelings arising from it. The soundscape fulfilled an important function in HMP Midtown, operating as an emotional barometer in prison spaces. One officer would frequently ask "How's it sound?" upon walking on to the wing, to which I would always respond with an indication of the mood (Mark, Officer). Feelings of discomfort, agitation or wariness could be generated by a range of sounds, or 'noise'. These weren't necessarily directly human (shouting) or emanating from interactions between humans and their environment (banging), but rather the general soundscape. Red described Midtown: "It's one of the worst jails, the very worst … everyone's on top of each other. If someone's distressed, you get interrupted sleep for days and you can feel the tension rising." Red's observation reveals how 'feeling' was made tangible when sound was accounted for, echoing the definition of sound as a 'modality of emotion' (Hemsworth, 2016). Discussions between the writer-in-residence[1] and I on a rather testy day illustrated how excessively loud music on an otherwise flat-feeling day could be sufficient to elicit concern: "Loud, what's it hiding? I can come on here and know something's up. See, I don't like that. Straight away, why isn't anyone telling them to turn it down?" (Bear). Loud music, or an abandoned television with the volume excessively high, could denote a number of activities associated with disorder such as testing the reaction and organization of the staff, displacing attention from something going on elsewhere, or a desire to irritate. Exuberant enjoyment tended to be accompanied by other sounds which distinguished it, such as singing in chorus. In this sense it was the collection of sounds – the key of the "tune" (Derek, officer) – as well as what was absent, which denoted a 'feeling'.

Conversation with one of the prison psychologists demonstrated how the soundscape was used as a means of gauging the 'feel' of the day: "It feels kind of feisty today, something's off" (Claire, psychologist). Claire's choice of language was interesting as it imbued the atmosphere with an anthropomorphized identity of its own. Exchanges like this demonstrate the extent of preoccupation with the emotional climate of those who lived and worked within it. The feelings elicited by a 'bubbly' atmosphere were a means of gauging imminent trouble and were therefore central to safety and wellbeing. While sound provided a means of assessing the mood of the day, it also impacted on the way others experienced emotion, sending waves of feeling around the community. Emotional responses could be heard, echoing around the wings in a 'ripple effect', reverberating on others and affecting group dynamics (Barsade, 2002). Sound, then, conveyed emotion which could influence other individuals: "It can make you suicidal. It can put other people's problems in your head, and you don't need that cos you got your own. It's very noisy. When it's quiet something's going on" (Pete). Emotions were transported on the soundscape, carrying around the wing and, where resistance was low, infecting others.

'Mood hoovers'

People's emotional state could, of course, be resistant to others. Whether the influence was likely to spread or elicit corresponding feelings depended on a number of factors including role of the individual/s in the community and the nature of the interaction: "Sometimes they're shouting at you like they're stressed. You can hear like they're stressed but what have they got to be stressed about?" (Ray). Ray indicated the tone of communication with staff could elicit a correspondingly agitated reaction. "The way they talk to you" (King) was a frequent point of complaint and grievance among the prisoners, although staff had similar complaints, sometimes directed at one another. Managerial staff also referred to one or two colleagues with a reputation for moaning and lethargy which sucked good feeling from the atmosphere as 'mood hoovers'. Working and living in close proximity with a relatively small team of colleagues perhaps heightened sensitivity to those whose emotional state had an adverse effect on the working environment. Transferring to another wing or unit was not an option in the same way as it would be in other prisons for staff or prisoners. There was often nowhere to go.

While emotion could spread rapidly around the prison community, it was frequently unintentional spillover of frustration or distress. Sound was also a site for exercising or contesting power over others, by exerting influence over others' feelings and shifting the emotional temperature. Banging was perhaps the most prevalent example of this. Depending on the force and context this could give rise to a range of feelings as previously discussed, from fear and anxiety to agitation, frustration, irritation. This could have a negative impact on order since it threatened the tone of social interaction which could then interrupt flows of activity (for example, if officers moved to incapacitate a prisoner and put them behind the door following a heated exchange, this would take officers from the host of other tasks they might otherwise be attending to). On one occasion, a disgruntled prisoner kept up his banging for the entire length of association. My fieldnotes are filled with references to it that afternoon – 'still banging … still banging … Beginning to fray the nerves'. I was speaking to several distressed people for much of this period, and listening intently, with a backing track of incessant, loud banging made for an exhausting afternoon. On another occasion I spoke to an officer as they were being whistled at who responded "Oh yeah, they know what they're doing. They can change a whole atmosphere" (Irfan, officer). Assessing the temperature of the prison community by reading the soundscape was an unacknowledged aspect of jail craft, requiring an ability to 'read the room' for signs of imminent disruption and/or threats to safety.

While prisoners were frequently confined to their cell, rendered invisible by the locked door they were stuck behind, they could make their presence keenly felt by assaulting others' eardrums, and thus affecting others' emotions. This adds complexity to the relationship between power and order by illustrating the diversity of forms disruption could take. Power could be exerted over another by imposing sounds which altered emotion and mood. Listening to the fluctuations of feeling in the soundscape emphasized the fluidity of power as it was exercised in the short term, through the day. Considering sound also leads to a closer examination of the significance of emotion in prison spaces. More usually emotion is treated as a means of considering individual experiences of prison and how this impacts their trajectory rather than the way in which emotion has a broader, social dimension. Utilizing the 'sociology of the senses', beyond the mutual gaze, reveals how the members of the Midtown community engaged in social processes of meaning-making which influenced the prison ecology.

Attuning to the soundscape provided an important means of assessing the collective mood and the likelihood of trouble. As my familiarity with the soundscape grew, so too did my ability to discern the rhythms of daily coming and going at Midtown. A good day had a number of variable but broadly harmonious components; a bad one carried a discernible discordance. What was coming might be unclear, but the arrival of trouble was clearly signalled by the arrhythmia of dissonance against everyday routines.

11

Arrhythmia

Recognizing signs of trouble was not sufficient to locate its source, nor prevent it. Identifying its qualities, however, provided a means of preparation. For staff this could mean taking extra care and deploying at different points around the wing; for prisoners – who often had a more developed sense of where it was coming from – this was similarly a cue for standing by. A variety of terms and rationales for taking the temperature of the day were used but reading the emotional range in the soundscape formed part of the daily routine for many at Midtown.

The soundscape offered a means of gauging the stability of the social climate and was integral to the ecology of survival for the broader community (Toch, 1992). Staff, uniformed staff particularly, as well as prisoners, relied on their ability to diagnose the likelihood of disruption as a means of keeping safe. These abilities were a vital, if largely unacknowledged, aspect of jail craft, allowing officers some sense of what they were walking into. The broader emotional climate could be discerned from the shifting soundscape, so too could disruption to stable rhythms and the onset of violence which threated the safety of all on the wing (Herrity, 2021). I draw from fieldnotes from two incidents to illustrate the qualities of bad days in which the arrhythmia of a disrupted regime rippled through the prison.

If a 'good' day has a particular set of sounds, so too does a 'bad' one: "The noise, innit like heat rises, noise rises" (Lugs). Arrhythmia refers to rhythms in a discordant state. Lefebvre defines arrhythmia as rhythms in dissonance: 'there is suffering, a pathological state (of which arrhythmia is generally at the same time, symptom, cause and effect)" (2004: 16). This is a useful means of conceptualizing what the soundscape of a bad day indicates:

> 'The atmosphere in the jail? Yeah, definitely. Yeah. I can relay a story to you. This happened on the 12th of July 2015, and we've got a lot of new staff ... and I was on landing three with one of the other more experienced staff ... and I walked on, and I said: "There's sommat not right here. It doesn't feel right." I said "Who are you working with

today?" and he told me, and I said, I says: "Look, I'll watch your back and you watch my back even though we're on different landings." And that morning I got assaulted three times, broke my ribs and was involved in five incidents … and that was just a feeling as I walked on to the wing. I don't know how I can explain that tension, or how you can feel that, but you could. Sometimes there is no sound. It's just a nothing. It's just a void but you sense it, you sense that there's something amiss. Because it's different. The noise is different.' (Officer Rose)

As Officer Rose confirmed, there was a different aural quality to the day which conveyed the emotional climate. Assessing its qualities provided indications of whether the regime was ticking over, or if disruption was likely. Staff knew well what this sounded like:

'An ordinary is sort of a nice, bubbly noise. You might hear a little bit of music in the background, and people are chatting and that. And sometimes the prisoners'll shout to you, and you know, it's a happy noise that is. But when things get a bit, you know, strained, it's a bit more, like I said the noise drops, and it's a different sort of noise. I can't explain to you what I mean.' (Kathleen, officer)

Officers sometimes expressed discomfort or exasperation when invited to describe what a good/bad day sounded like. Officer Rose in particular (who I came to get on with quite well) got rather grumpy with me, dismissively suggesting there was no way to identify a bad day. He then proceeded to describe these qualities with considerable thoughtfulness. Despite some resistance to this line of enquiry they were all able to identify sounds which signalled the 'mood' on the wing, both in interview and conversation. Given the near unanimity with which people in HMP Midtown were able to describe feelings, emotions, moods in terms of sound it seems more likely initial discomfort stemmed from a lack of immediate vocabulary for doing so, and the unusual nature of the task. They frequently spoke of a 'feeling' before reflecting on its aural qualities. Both staff and prisoners elaborately articulated what it sounded like when things went wrong:

'Sharp, sharp sounds. You can feel it. The wing feels there's a bit of a stress … people walk around differently, there's certain prisoners who walk around in a certain way. There's certain sharper, louder sounds that are out of sync with everything else … cos when everything's running correctly there's like a pattern of noises that just fit in together; people are moving around all this kind of stuff, and then if something kicks off, if someone kicks off then there's a peak in that noise and then certain, in a certain pitch and you. Bang. Straight away, you know? Oi YOU.' (Derek, officer)

'You just see everyone running, watching the fight. And it's just stupid. And then you see the way it is, so the atmosphere goes quiet, and after they start going "Raaaa", it goes up.' (Jack)

Particular varieties in movement indicated something was afoot. Lots of activity back and forth along the landings, huddles in corners, constituted rhythms discordant with the routine. These behaviours disrupted the usual rhythms of everyday life inside, providing cues to potential threats to safety. There was a discordant symphony of sounds which indicated trouble or shady activity. People clustering around the door to the First-Night Centre generally indicated the anticipated arrival of someone packing.[1] These huddles would happen during the evening meal, when those on the First-Night Centre came through to collect their dinner. The effect was marked as it disrupted the rhythm of men moving between landing, to servery, to landing, to cell. These behaviours were not absent on a more stable day, but rather worked within and around the daily routine rather than against it.

Rhythms of violence

A violent incident had its own soundtrack. Hushed, prickly quiet, subtle changes in movement and disruptions of rhythm followed by a whoosh of voices and action. Men's voices, rubber soles struggling for purchase on shiny floors, congregating in groups and corners. Much 'business' was conducted behind cell doors, away from cameras, prying eyes and the risk of punishment, as indicated by testimony of numerous prisoners. What could be seen was either a spontaneous flare-up or performative – instrumental at least as much as it was expressive. Staff were not immune from this – a hard line taken in a rushed moment would have to be backed up with action to ward off the potential for loss of face. Feet on lino was a significant aural marker of trouble since there was very little reason to rush. No one was going anywhere (and the few who attempted this were decked out in humiliating, harlequin like clothing to indicate they presented an escape risk). Staff shoes, being part of the uniform, are made from a narrow range of materials. When they moved in to twist someone up[2] they scuffed on the floor, chains jangling as they worked in concert. It was also apparent when the rhythms of the day had been disrupted to the point of interfering with staff's ability to work together: 'Not in rhythm with themselves. Bumping into one another. Not working in concert, desynchronized' (fieldnotes).

'Sitting in the office in the Segregation.[3] And, you can't hear what people are saying if they're on the threes, but when there's a certain sound of, erm, jeering I suppose ... Jeering is just never good. So you're trying to respond to that, you can identify that quite quickly. And then the movement of feet. The rapid movement of feet. So literally when you're downstairs you can hear somebody upstairs moving faster than they should, so you start to pick up on it.' (Tone, officer)

Officers at Midtown listened for anomalies or disruptions to the usual rhythmic ebb and flow, for movement out of speed and out of place. While unacknowledged, listening formed an important part of the officer skill set. Sound was used to interpret aural cues to action for staff, implicating sound in processes of security and safety, integral to the ecology of survival for staff as well as prisoners. Sound alerted staff to the precarity of their circumstances, though they were not necessarily as attuned to the same aspects of the sonic environment as those who lived within it.

While Jack maintained the response to violence was determined by its recipient, observations and discussions suggested this was an over-simplification; an 'us and them' which reflected Jack's poor relationships with many of the staff (and in Jack's case it appeared to be reciprocated). Violence might be part of the fabric of prison life, but it had a complex moral code attached, as Stretch illustrated. This code had an aural quality too. Depending on the circumstances it could reset the tone of the community or ratchet up tension. The precise conditions that determined which days were ones where things settled and 'order' was resumed quickly, and when 'bubbliness' was sustained, remained a puzzle. From observation, this distinction appeared to rest in whether the arrhythmia was caused by anticipation of a specific incident (for example, a potting, or score settling), or if incidents were symptomatic of a broader malaise. Differences between sustained bouts of disorder and disruption, and isolated incidents aside, a bad day had a sound and both prisoners and staff were able to tell me what it sounded like:

'Like a rattle Cccggghhrrr ... like, imagine a radio that's not on the right station. And you got to pick through it. I can decipher it some way. I don't know why. I can decipher it. I was on the fours last night yeah and it was kicking off downstairs. No one else could hear it but I was like – " the block's getting smashed up". They went "shuddup". They went "how dyou know?" And I were only leaning on the wall. I was leaning but I knew from the vibrations, cos there's different vibrations from music to damage and they say to me "how can you?" And I can smell things as well. I smell trouble. I'll stand there and I don't know why but I'll start sweating and then I'll be – there's gonna be an incident.' (Stretch, prisoner)

In a place where violence is commonplace knowing what is going on and where was key to avoiding harm. Sound performed a useful means of alerting members of the community to changes in the emotional climate as well as conveying violent interactions in process through the walls, pipes, floors and so on. This seemed to hold for those who had been inside for some time, whether their preference/role was to get stuck in, or – "nothing to do with me" (Will) – to avoid confrontation.

I took extended notes of incidents where events conspired to disrupt the normal regime. These were among the limited occasions I was free to write, removed from the steady routine of a better day and the stream of chat and conversation which characterized one.

On the netting

> Lone figure at height, loitering, bouncing on netting. Pacing. Tense waiting. Peering. Speculating. Men remain behind the door. Growing frustration as day is disrupted. 'Fucks with your mental health when you have people like that twat' mutters Finchy as he passes (a cleaning orderly). 'Get off the fucking netting!!' a disembodied voice shouts. Bang. Bang. Bang. 'Okay, go and get kitted up and then round the back way' staff murmur to one another, as they strategize his forced removal, patience exhausted, time spent. Angry voices, agitated. 'Do me a favour, go sweep him off the netting would you?' Orderly says to officer, he replies: 'I'd love to, he'd come straight through like a chip.' 'As soon as he's off there it's all gonna kick off!' And then he toddles off as unremarkably as he walked on. Talked and gently walked ... ten minutes later, music resumes. Only then do I realize the absence of sound. Men listening behind doors for cues to regime. Non-conversations resume. Irked boredom between doors. Two fights, both on the threes. Rhythms erratic today. Residual tension. (Fieldnotes)

'Going on the netting'[4] was classed as an incident at height, which set in motion a whole chain of action, not least of which was restricted movement and suspension of the regime for most of the prison. The gap between landings, or spurs, on higher floors was covered by anti-suicide netting. This was also used as rubbish disposal, temporary storage or a means of alleviating boredom and/or distress for those venturing on to it as a statement (orderlies often hopped across it in the course of their duties and a blind eye was turned, or warnings issued because the intention was to facilitate rather than disrupt the routines of the day). Prisoners tended to have little sympathy for those engaging in this behaviour because of the disruption it represented. The day ground to a halt, eliciting impatience from staff and prisoners. There was little movement, but audible tension (often very literally in the sound of staccato expletives issuing around the landing). Here there was a convergence in the irritation between staff and prisoners which served to reinforce a sense of community. Everyone wanted to get moving. Humour was often exchanged between prisoners and staff. In this way incidents at height could offer a means for staff and prisoners to express solidarity and shared purpose, minimizing the social breach such events represented.

Cell fires were less common than going on the netting and elicited a significantly different response given the higher stakes involved in deliberately setting your own cell alight (with you in it).

Cell fire

Officer comes in, meeting suspended, all back to cell. Distant panic sounds, disruption to routine. We re-enter unit and stand around. Library suspended. Cell fire, Lugs as he walks by: 'Says he wanted to kill himself, poor sod.' More sympathy than I expected. Banging. Lock in. Feet on metal … most away, just a few dawdling … subdued. Not the noise I anticipated. Davey says: 'My cell's right by there, I don't want to get locked in' as he drags his feet towards his pad. All is hushed when last men away. Taut, waiting. Officers in fire hoods, obscuring features, banging on door to get in. Roof opened but smoke gets around quickly. Stings my eyes, bitter in my nose. Staff taking it in turns to wear hoods ('It's hot under there'). Still battling to get in. Hose makes sound as drips on to floor below where one or two wait to mop it. Fire brigade troop in but will not enter cell until prisoner has been removed. Staff will douse him with water/extinguisher along with everything else, someone tells me. Four officers in full control & restraint (riot) gear approach. Banging against the door. So quiet … all listening. Everything suspended. All focused on this scene. Battle quick, hard, brutal. They are in. I can't hear much from my vantage point: 'MOVE THAT FUCKING MATTRESS NOW. MOVE IT. THIS IS HOW WE DO IT.' Prisoner brought out of cell, bare-chested, shaven-headed. Small next to uniforms. 'I'm not even resisting though. I'm not resisting.' 'FUCKING SHUT UP. JUST BRING YOUR KNEES UP IN TO YOUR FUCKING CHEST.' Prisoner taken, twisted up (head immobilized, arms behind back) to Segregation. Quiet. Chatter subdued as men reappear. 'Now they're going to try and put the smoking ban forward' someone mutters. (Fieldnotes)

Here there is less convergence between staff and prisoner motives though it is reasonable to assume that most would prefer to avoid burning alive. The presence of fear, the silence as men listen behind the door renders power asymmetry palpable (Warr, 2022). Every man who is behind the door is reliant upon officers to unlock them, or leave them to burn, in the event the fire spreads. At this point, listening is the only means of gauging threat for those behind the door. The disruption to normal operations was here linked to fear and distress. Staff were antsy and agitated, prisoners subdued and anxious. It took me a moment to understand why there was an absence of shouting out for information or for unlock; the men were listening. The rhythmic rituals of the regime were disturbed, the emotional climate heavy and uncomfortable.

12

Polyrhythmia

For all the complexities of everyday life at Midtown, it had a discernible rhythm, its components the different musical parts in a series of pieces played over themselves in competing time signatures. A 'good' day was not one in which temporal and spatial experience united but one in which its non-linear multiplicities were in harmony; a 'polyrhythmia' (Lefebvre, 2004). Uneventful visits, correct and accurate counts, prompt meal service and good humour combined to carry the day.

Lefebvre (1991) identifies three dimensions to how we experience space. We think of spaces simultaneously in terms of their representation on maps and blueprints, how they come to signify ideas of form and meaning, and the way these simple understandings are complicated and undermined by the realities of everyday life as it moves through their corners. These ideas help to decode the various levels and forms of prison life. There was the prison as it was rendered by what cab drivers told me they had read in their morning papers; places of punishment/holiday camps that undermined/reinforced our sense of law and order. Prison life as it was detailed and specified on prison service orders and instructions issued by senior management or commanding officers. Then there was the thrum and bustle of bodies busily remaking social spaces through ingenious dallying, in tension with the commands bellowed around the wing, and the periodic clang of the bell. These 'triadic' notions of space corresponded to the rhythms of regime in theory, on paper and in practice. Attuning to their meaning revealed the complexities of temporal and spatial experience, as well as how this was woven into the various activities that comprised a stable, orderly day.

A 'good' day

A good day in prison has an immediately identifiable soundscape. When asked what a good day sounds like in interview people offered remarkably similar accounts. Prisoners tended to be more location-specific and their response to depend on where they wanted to be, though remarkably few told me there was no such thing. The degree of agreement between some staff and prisoners over what constituted a 'good' day is illustrated by comparing responses to this enquiry. This revealed a broad convergence in the desirability of a day passing predictably:

> 'Long as I know everybody's away and I know them females are going home, or them males are going home to their children, cos they're only here doing a job. I can go to my cell and lay down and know the day's gone smoothly. Even if there's been an incident, as long as everyone's gone home, I'm happy.' (Stretch)

> 'So when I ring that bell for that last time, get everybody behind their doors, everybody comes in and signs for their numbers, it makes you feel good ... Nobody's been hurt, staff or prisoners, we've got the right number of people we're supposed to have, job done.' (Officer Rose)

Not only was a 'good' day discernible but also so was a return to a steady rhythm following disruption. Lefebvre assigns the concept of 'polyrhythmia' to the everyday rhythms of life: 'The analytic operation simultaneously discovers the multiplicity of rhythms and the uniqueness of particular rhythms' (Lefebvre, 2004: 16). Polyrhythmia refers to the unity of living rhythms in healthy, normal, 'everydayness'. The state of a steady multiplicity of rhythms working together was a good day in prison. Staff worked to keep the regime to timely order while offering sufficient slack to accommodate the men's dawdling, tactics of diversion and legion queries (Jewkes, 2012). In music, polyrhythm may refer to the simultaneous combination of contrasting or conflicting rhythms within a piece of music, not necessarily working in harmony (as in polyharmony) but nevertheless comprising one piece (Cowell, 1996). These multiple, independent rhythmic lines can be discerned when listening to a 'good day'. There is room in the tune for complimentary rhythms, and constructive unruliness exists alongside cooperation, bartering and bantering; a rhythmic 'give and take'. In the sense that this was broadly interpreted as an instance of rhythmic cooperation the extent to which power and authority were present was not clear:

> 'I used to enjoy lunchtimes cos you get the men out and the staff are working and I'd be standing at the top of the landing and you're almost like a conductor because you're getting the staff in certain places, and you're moving them down and you're unlocking in certain areas, and you're getting the regime going and you're driving the regime,

and it's great and you're seeing the prisoners and they're bouncing off you.' (Derek, officer)

Derek likening his role to that of a 'conductor' echoed Officer Rose's assessment: "If you're on the wing then it's your job to drive the regime. This gets done then." Observations written in my fieldnotes recount a good, lively day where everything appeared to be ticking over as expected and the mood was generally positive.

The regime

The regime, as it exists on paper, has different schedules which cover Monday–Thursday, Friday, Saturday and Sunday. Since Monday–Thursday covers most of the week I have included this one rather than the various variations and disruptions to the theme (for example, every first Wednesday is staff-training day and much of the usual regime – itself given to disruption – is suspended, and similar applies to bank holidays). This is the form of the prison day as it is listed on the wing office wall:

7:30: Roll check/courts unlock
7:45: Auditing/ briefing
8:00: Unlock, treatments, moving, domestics
8:35: Clear landings, kitchen workers to work, all others lock up
8:45: Education and Work according to lock-up/activity lists
9:00: Domestic period, IDTS (integrated drug treatment system) – move only
10:00: Exercise – all others locked up
11:00: Cease exercise. Lock up
11:20: Serve lunchtime meal
11:45: Return from activities
12:20: Lunchtime roll check
12:30: Staff off duty
13:30: Staff on duty, movement to education and work according to lock-up/activity lists
14:00: Cease activity, movement. Commence domestic period
15:00: Commence exercise, all other prisoners locked up
15:30: Early finish kitchen workers, showers and phone calls
16:00: Cease exercise, lock up
16:00: Tea, meal and treatments
16:45: Movement back from activities
17:45: All prisoners locked up
18:00: Staff duty
18:00: Commence kitchen showers

18:30: Cease kitchen showers
18:30: Complete any agreed phone calls via apps, auth Oscar 1
19:00: Cease evening duties, final roll check
19:30: Staff off duty
19:30–20:45: Court returns, FNC duties and patrol
20:45–21:00: Handover to nights
(Tues, Wed, Thurs, Sat, Sun. Visits 14:00–16:00)

Ostensibly the prison ran on this strict schedule with no deviation, the day shaped by lists and counting, punctuated by the bell, keys in locks, shouting and movements around the prison. The ideal prison day adhered to this routine. The reality differed markedly; staff numbers and experience fluctuated causing disruption. Lists reflected a version of entitlements which may or may not differ from agreements or prisoners' expectations (cue daily round of banging), and prisoners worked to impose rhythmic variations on the theme of the daily regime. Graham, an officer who left towards the end of my time at Midtown, described the day shift as: "like tipping up a box of frogs and trying to get them all back in again … It's a small space but there's plenty of places to hide". Despite most of the prison sharing one, large space, prisoners were adept at keeping a low profile if their priorities differed from those of the routine. Some members of staff were similarly adept at disappearing from view. As Ket observed, everyday hustling to get by involved a fair bit of ducking and diving on all sides. Mealtimes, the loudest points of the day, were subject to the most audible riffs on the regime as men rushed to obtain sought-after items, conduct business and socialize. Many expressed a dislike of the food and cooked their own meals in cell via kettles (noodles and/or mackerel and curry were popular). In short, listening to the rhythms of the day provided a means of demarcating the distinctions between these different spatial experiences, which made the 'tune' of daily life at HMP Midtown more discernible (Lefebvre, 1991, 2004; Lyon and Back, 2012).

While the regime offered some distraction and shape to the day, it was perceived as far from sufficient to keep the men occupied. Keeping busy, and finding ways to do so, within and outside of the rules, was a full-time occupation, but recognized as essential: "You have to keep yourself busy, else your head will pop" (Mooch). The successful 'doing' of time, involved some ingenuity and innovation. It sometimes appeared that getting away with it, or bending rules, was at least as central as any specific reason for doing so. Prisoners regularly thanked me for helping them 'kill' some time. Lugs was quite adept at keeping busy: "I like being banged up most times. Sometimes I don't like getting banged up if you've noticed. When they shout bang up though, I just put my gloves on and go and collect something then walk back down." Lugs was a cleaner when he wasn't working in the laundry. Like a number of others, he carried a seemingly endless supply of plastic gloves wedged in his pocket for lending his dawdling the appearance of legitimacy.

The alternatives to keeping busy out and about were finding forms of amusement in cell. These included an array of activities:

> 'People just want drugs in this place to get them, it takes the bars away for the night. Does that make sense? … If I was smoking drugs, I'd just want to take them bars away for a day or two, or three, and sometimes it does. It goes rapid sometimes, do you know what I mean? Behind the door.' (Lugs)

Drug use was rife and could often be smelled upon entering the wing. Those in an affected state had their own rhythms of movement; slow, sluggish and distracted. Mooch and Harry sometimes emerged from all-night betting-based activities bleary-eyed and out of sorts. The lived reality of the regime was markedly different, more messily complicated than it appeared on paper. Spatial practices of everyday living bore little resemblance to the imaginary order of the prison.

Polyrhythmic variations of daily life at Midtown revealed divergence between staff's use and experience of time and that of prisoners. Adherence to the regime was the goal of a 'good day' for staff. While prisoners wanted predictability and order, some sought latitude and as much time out of cell as could be eked out from whatever slack could be utilized from the regime. Upsets to daily rhythms sounded discordance between the intermittent goal of exercising agency within the constraints of the prison and the comforts of security offered by a predictable routine. This reflected a wider difference in the way these groups were situated in time. Staff largely operated in the present. The No. 1 governor expressed frustration with his staff sometimes failing to dig at underlying reasons for behaviour: "There's often an ulterior motive but staff don't always see that. Staff will see a behaviour and respond to that behaviour without necessarily understanding the cause." Staff culture imposed a particular emphasis on the now; dwelling on past mistakes was frowned upon: "Yesterday's in the past, it's history, it doesn't exist, let's deal with today" (Officer Rose). In contrast, prisoners were focused on past mistakes, the steps that brought them there and hopes and anxieties about the future. Staff sought to guard against what Giddens (1984) terms 'time-space distanciation', while prisoners sought to enhance it. This refers to the expansion of relations over space(s) and the contractions of time, represented by interaction with people who are physically absent. Tension between the temporal experience of staff and prisoners was a significant site of power contestation. Absence and presence of control over time and its disposal was the source of continual conflict: it was often the rhythms of this temporal dialectic which determined the pace of the day.

'Feeding time'

Standing in the midst of activity on the wing demonstrated how far removed the messy, human hubbub was from the shabby-cornered, typed itinerary taped to the office wall.

> The bell is rung signalling evening meal. Men go to collect their food half-landing by half-landing, queuing in an ever-moving line into the servery, slurping stray peas and surplus gravy from the sides of impractically small, plastic, prison-issue plates as they emerge from the other end. More practised hands carry Tupperware boxes in which food can be more confidently swaggered back to cell via snatched conversations and hurried business meetings on route. Crescendos of dawdling ... officers shouting, footsteps – officers purposeful, measured rubber-soled boot on metal, scurrying prisoner plimsoll, elusive two-at-a-time step with surplus energy, swerving and scurrying for snatched conversations. Cheery greetings as men pass me, making their way down the stairs to join the queue. Down, around, in the servery entrance, reappearing with collected food out the other end and back to cell in a seemingly endless stream of institutional greys, splashes of colour, expensive trainers, and institutional blues. Huddles and murmurs, hurried exchange of cigarette papers before bang-up. Bartering, bustling, hustling and hanging back. Jostling at the medical hatch, some vaulting the gate on the walkway between meds and servery, positioning themselves mid-queue; slow moving and loud. Gravy in spilt, interrupted trails, on floor, on rails, stairs, surfaces, inexplicably appearing on officers starched, white shirt arms as they cajole and shunt the men back to cell. A prisoner slips on stair spillage, his cheery hello supplanted by anger at being laughed at once balance is regained: 'If I wanted to fucking split my head open then I'd come down there and do it to one of you!' Budging along on the ledge to accommodate another for a moment of snatched sociality, a row of men, convivially chatting, precariously balancing plates on the thin ledge. Snatching up chips. Using hand to scoop while other holds on to plate. 'Come on, move along. If you've got your dinner back to your cell. MOVE IT.' Bang. Bang. Bang. Only when quiet descends, 'feeding time' is over and all are behind the door are the Veeps escorted up from the bowels of the prison to collect their meals. (Fieldnotes)

This was a good day. A bustling, 'organized chaos' that characterized the ebb and flow of daily life in HMP Midtown. The men snaked around the prison, between landings, stairs and servery. Banter and business were conducted in good spirits (as far as could be heard). There was sufficient confidence in the sturdiness of the day's rhythms to accommodate the counter rhythms of ducking and dawdling; last-minute searches for Rizla before bang-up, the redistribution of various necessities, shady dealings. Rare opportunities for snatched moments of commensality were accommodated – fundamental to social life but hard to come by in prison (Kerner et al, 2015). While a good day had an ordered rhythm of sorts, this did not indicate a singular pulse but various, steady rhythms accommodating one another within a shared sense of collective daily life. The greater whole was working in concert, albeit to a multitude of time signatures. The mood was positive and generally harmonious as these rhythms worked within, around and through one another: a polyrhythmia

On a smaller level, Ket talked about the difficulty of maintaining harmony in the laundry. Particularly fastidious prisoners – such as Lugs – were often drawn to this opportunity for work. For a time, Stevie also worked there. In contrast to established laundry orderlies who guarded their respective piles and systems with regular threats of violence, Stevie had ADHD and anxiety among other conditions, and as a result had a rather chaotic approach to work. He was also rather boisterous. Ket told me: "He's just too much, I told them we were pretty much finished just so I could have some peace and quiet … they complain to me – 'He's messed up my pile, I can't deal with it' – and I tell them 'You have to tell him'." Having observed militaristic operations between the prisoners in the laundry (violence was narrowly avoided when a dispute over sock piles erupted) it was clear how Stevie's manic chaos might threaten harmony. His unpredictable spirals into distress and self-harm, however, meant that he needed to be out of cell and occupied as much as possible. This presented a challenge. Nevertheless, these rhythms within rhythms were discernibly harmonious in that the plates were kept spinning, just.

It is this multiplicity of living rhythms to which people refer when asked what a 'good' day sounds like. In the social context polyrhythmia acted as a means of affecting social cohesion, setting a predictable pace for the daily rhythm. The reassurance this provided for members of the community proved contagious, maintaining a steady equilibrium to the emotional climate on the wing. A 'good day' was "just everybody getting along" (Davey). In this way, sound was a source and indicator of social cohesion, reinforcing the mechanical solidarity which enabled the prison community to rub along together.

The stultifying regime made it easy to overlook the significance of days when nothing much happened. Standardized days of drearily predictable routine could militate against recognizing what 'everybody getting along' signified, but this was the marker against which departures from the ideal were measured. Amid the drowning cacophony of comings and goings, the significance here lay in what was not happening. The deafening intrusions of longing for out there did not impinge upon the polyrhythmia of getting on and getting by inside. Humdrum hustle and bustle was not brought to a clattering halt by life-threatening violence, or the demands of administrative necessities. The day moved along to the rhythms of the everyday tune.

13

Jingle Jangle

'Those keys, can't forget where you are.' (Prisoner, fieldnotes)

As different rhythms of everyday comings and goings unfolded within the prison soundscape, the nuanced complexity of flows of power between people and place became more apparent. The jangle of keys and clang of gates reverberated with the potency of the prison, a symbolic violence upon those who felt the weight of its meaning.

The Midtown soundscape signified the extent to which power flowed in a broader relational sense than is depicted from within the constraining peripheries of vision. Officers enacted power over prisoners by evoking symbols of both their relative status and that of the prison. The sound of keys echoed with their literal function, but also jangled with symbolic representation of broader social censure. The prison soundscape reverberated with the power to punish that was felt in multifarious ways, most keenly by those stripped of their freedom, but also by those who worked in these spaces. Different individuals and actors were more or less disturbed by particular elements of the soundscape; I focus on a selection of examples to demonstrate what impact this could have, and what it says about operations of power and the violence in which it manifested.

Power flowed through the soundscape, both in its making, and the wider potency of the prison it signified. Nathan, interviewed for my undergraduate dissertation, described being held in Seg while in a young offender institution (YOI). An officer had left a radio on to keep the young men company through the night while they were held in isolation. A second officer walked through and shifted the dial a fraction, so they were left with white noise all night long. The mean-spiritedness reported here bears no comparison to the thoughtlessness of clanging gates at unsociable hours that many reported at Midtown. Power ran in electric, invisible lines, so often wielded carelessly. When it was not, the effect on relationships could be profound. Much noise emanating from routine practices was attributable to institutional thoughtlessness; 'the ways in which prison regimes (routines, rules, timetables, etcetera) simply roll on with little reference to the needs and sensibilities of [prisoners]' (Crawley, 2004: 350). Sonic intrusions arising out of institutional practices, and responses to them, were often reported as being experienced as a symbolic violence, partially because of their inescapability. Lack of control over exposure and ability to curate the sensory environment amplified the loss of agency (Wener, 2012).

Keys

Given their association with loss of freedom, autonomy and security, keys are perhaps the most evocative symbol of imprisonment and the loss of freedom it denotes. For Midtown prisoners, much of their power rested not in their physical form – keys often cannot be seen at the point of greatest significance; behind the door – but in their 'jingle jangle' (Behan, 1954). That "you can always hear keys, always" (Marcus) speaks to the important symbolic function of sound in the context of prison (Chion, 2010). While the sound of keys was particularly significant for those locked in, staff's awareness largely extended to a practical consciousness of their operational importance (Giddens, 1984). Aspects of the soundscape derived their potency from the context of prison, as well as the social position of the listener. Tommy, a lifer caught at Midtown while awaiting an appeal date, described entering an unfamiliar prison for the first time: "You want to speak to someone new then. I've felt it myself. When you hear those keys coming and you're in a new nick and you don't know who's out there … are they coming for you? What's happening?" For him, keys induced anxiety about exposure to what awaited on the other side of the door, inviting apprehension at the unknown. Keys enhanced feelings of uncertainty and lack of control, heightening fear about who is "out there", "what's happening" and whether "they" are "coming for you". Feelings of discomfort have the potential to endure regardless of proximity of others (if in single-cell occupancy) or how limited is the line of sight, because there are no barriers to the institutional soundscape. The sound of keys reinforced the sense of precarity, serving as a reminder of vulnerability to the caprice of the keyholder. Hearing that jangle alerted prisoners to their position, not only powerless to control their movement beyond the cell, but also from exposure to what lay beyond.

The potential violence of sound becomes clearer by considering its uses in states of war. Sound features in increasingly sophisticated techniques in warfare, used to induce fear and induce ontological insecurity in targeted populations.

> Fear induced purely by sound effects, or at least in the undecidability between an actual or sonic attack, is a virtualized fear. The threat

becomes autonomous from the need to back it up. And yet the sonically induced fear is no less real. The same dread of an unwanted, possible future is activated, perhaps all the more powerful for its spectral presence. Despite the rhetoric, such deployments do not necessarily attempt to deter enemy action, to ward off an undesirable future, but are as likely to prove provocative, to increase the likelihood of conflict, to precipitate that future. (Goodman, 2012: 14)

Sound is heavily interwoven in the creation of an 'ecology of fear' through sensory onslaught. In Tommy's account of his first time inside he refers to the fear of uncertainty generated by sounds from unseen sources:

'I remember waking up in the morning and I was in a cell with my cousin Ciaran, and he was like "Oh, what's it gonna be like?" And I was like "Will you shut your mouth, I dunno, I've never been before!" Opened up in the morning and, I think the build up to that door being opened is when you feel … but the sounds. It was the dogs barking in the morning that I remember. And then you can hear people shouting.' (Tommy)

Tommy's account echoes Crewe et al's (2014) description of the effect of living with the potential for violence as affecting a state of Hobbesian diffidence, or 'consumptive wariness'. Jack attested to this sense of apprehension: "This environment can be very, very, it can be very scary, it can be very intimidating. It can be very push-comes-to-shove if you know what I mean? Like they say there's three ways, what is it? Run, stand or flight?" Sound was implicated in the consistent maintenance of a sense of tenseness, its effects reverberating with experience and expectation. 'Tightening' strategies of confinement were amplified by associations with, or recollections of, other sites or states of violence (Canning, 2021). Eleanor March (2021) makes explicit parallels between these spaces in analysis of prisoner writing:

The WHACK and THUMP recalls the CRACK and THUMP of the deadly weapons in the battlefield scene, in an aural embodiment of the violence of prison, enacted on human flesh. In this scenario, the language of proximity conveys the forced, unwanted physical proximity of prison life. Ultimately, the narrator's inability to decode the prison soundscape leaves him unable to adapt to prison life, and the story ends with his suicide.

The source and function of sound could be entirely divorced from its effect, and in that sense was irrelevant to how it was felt and interpreted as a violence. Several prisoners explained that the incident alarms (which did not sound terribly often) were designed specifically to incapacitate: "You know that's made to put you on the floor?" (Lugs). Few emergency alarms sounded on the main wing during my time there. When it did the effect was significant. I wrote at the time (I was in mid-interview) that I had felt unable to think, my discomfort sufficient to prompt the prisoner I was with to express concern.

Some prisoners interpreted aspects of the soundscape as punishment. Lugs was a local and had spent much of his adult life in and out of HMP Midtown. He had a local inhabitant's familiarity with the culture and soundscape of the place which corresponded with his identity as a member of the community outside:

'That bell, and that alarm, that just does me. It's mental. That's how, it weren't like that a year ago. It used to be dlaalala and now it's drrr. And you know if you misbehave? You been downstairs? They got a noise. If you're misbehaving, they'll go and press that button so that noise is out your door, and you'll be like "I'm behaving turn that fucking thing off". And they're "Wait til you're calm Lugs or put some earplugs in" they'll say. "Fuck off, turn it fucking off or I'll chin ya!" That noise does me!' (Lugs)

Prisoners reported experiencing these aspects of the soundscape as less about interpersonal power relations between themselves and individual officers, and more about being at the sharp end of the disciplinary purpose of the prison. A number of prisoners recognized that staff were "Just doing their job" (for example, Will, Davey, Stretch and others in fieldnotes). Sharp distinction was drawn between these individuals and the deprivations of imprisonment. While prisoners had a host of experiences of negative (and positive) interactions with staff, these types of sounds (keys, clanging, alarms) were often interpreted independently of the individuals responsible for making them. The sounds emanating from an individual's interaction with the environment were indivisible from the potency of the institution, lending gravity – or 'sound weight' – to its experience. As Lugs explained, these sounds were interpreted as punishment, both in form and content, often signalling the impending use of coercive force.[1] They were interpreted as unpleasant by design, meant to elicit discomfort in the listener and amplify a sense of powerlessness. Power, then, flowed through aspects of the soundscape, imbued with the semiology of punishment and remaking the social relations on which its force was dependent.

The ability of sound to traverse time and space maximized its potency by eliciting and reconfiguring memory. While the prison soundscape could evoke memories of other times and places, it also retained its potency through recollection:

> I knew I would have to submit to a cavity search, but it wasn't the strip search that dominated my memory of this event. It was the noise.
> Since concrete and steel do not absorb sound, the clamor and voices from within just bounced around, crashing into each other to create a hollow, booming echo that never ended. It sounded as if someone had placed a microphone inside a crowded locker room with the volume pumped up, broadcasting the noise all around the sally port. It was this deafening background noise that would lull me to sleep at night and greet me in the morning for the next five years. Though I have been out of Graterford for many years now, its constant din still echoes in my ears. (Hassine, 1996: 6)

The prison soundscape permeated memory, eliding distinctions between the prison and other places:

> 'dreaming of keys, I thought I was back in here! But what was worse, was when I was back in, I dreamed of the sounds of home, hearing my brothers and sisters running about, kitchen sounds, breakfast being made ... but when I woke, I was banged up.' (Ian, conversation in HMPYOI Aylesbury)

This effect was also experienced by staff, though the source was often different (for example, hearing alarms in their dreams, or raised voices on the street [Joanne]). Sound was also a source of knowledge; an ability to navigate the sonic environment was bound with strategies of survival for both staff and prisoners.

Brut and Old Spice

Unbidden sensory intrusions worked to compound past trauma with current, carceral experience, amplifying and distorting the significance of detail which could only be understood in the context of personal narrative. During our interview, after talking about taking refuge in the shower as an abused child, and the compulsion to wash "the dirt off me", Stretch related a past exchange with an officer:

> 'If I smell Brut or Old Spice it gives me a panic attack. I had to ask one of the members of staff the other week "Could you stop wearing that aftershave in prison please?" He said "Why?" I said "Cos I'll have to do something to you." He said "What do you mean, it's aftershave?"

I said "Yeah, but it reminds me of my past, when I was raped." And respect to him, he doesn't wear it no more in prison.'

He did not tell me which officer it was, and I did not ask. I suspected though, that respect for Stretch's request was partially derived from shared local knowledge about his story and circumstances. My starting point was sound but focusing on social aspects of auditory experience also worked to heighten sensitivity to the ways in which the sensory worked as a conduit for power. Unable to curate sensory experience, to be surrounded by sounds, smells, tastes, feels of one's choosing, amplified loss of agency. Past recollections merged in discordant, jarring tones of the prison environment in the present. In the absence of a deep understanding of individual circumstances it might have been easy to dismiss his visceral response as confrontational aggression, in ways which might have dire repercussions for his trajectory (Stickney et al, 2023). For Stretch, this was a matter of self-preservation. As we write elsewhere 'it would be a mistake … to situate these sensory and symbolic tussles solely within prison daily life … the prison leaves its mark in sensory traces that linger long after the prison sentence has formerly ended and frequently follow its staff home too' (Herrity and Warr, 2023).

"I hear a lot of things, me"

The panopticon model of prison design is broadly understood as facilitating greater control over those locked within it by allowing perpetual surveillance. Power functions broadly within the peripheries of vision. When Foucault adopted the panopticon as a metaphor for charting the operations of power and social control in the modern age, there was no place for sound, though Bentham acknowledged its significance by incorporating it into his original design (Bentham, 1767; Foucault, 1977). Mooch was demonstrating status by telling me "I hear a lot of things, me". It was important to his presentation of self that he was recognized as being in the loop, having his finger on the pulse of prison life: "I know what goes on in here man" (Mooch). He was not alone in recognizing the importance of sound as a means of keeping abreast of developments in the prison. Both staff and prisoners repeatedly referred to sound as a source of knowledge.

In an environment where goods are scarce, freedom restricted and the cost of being found in possession of forbidden items can be high, information is a valuable commodity. Both prisoners and staff used prison sonar to save time and legs. Conversations with Lugs were frequently interrupted by shouted responses to calls for him, inaudible above the general din to my ears: "Yes, what you want Finchy?" Staff did the same, frequently shouting around the wing for some elusive prisoner or colleague. Information also took more conventional forms of course. Reputations could thrive or falter on the back of it: "Want to know the loudest thing in here? It's the whispers" (Karim). "Loose lips sink ships" was a phrase repeatedly uttered in my presence, usually after some rash disclosure.

While physically constrained for much of the day, prisoners' soundscape extended far beyond that of staff since their aural vantage point presented a greater number of sources of sonic information. At a perpetual disadvantage in this respect, staff constantly battled to interpret the deluge of information from the immediate environment as well as the control team, via their earpieces. Juggling the dissonance of information as it unfolded in their environment, with the delayed report being relayed via radio. At the same time, they were keenly aware of being subject to the scrutiny of many (Mathieson, 1997). "I suppose mischief heightens your senses greatly (laughs) ... They know. They know a hell of a lot. They're in tune to wherever you are" (Officer Tone). A number of staff were identifiable by their movements. Joanne, for example, walked with sticks which made a distinctive sound as her chain bounced off them. One officer had a particular way of walking which swung his hips causing his keys and chain to chime rhythmically against the bars on the walkways. Another whistled the tune from 'Kill Bill' repeatedly (from a film soundtrack called 'Twisted Nerve' [Herrman, 1968]). This reverberated with Tone's memory of a former fellow officer's habit of whistling 'Zippety doo dah', offering staff their own reassuring sources of ontological security. Accounting for the role of sound in processes of surveillance reveals the extent to which power is diffused through multi-directional aural interactions. Exerting power through the emphasis of presence in the environment was necessarily compromised by the responding scrutiny invited by it. If sound was a source of knowledge, and knowledge was power, it was necessarily spread among those operating within the Midtown soundscape.

The task of keeping on top of developments was made harder by the balancing of sometimes overwhelming streams of information. While staff reported an ability to "just numb it out" (Lena, officer) over time, the demands of wearing a radio while on duty sometimes showed:

> 'I can't think, I can't concentrate. It affects my ability to work. Trying to reason with people while there's this row going on. Making a difficult situation worse. I end up shouting at comms and they're only doing their job: "Yes, I'm fucking here!"' (No. 2, deputy governor)

It sometimes appeared the stream of information coming through radio communications constituted a sensory overload making it more, rather than less, difficult for staff to effectively operate. It was also unclear whether this contribution to personal soundscapes enhanced tension rather than diffusing it.

Officers repeatedly encouraged me to wear a radio for a shift, which clearly indicated the degree to which they felt this was a significant component of their working day. I was reluctant to draw more attention to my presence but observing staff juggling communications with colleagues, interactions with prisoners and the stream of information feeding into their ear was instructive. Conversations were frequently interrupted by muffled flows of instruction and information over the radio. Staff looked away to concentrate, a widespread habit which betrayed the nature of information they received (as Stretch noted) and could be interpreted as an act of considerable disrespect by the prisoner who had lost their attention. I was frequently subject to this, which taught me about the practicalities of an officer's working day but was profoundly frustrating as it indicated the premature conclusion of a conversation. Invariably, despite assurances to the contrary, this signalled the termination of our discussion. This aspect of staff operations often seemed to provide more interference than assistance for all concerned.

Attending to the significance of keys jangling, and gates slamming for those who could not escape their shuddering echo made different aspects of social experience audible. The jangling keys worked to remind the prisoner of their circumstances, while they could be a source of comfort for an officer, a reminder of their position, their identity and their role in the broader matrices of criminal justice practices. Sound seamlessly traversed interactions between individual agents, their role and relations to Midtown, and to the weight of social significance the prison's structural function carried, reinforced by the jingle jangle of the keys. Various aspects of the prison soundscape served as auditory signifiers of power, resonating with the asymmetry they derived their force from. The social meaning of the prison was reconstituted in their hearing. While the soundscape was a key site of power relations and ongoing quests for auditory knowledge which formed their battleground, those bangs and clangs resonated with a force which reverberated far beyond their hearing.

Sound forms a key component of power maintenance; auditory signifiers of power resonate with the privilege on which it depends, and social memory is reconstituted through it. The clanging of gates, jangling of keys reinforce the power and privilege those working for the prison have over those imprisoned within it. Those bangs and clangs resonate with a force reverberating far beyond the present, in memory imagination, and expectation.

14

Disentangling Power and Order

Inviting people from the Midtown community to reflect on the soundscape revealed complexity and nuance to the various flows and channels of power, mediated and amplified by the clangs, bangs and jangles of the prison. Listening, rather than looking, altered perspective. Asking what others were hearing allowed for an understanding of how power operates within the community, between people and place. Like peeling and segmenting an orange rather than observing it in a bowl, as the pieces separated, various textures and states of matter were revealed. The impacts of individual strains of the soundscape were interpreted in the context of various associations with temporal and spatial experience. These readings transcended immediate relationships between people and place, recalling memories of other times, interconnections and locations. Recognition of the various ways in which power flowed through various conduits, as well as from them, challenged any straightforward notion of authority. Or rather, acknowledging this deeper complexity in flows and effects of power highlighted distinctions between enacting the capacity to make decisions and an answering acknowledgement of the right to do so. Correspondingly, direct associations between authority and cooperation were attenuated. There were various reasons underpinning the decision to hum along with the everyday tune, and, far from being moot these were central to the work of keeping it playing.

The soundscape rattled and clanged with the potent charge of punishment, and thrummed with the routine activity which comprised an orderly day. Listening to these aspects of prison life added respective definition to what was being heard, challenging representations of these complex phenomena as interchangeable. Learning the soundscape from within the community allowed for various accounts of power, as well as order as they featured in everyday life. Staff recounted practice which was more about maintaining control and cooperation than exercising power specifically. Officers, and other staff, rarely spoke about operations of power, nor reflected on their roles in this way but it was also less apparent in group activity than might be anticipated. The process of learning familiarity with the rhythms and routines at Midtown attuned the ear to the vagaries and variations of an orderly day, and what lay at the heart of its maintenance.

Bottom up

Situating myself within the community allowed me to hear a broader range of experience. Rather than observing from outside, immersion in the soundscape brought different elements of social experience to the fore. There was a levelling process in asking similar questions of all those I spoke with as well as interviewed which allowed for an assessment of the convergence and divergence of experience. Aural lines of enquiry exposed a greater complexity to people's understanding of power and its flows, individually, collectively and structurally. This had a corresponding effect on how power was understood in relation to the maintenance of the rhythms and routines order depended upon. Hendy's characterization of interactions between sound and power also work to decentre power sufficiently to add nuance and contingency to its broader operations:

> It is therefore a force acting upon people, for good or ill. At the same time sound never bestows absolute power on anyone, since by its very nature it is hard for sound to be entirely owned or controlled. Its natural tendency is to move freely through the air. And although human ingenuity is such that sound can always be manipulated, sound is also too intangible and slippery a thing to remain in the service of elites without also being available for use in inventive and subversive ways by the dispossessed. (Hendy, 2013: xiv)

Order could be undermined as well as buoyed by various members of the community. The degree of official authority with which individuals engaged in these processes (and therefore the forms these behaviours took) depended on their role and relationships but did not determine involvement. A prisoner would be hard-pressed to declare a successful count, or the beginning of dinner – markers of a day going according to plan. However, they did engage in activities which infected the social emotion on the wing to relieve tension and engender conviviality and cooperation. Singing, laughter, kindness all helped to spread a sense of goodwill. There was a force in these everyday human practices and listening to them disarticulated complex flows of power from the polyrhythmia of a good day. Order, contingent, fragile and precarious, was comprised as much of efforts from those without formally appointed power as with it.

Staff were not immune from the effects of power flowing from the place as well as alternative streams of authority. Balancing streams of information from the environment and colleagues beyond, could work to undermine a sense of security rather than shoring it up. The deluge of things – and people – requiring simultaneous attention heightened awareness of the currency of information as well as the limits of its value. Perpetual preoccupations with security and surveillance made staff only too aware that they too were watched and monitored, creating a sense of precarity and exposure. Maintaining a semblance of order was less about power than preserving some appearance of control.

Conducting the noise

As mentioned previously, when reflecting on presiding over a 'good' day, Officer Rose echoed Derek's explanation of his role as a 'conductor'. Derek had clearly given our pending interview a lot of thought, and his considerations of sound led him to make various parallels with music and his relationship with it. This was both literal in terms of his use of music to strengthen the membrane between work and home, and in terms of organized sound, or the rhythms and strains that comprise the soundscape of prison social life. His analogy was in keeping with the themes he consistently referred to throughout our conversation, but his assessment of his role was deeply informative: "You're getting the regime going and you're driving the regime, and its great and you're seeing the prisoners and they're bouncing off you." Derek's description revealed much about his perceptions of order. As the conductor his role was, of course, to stress the metrical pulse of the regime. He was charged with keeping rhythm, but as a conductor, was nevertheless part of the orchestra and every bit as dependent upon his fellow musicians. Prisoners were not mindlessly following but rather "bouncing off" him, their rebounding force a necessary counterpoint in the rhythms of the day.

Derek's depiction of a mutual effort in "driving" the regime suggests securing cooperation was as much a matter of expertise as authority. In keeping the plates of the regime spinning, Derek was managing to keep control over its running rather than impose the power of authority. He was also operating as a 'conductor' in the sense of channelling the collective through his jail craft. This distinction is important for what it reveals about the difference not only between power and control, but also between power and regime maintenance. Power and order are frequently depicted as being inextricably intertwined. Accepted as an explanation for the endless conundrum as to why those vastly outnumbering officers charged with putting them behind the door comply. In presenting a means for examining the composition of order from within, the soundscape offers a corresponding alternative means of theorizing about its basis, absent the force of authority with which it is so often intertwined.

Order is a concept closely aligned with power; the ability to influence and to impose control (Hearn, 2012). Examining the meaning and effects of the soundscape broadened understanding of how power operated. Given much social theory is concerned with understanding the role of power discourse in the practice of government (Hindes, 1996) it is unsurprising social theory is used in attempts to excavate conditions for, and disruptions to, order. This has the effect of closely aligning what are distinct and complex phenomena. Listening to the ebb and flow of daily rhythms as well as exploring the force of its elements revealed additional complexity to this relationship. Power flowed in multifarious ways, transcending layers of social life as well as temporal and spatial experience. This worked to disrupt and worry at presumed relationships between power and order which had corresponding implications for how social stability was understood.

The assertion that prison embodies prevailing ideas about social order and that these offer powerful instruction about the wider social world and its organizing principles is a familiar one (Foucault, 1977; Ignatieff, 1977). The reverse – that broader ideas in social organization can be useful for understanding prison life – is also a fruitful field for exploration. Weber looked to organized sound – via the sociology of music – to explore his theory of rationalization. He argued that particular forms of musical theory and composition echoed developments in social organization (Weber, 1958 [1920]). Attali (1977) asserted that cultural practice – specifically music and the arbitrary social processes which determine its classification as of cultural value, or 'noise' – provide a valuable lens for shifts in the political economy. These are valuable explanations for exploring change in penal culture and its manifestations, as well as how particular ideations of punishment are conveyed through the soundscape.

Daily practices of power were aurally discernible. Listening to them, and reflecting on what others were hearing, disrupted an immediate and unassailable parallel between these levels of social experience. Focusing on sound detached and redefined the relationship between power and order. Order is too often depicted as directly flowing from consistent power, resting on the degree to which legitimacy of its conduits is accepted. Experiences of living and working with the echoing effects of the clangs, bangs and shouts of the prison soundscape reflected the need for greater complexity in conceptualizations of power. There was a need to differentiate between its various facets and operations which also served to detach it from order (Hearn, 2012). Power and order are often treated as synonyms in prisons literature – a shorthand when attempting to capture the texture of relationships, but one which obfuscates and distorts understanding of their respective complexities.

Listening to legitimacy

The tendency to assume prisoners comply with the routine because they are compelled to do so necessarily places the exercise of authority at the centre of its logics. This results in an entanglement of order and power. Focusing on the ways authority is exercised reinforces the assumption it is present, and assumes the salience of legitimacy; the recognition of reasonableness, validity and acceptance of authority on these grounds. Rooted in political theory this conceptual framework loosely refers to the 'variable conditions which render it more or less likely that prisoners will accept, however conditionally, the authority of their custodians' (Sparks and Bottoms, 1995: 47). Too often this rather abstract concept is conflated with legitimation (Carrabine, 2005) – the processes by which actions become accepted rules and standards. That an action is accepted does not necessarily signal assent, an observation echoed by Sparks et al (1996: 82):

> Whether prisoners too have an interest in the reproduction of the routine (either for the sake of 'ontological security' or more pragmatically for the reliable delivery of services they value, like food and visits) is a moot point. We suspect that very often they do, and hence co-operate more or less willingly in the running of routines.

Listening to the ritualistic rhythms of the prison day illuminates an additional dimension to processes of order maintenance in which power gives way to the comfort of predictability. This is significant for what it intimates about the co-produced nature of order. Listening from within, rather than observing practices of regime enforcement, shifts our understanding of the basis for compliance and cooperation. Legitimacy has undergirded much of the most significant work in prisons literature for the last 30 years and remains one of its most enduring and influential ideas. This represents a drift from Beetham's assertion of the basis of power as stemming not from a belief in its legitimacy, but successful incorporation into wider belief systems (Beetham, 1991). This has consequences for the way order and its maintenance are understood, as well as the extent to which we are inclined to accept that legitimacy is inherently problematic (Carrabine, 2005). Power lends prison order its form, and sets it in the fabric of prison life, but it is less pronounced in the interactions and activity which form its daily substance. Exploring the rhythms of everyday life reveal additional dimensions of experience in which power and authority are de-articulated from order and its maintenance.

Listening to order

'Order' is a deceptively complex term, particularly in prison spaces where its range and significance conceal the various levels of practice which compose it. Order relates to the portioning of time and activity; the delivery of the regime. Its potency lies in the extent to which stability and safety rely on its maintenance. There are vast distinctions in the forms it takes, the means of imposing it and how it is defined among different places and populations: 'both the means used, and the conception of order sought or imposed can vary significantly from one prison system to another, and even in different prisons within the same system' (Sparks et al, 1996: 1). Derek's account takes this further:

> 'So when you go to a particular department, not necessarily a prison … you could be in a classroom, you could be on another wing … you'd know that tune. And if something's out of sync you'll know.'

For Derek, order has discernible qualities unique to the specific environment not just of the population or the prison, but also in different spaces within it. Liebling and Arnold's definition is sufficiently commodious to hold these distinctions: 'the degree to which the prison environment is structured, stable, predictable and acceptable' (2004: 291). Their definition incorporates both the regime and the state of relative security arising from its predictable maintenance. Necessarily, sustaining daily routine is dependent on a variety of community members fulfilling designated roles, adhering to patterns of formation in relation to one another. In this sense order also refers to prison social structure, hierarchy and the identities this imposes. In the sense that order refers to the predictable patterns of daily life, stability is a matter of balance and negotiation; correspondingly, order is neither fixed nor unchanging but is rather a continual process of re-making (Sparks et al, 1996).

Examining the audible dimensions of the rhythms of daily activity revealed the various components of the ebb and flow of its routines (Lefebvre, 2004). Increasing familiarity with these spaces, the life that rumbled within them and the individuals who lived and worked here unveiled various contributions from people and their interactions with the environment. I became used to certain voices and modes of communication. I could identify individuals working within it, the soloists and virtuosos, the bum notes and crescendos of movement and meaning. Too often order is depicted as flowing unproblematically and simplistically through power, its direct and unproblematic corollary. The ebb and flow of the everyday tune was a complex concerto of call, response, variations and deviations. I was not at Derek's level of familiarity, but I was beginning to understand this aspect of his craft: "Like a musician listening to a song, they can hear all the bad notes."

Solzhenitsyn's (1970) semi-autobiographical *One Day in the Life of Ivan Denisovich* opens with the jarring reveille which begins the prison day. He draws on this sound to bridge the distance between the world he writes of, and that of the reader. Using sound in this way works to depict the lived experience of the gulag. Its sounds and rhythms impose effects on its inhabitants in ways which underscore interactions between the social meaning of carceral spaces and the experience of daily life within them (Lefebvre, 2004). It is noise which imposes shared patterns of behaviour, marking time for routinized activities which shape daily life within the prison's acoustic community. Sound lends shape, form and substance to the rhythms of the prison day, inextricably intertwined with the order which characterizes the daily regime. In prison spaces, sound is a means of mediating power, control and inclusion for those within its soundscape. Sound is a site for exploring the composition of order which characterizes the prison day. The soundscape provided a means for exploring the rhythms which characterized the regime, separate from the potency which imbues it with meaning.

Solzhenitsyn (1970) uses the prison soundscape to evocative effect, drawing us into his prison day. In so doing he emphasizes the role of the reveille in shaping daily life – at once a reminder of his circumstances, a call to order and a means of elucidating the deprivations of living under a repressive regime. The significance of the prison soundscape in his account lies in its effects on the eponymous character and effectiveness for characterizing an institution. Prison life echoes with routinized sounds, imposing a sense of order both comforting in its routine and inhibiting in the restrictions on freedom and movement it signifies. While power and order are not unrelated, there is no immediately apparent cause and effect between the power to punish and imprison, and motivations compelling adherence to regime. What is explicit is the connection between following the regime and survival of those subject to it. Survival in this context relates primarily to the threat to existence posed by gruelling life in the prison labour camp. The particular nature of deprivations within the carceral environment is less important than the degree of power disparity denoted by preoccupations with survival. Whether this relates to literal preservation of life and limb or the rather more nebulous stability that comes from maintaining a solid sense of being, the necessity of seeking existential comfort from the regime militates against interpretations of compliance as emanating from acceptance of the system's broader legitimacy (Harkin, 2015). Living – and working – within a steady emotional climate was a source of personal as well as collective stability.

> The maintaining of habits and routines is a crucial bulwark against threatening anxieties, yet by that very token it is a tensionful phenomenon in and of itself ... The discipline of routine helps to constitute a 'formed framework' for existence by cultivating a sense of 'being' and its separation from 'non-being' which is elemental to ontological security. (Giddens, 1991: 39)

Motivations for participating in the regime are multifaceted, contingent and fluid. Conducting the stuff of daily life was also rarely accompanied by deep reflections on the nature of compliance or degree of perceived legitimacy. Just as people in other circumstances go about their daily lives without continual reflection on the nature of existence, so too did those inside, navigating frustrations and deprivations as they arose. Using sound to evoke carceral experience also goes some way to addressing the divide between social life, the micro interactions that characterize its character and structural aspects of social experience that lend and reinforce its form and meaning.

The process of learning the soundscape added texture, contour and complexity to processes and practices of power and order. Listening to the audible components of the day shifted perspective as I sought to hear the rhythms of daily life from within, to gain insight into how this was experienced and what it meant to those participating in it. Shifting position in this way revealed the flattening effects of treating power as if it is inextricably and simplistically intertwined with order as at once its cause and effect. This greater complexity could only be accommodated by a partial detachment between power and order. So frequently used interchangeably in the literature, listening to their forms and function resisted attempts to impose a simple framework of understanding. Power corresponded to a wider field of social experience than action, cause and effect. Its audible navigations were exercised through the bangs of frustration. Clangs of doors that resonated with the collective weight of social censure and the many souls locked behind them. In the interference of radios which hampered relationships and confused as much as they secured. Order and motivations for upholding it were correspondingly multifaceted. Immediate temporal dissonance sounded through feet scurrying to enact illicit deals, or snatch moments of commensality but conversely contributed to the polyrhythmia of a good day well conducted. Comfort, coercion, camaraderie and cooperation were audible strains in the concerto of an orderly day.

15

Learning the 'Everyday Tune'

As various strains of the soundscape became more discernible, so too did the 'feel' of the day. Derek, a senior officer with 27 years' service likened a normal day to a piece of music – what he termed "the everyday tune that's normal for here".

> Noise. Noises. Murmurs. When lives are lived and hence mixed together, they distinguish themselves badly from one another. Noise, chaotic, has no rhythm. However, the attentive ear begins to separate out, to distinguish the sources, to bring them back together by perceiving interactions ... A certain exteriority enables the analytic intellect to function. However, to grasp a rhythm it is necessary to let oneself go, give oneself over, abandon oneself to its duration. Like in music. (Lefebvre, 2004: 27)

While the audible components of a good day were complicated and sometimes contradictory, there was broad agreement between various actors about what this sounded like, as well as the significance of learning to read it (Lefebvre, 2004). The implication of Derek's account was that the components of an orderly day were discernible and, much like a more conventional example of a 'tune' could be learned. Various accounts of the soundscape indicated this process of acclimation and attunement was central to successful management and control of the environment. By extension, and despite its broad absence from other accounts, 'reading' the soundscape was an important aspect of jail craft.

> 'If it was pointed out to you, you'd think yeah, right, that *is* wrong. But then a musician, they'd know straight away. Every member of staff there is almost like a musician at different stages, some will notice it before others, some will notice other things before others, depends on what instrument they're listening to.'

Derek's account emphasized the importance of learning the environment, but also attending to the strengths and skills of colleagues. His reflections revealed the centrality of deep familiarity with the ways of listening adopted by colleagues. An intimacy near impossible to attain in the current climate of staff shortages, inexperience and attrition. Order was audible and it was an orderly state that provided the point of reference for understanding deviations from the routine (and the disruptions and disorder this denoted). While both better and worse days could be identified from the soundscape, it was a good day that was used as an instructive means of understanding and maintaining stability. Prison studies, often influenced by concerns of the day (which understandably tend to centre around safety, however narrowly defined), use disorder as their point of focus. Attending to the soundscape illustrated the value of taking the lead from those who lived and worked in prison spaces. This echoes and elaborates Carrabine's (2004) assertion that order, and disorder, are not accurately represented by simplistic binaries. Nor are the conditions for the breakdown of order a sufficient or accurate explanation for the maintenance of stability.

"The noise of the place"

As Derek explained, the polyrhythmia of a good day was audible, and listening was part of the daily practice of 'reading' the environment for signs of threats to stability and the safety this rested upon. This was a recurring theme in staff and prisoner accounts. It was a 'good' day that provided the point of departure for anything wrong or out of place.

> 'The everyday tune that's normal for there. Everyone'll interpret that different. But you got to learn that tune. Learn the tune that the establishment's playing. And anything that's out of sync, any noises that are out of sync. Any shouts, or screams, or rumblings, you pick up on that, erm, and you'll subconsciously do it as well, there'll be staff that have worked in a particular place for ten, 15 years, and they won't know, they won't consciously learn the noise of the place but if anything's out of sync they'll be like that: "What's he doing there?" "What's he doing up on the threes?" They'll know. But if you try to explain it to 'em they'll be like: "You whacky, what you talking about, tunes 'n noises? What you talking about?" But people won't understand, but that's how it is. That's how we react.'

This everyday tune of the normal day – a steady, predictable regime – echoes Liebling and Arnold's definition. Order had an audible rhythm to it, a marker for a good day and a baseline against which deviation was measured, as Officer Rose confirmed:

'Some normal, chaotic unlock, everybody'll go back to their cells so I can progress with the regime. Get everybody off to work, get those out that need to go out, they'll just have their bitting and bobbing. Just general chat, noise.'

While disorder – and the threats to safety it posed – were central to concerns around which Midtown organized and operated, it was order that assumed the instructive point of reference. In contrast, disorder frequently forms the focal point of academic enquiry. Shaped partially by the wider political context of the time, and the research brief to 'consider the social context within which control problem behaviour arose', disorder has been the preoccupation of a number of prison studies emerging in the wake of the Strangeways riot (for example, Sparks et al, 1996). Order is studied in negation, its absence providing insight into what has gone wrong. This raises questions about how using a 'normal' day as a point of comparison, as both staff and prisoners at Midtown did, alters the way we understand processes of social organization:

'It's your own prison in my experience ... You get a sense of a normal day. You know what the day is, you know how it's gonna pan out, you just know. You have your normal noises, your regular sounds, your normal behaviours, and then if something's different, it's noticeably different.' (Officer Rose)

This was significant both for what it indicated about the nature of order and what it revealed about life at HMP Midtown. A focus on disorder deviated from the practice of those I spoke to and aligned order more closely with processes of power and its maintenance. Social life at Midtown was fluid and complex, the relationship between order and disorder were far from directly antithetical. Rather, order was characterized by the multifarious activities and interactions which characterized the ebb and flow of social life on a 'good' day. At HMP Midtown, order was a complicated business. Not only did it require being 'worked at' as Sparks et al (1996) identify, but that work took many forms and was undertaken by numerous members of the community. Within the expanse of variety between a perfectly attuned day and one in which all semblance of control has been lost, was the rich assortment of distinctions within the broad range of an ordered day. Keeping the 'everyday tune' playing, in rhythm and key, was the main preoccupation of staff on the wing. While prisoners were often understandably ambivalent about unquestioning compliance, their participation in shared rituals of meaning-making signalled assent to joining in with the chorus, albeit with personalized lyrics. While it was clear that the forces at work compelling compliance were present (Crewe, 2007), there was a considerable degree of cooperation in setting the pace for an orderly day. There was comfort and companionability in contributing to the rhythms and routines of the day, which, while not unrelated to the fear of violence – both in the form of physical threat and the risk of additional deprivation – was also motivated by the desire for a 'good' day. Compliance and cooperation with order was explicitly linked to remaining in one piece, and the desire to get everyone away safe. This was linked to survival in a broader sense; the desire to prevent 'meaning deprivation' and retain a sense of normality, of 'just everybody getting along' as well as avoidance of physical harm.

Orderly disorder

'Arrhythmic' states were also complicated, the result of shifting recipes of personalities, moods and events. I found this underlined the broad range of behaviours and incidents which, at times, fell under the umbrella of 'disorder'. While 'disorder', strictly speaking, refers to concerted acts of 'disobedience' or 'indiscipline', at times it was elided within a wide spectrum of behaviours. It is also worth noting that, on occasion, acts which were technically against the rules and therefore 'disobedient' or 'undisciplined', worked to re-establish order and relieve tension. This amplified the delicate balancing act undertaken by staff as they sought to maintain or re-establish a polyrhythmic state to the day. Recognizing the value of behaviours working to improve the emotional climate could involve an absence of authority. Rather than exercising discretion or 'good authority', this reflected the wisdom in a willingness to relinquish control, and one which often partially rested on what could be heard.

When asked what a good *prison* sounded like, many I spoke to had difficulty and often fell back on the rather vague 'quiet'. There were exceptions to this, such as Lamar who was keen to move on and having various issues at Midtown:

> 'Calm quiet ... where everyone's calm. Everyone's not crazy in their heads or running about like headless chickens for mamba. That would make things a lot more levelled ... Cos I've been to prisons that are quiet, and you feel a lot more at ease.'

Generally, those I spoke with found a good *day* considerably more tangible and tended to respond with thoughtful reflections:

> 'You know it's running well cos everything's going to plan. Everything's happening on time, or certainly within a few minutes of on time. Without any interruption, er, without anybody sort of messing about and doing stupid things, just everybody behaving and doing what

they're supposed to, staff as well. Not just prisoners behaving but getting staff to do their job on time, and do it right as well, but yeah, it just all drops into place.' (Officer Rose)

For Officer Rose the process of understanding and managing the rhythms of everyday life was dependent on a familiarity with what a 'good' day sounded like. His account resonated with the disappointment expressed by some Midtown officers at what they interpreted as a reluctance to assimilate among a group of new staff from a closing prison. A number of these incomers expressed discomfort at their new workplace, stating a preference for "order" (the inference being that this was absent from Midtown). They settled in after a time, but initial unease was caused in part by a lack of familiarity with the "everyday tune that's normal for here". They mistook their unfamiliarity – and difficulty 'reading' it – for an absence of a tune to learn.

Officer Rose's account of a good day, with "everything going to plan", echoed the centrality of predictability. The importance of knowing what was coming, and its association with order were recurring themes in interviews and conversations with both prisoners and staff: "It would be better if there was more order. More things to do ... if there was more of a structure. There has to be more order or else nothing's gonna get solved" (Tommy). Tommy clearly identified order with purposeful occupation. For him this was the bedrock of solutions to prison problems. Again, routine and structure were identified as key (and related to survival – Cohen and Taylor, 1981; Liebling and Arnold, 2004; Tait, 2011). Davey reinforced this sense of importance. While he anchored predictability in knowing in advance so he could organize himself, there was a comfort in predictable rhythm: "I prefer to know what's going on. I just don't like not being told. Say, if there's bang-up for one day, I like to know there's bang-up before that day so if there's things I need I can get them" (Davey). Like being stuck in a tunnel on the London tube, sitting in uncertain silence ratcheted up anxiety, which was greatly alleviated by the driver explaining the reason behind the delay.

Rituals and routines

Routine and rituals were a source of ontological security; a means of deriving comfort and meaning from the day. People engaged in the routine not because of an adherence to the ideological principles which founded it, but because security was derived from engaging in familiar spatial practices (Giddens, 1984). This provided an explanation for consistent difficulty in obtaining an answer to questioning about what a "good prison" sounds like (beyond "there isn't one", "there's no such thing"). Legitimacy rarely featured in conversations with anyone in the community beyond the abstract application to the plight of others, or the reasonable acceptance of a fair refusal from staff. Processes of legitimation on the other hand, to the degree that rules and routines became accepted in to the everyday, were commonplace. Predictable practice formed the rhythms and routines of a stable community which united its members in reaffirming a sense of mechanical solidarity at HMP Midtown.

What does this mean for how a good day is understood? Underpinning a number of accounts of the maintenance of order in prison are particular conceptions of legitimacy. Sparks and Bottoms draw heavily on legitimacy as a source of disorder, quoting Woolf: 'They [prisoners] felt a lack of justice ... the failure ... to act with justice created serious difficulties in maintaining security and control in prisons' (Woolf, 1991: para 9.24, in Sparks and Bottoms, 1996). This intertwines order with conceptions of authoritative modes of power. Order is maintained because those subject to it broadly acknowledge and accept the fairness of the regime and thus the authority of those who maintain it to do so. This was not a clear factor in accounts of cooperation and/or compliance for those I spoke with at HMP Midtown. Rooting enquiry within the soundscape replaced a top-down reading of these motivations with one from within the community:

> 'A good prison sounds like officers on the wing with a positive vibe about 'em. Yeah, like when you first hear in the morning "Alright lads, alright", "Morning mate, morning mate" that sets the tone. But when you got the wrong screw opening the door, that can set the tone like ... fuck I've just come out my cell and that can set a bad, you know what I mean? 'Specially when you're in a bad mood as well ... the best jails are when staff sound positive, cos it makes the vibe come through the prison. Yeah, we're here, we don't wanna be here and you don't really want to be as well, but it's a job and we've all got to get along ... let's just get on with it.' (Tonk)

Tonk's circumstances made perceptions of legitimacy less likely (he was recalled having been released after serving a substantial indeterminate sentence for public protection). It is significant, however, that he viewed questions of legitimacy as somewhat separate from his interactions with staff. Prison, for him, was far from ideal for all within it. Despite raging about the injustices of his case and subsequent treatment at the hands of "the system" and its agents, Tonk was resolutely stoical about "get[ting] on with it". For him, this was key to surviving an indeterminate sentence with his sense of self intact. Tonk perceived a connection between positive sound and spreading a sense of good feeling. For him, shared cooperation and sense of community were conveyed via the soundscape, and central to a good day and the order it denoted. This interpretation of what made a good, ordered community was not limited to prisoners, but could also be seen in staff accounts, where the rhythms of a good day depended on a shared sense of cooperation and community:

> 'The staff there, even though they were hardcore, they made it safe ... they all had their back, they worked together, they all knew what was going on ... run so smoothly ... so smooth. I've never known anything like it, and I just thought, wow, this place is different ... the prisoners knew where they stood ... They knew what, who to speak to, who not to speak to.' (Ket, officer)

There were, of course, multiple reasons for compliance among those held at Midtown, many of which related primarily to a pragmatic awareness that this was more likely to ensure rights and privileges were accessible. Lugs illustrated this succinctly when, during our interview a man lumbered past the room shouting: "Everybody riot!!" Lugs responded: "Why do that when everybody'll get banged up? Why do you want a riot mate? Idiot." Jack illustrated how this could work the other way when, in another prison, he had attempted to lead a riot, only to find he was on his own. What was not clear from talking to people in Midtown, was that legitimacy – perceptions of fairness or acceptance of authority – were necessarily connected to order, though this was cited as a significant factor in relationships with individuals. "If they say something they'll keep to their word. Like that's what a good officer is, innit" (Stevie). "If it's 'no' then fair enough" (Mooch). "If they're entitled to it, I'll do it. If they aren't, tough" (Officer Rose). Repeated identification of even-handedness as the mark of a good officer echoed Mathieson's (1965) assessment of the importance of regulated staff decisions, but also further underscored the desirability of consistency. These accounts reinforced the sense of an overarching importance of predictability as a basis for maintaining order and the stable emotional climate with which it shared a symbiotic relationship.

Using legitimacy as a conceptual framework for exploring order relies on a particular understanding of the relationship between power and order, and authority; the form in which much power in prison is assumed to manifest. In contrast, the social life at HMP Midtown flowed on the predictability of ontologically reassuring rituals and the emotionally stabilizing soundscape which lent them social meaning. This is not to say that perceptions of a deficit of legitimacy were insignificant in providing the impetus for acts of 'disobedience' or violence. Fieldnotes and interviews include repeated references to inconsistencies in treatment or unfairness. Those I spoke with at HMP Midtown indicated that legitimacy was not a predicate of order. Crises in processes of legitimation might feature in concerted disorder at Midtown as elsewhere and there is much work to suggest this would be the case (for example, Carrabine, 2004). It was less clear that the reverse held.

Listening to the rhythms and routines of the day expanded understanding of the multiplicities of power relations at work in their maintenance, mediated though auditory interactions between people and prison spaces.

Reconsidering the relationship between order/disorder and legitimacy allows for a more nuanced consideration of the array of behaviours which are loosely characterized as threatening order. Many of the instances of violence I witnessed or discussed with staff and prisoners were explained as working to uphold or maintain order, rather than seeking to undermine it. While this reflected the omnipresence of violence in prison, and its broad acceptance in prison culture, it was also the case that some instances of this behaviour were about restoring social breaches (perceived discourtesies or wrongs) as a means of maintaining social order, rather than in an effort to disturb it. Much of prisons literature explores disorder and disruption as a means of understanding order, but this obscures the broad continuum of behaviours which were associated with both. Attending to these complexities revealed the partial understanding allowed for by a reliance on a crude dichotomy between order and disorder.

16

Listening to Power

'Every time that bell rings yeah, it's like a reminder you ain't got no liberty.' (Duke)

Navigating the cadence of the soundscape was intimately entwined with the ecology of survival. Learning to hear where power was less implicated in motivations for behaviour added clarity and definition to understanding where it *was* more keenly felt, and by whom. Charting this process with others extended understanding of how this shaped relationships between people and place.

The nuance, significance and delicacy of relationships between prisoners and staff, as well as within respective groups, reflected complexity in the recognition of distinctions between different levels of experience. While this depended somewhat on circumstances, prisoners differed markedly in their feelings about the potency of the broader institution, the 'system' and relationships with individual staff. This was instructive for understanding distinctions in the forms and flows of power between individuals, the institution and broader conceptions of 'the system'.

Every contact matters

Difference between relationships with the broader institution and those which comprised the stuff of daily life was a recurring feature of conversation. Stretch had developed a deep familiarity with both the institution and various members of its community. The profound demarcation of his respective feelings for people and place was a powerful indication of how deeply these distinctions forged his relationship with Midtown. He had little affection for the prison (though described it in terms of territorial belonging elsewhere): "Just blow this place off the face of the earth ... This is inhumane. This place is inhumane." He used a range of expletives to refer to some members of staff, so his fondness for them was far from universal. However, the significant degree of attachment and mutual care he expressed for others was profound and affecting. His fondness extended to assigning some members of staff quasi-parental roles. This spoke both to their significance in his personal narrative and the care and sensitivity with which these individuals conducted their job: "I'm lucky I've got Miss F, Mr S, Mr P on the First-Night Centre. They just pick me up and they're like me parents, literally." If the soundscape reverberated with stark power asymmetries between people and place, it also hummed with interactions forged by concern and understanding. When, towards the end of my time at the prison, Dermot died, the loss rippled through Midtown in ways that reflected the relative intimacy and 'local' character of the place. Dermot was a well-known and frequent resident. Boisterous and good-natured it was hard not to warm to him. Having been moved to another prison he suffered a relapse and overdose he did not survive. The loss of him echoed through the community among staff, prisoners and beyond. Few of us were left untouched by his dying.

Power within prison flows in complex currents between people, place, expectation and experience. While it was present in relations which buoyed stability, listening to the tone of interactions which were genuinely rich in affection and familiarity emphasized informal and multi-directional flows of power. Midtown shaped the form these relationships took, but their content less so. The appearance of these relations was specific to the prison, both in terms of its asymmetry and structure (for example, additional sanction, systems of 'punishment', threat of movement (Goffman, 1961; Sparks et al, 1996). Their form belied far less stark and unequivocal distributions of power. Rather, the daily routines were forged on unofficial cooperation and compromise between prisoners and officers (Sykes, 1958). Power in prison, Sykes contends, is not based on authority (which relies on legitimacy and duty for its operations) and comprises 'something more than ... outward forms and symbols' (Sykes, 1958: 45). Power flows in multiple directions, is partial, fluid and unreliably distributed which make it a poor means of securing order. Rather, order relies on a system of informal and illicit agreements with the population which form a necessary corruption of authority (Sykes, 1958). Familiarity and care underpinned the exercise of discretion, and the nuanced application of informal accommodations which characterized perceptions of the 'good' officer (Liebling, 2000; Arnold, 2016).

Banging

The lexicon of banging represents one of the most explicit demonstrations of sound as a system of signification in prison (Chion, 2010). Prison offers limited access to goods and services. Mobility and, consequently, vision were heavily restricted for much of the day. In this environment banging (most often on the inside of a locked cell door) was a means of compensating for lack of visibility behind it – a means of being heard and form of social exchange. Imposing a presence on the soundscape challenged the constraints of being 'behind the door' and the powerlessness this represented. Quantity of banging, as well as tone, frequency, context and quality denoted the wider emotional climate: "A bad day, I s'pose the sounds that relate to a bad day is banging, constant banging, unified banging is terrible, that is, it's not a good sound" (Tone, officer). Some I spoke to claimed it always meant the same thing ("to get out, mostly to get out. It don't have no meaning, it's just to get out" [Robert]). Others recognized the wider set of meanings banging signified, depending on the social context of their interpretation:

> 'You could hear banging now and it wouldn't necessarily bother you, but in those situations when you're walking on the landing to drop something off, it's a different type of banging. It can be quite intimidating. It's just the type of bang, isn't it, and you know, the atmosphere when there's been lots to go into that full lockdown.'
> (Joanne, substance use support worker)

Conversations elicited in response to banging while out on the wing prompted discussions on who was banging and why. These conversations functioned as assessments of the emotional temperature. Banging represented an act of insistent communication in opposition to the constraints of the physical environment and in that sense constituted an act of resistance which covered an array of meanings, and messages. Diane explained:

> 'I always find, in the Seg it feels different ... I find it personally quite disturbing really, and I think the prison staff probably do as well because I think they're often dealing with people who, you know, have severe mental health issues and you know, it obviously isn't the best way to treat people, to put them behind doors. And I find that, again, quite upsetting really. I think there's a difference between that and people just kicking because they want to be unlocked.'

Diane's explanation illustrates the centrality of context to what was being conveyed. It was also clear that Diane and Joanne could discern different meanings (Chion, 2010). What follows is by no means a comprehensive key. Specific meanings vary according to context of regime and individual circumstance, but these were commonly heard examples at Midtown.

Rapid, rhythmic: Bangbangbang

Denotes frustration and irritation. The banging may indicate the regime is running a little behind, that the person within has urgent business to attend to, and/or wants out. Frequently this banging erupts in short bursts. It may be echoed by a number of cell occupants depending on what else is occurring. It can go on for prolonged periods of time, particularly if items are used to do the banging rather than fists or feet.

Slow, rhythmic: Bang. Bang. Bang.

This expresses more focused and intense displeasure. The effect can be disconcerting, especially if other prisoners join in. The intention is to enforce a sense of power in number and strength; to intimidate. Officer McKie illustrates how this can be experienced by staff:

> 'I remember being on the twos landing ... and a small number of prisoners started banging on their doors, and a large number followed the cue and joined in. And we were standing there on the twos looking at each other, everyone was locked up, but it was genuinely frightening. It felt like the wing was shaking with this banging on the doors. And I guess we were standing looking at each other thinking fuck, we're going to have to unlock these for tea. And there was such a ... you could cut the atmosphere with a knife. There was a noise that was quite intimidating, and I was thinking I've seen this before, you know, I've done a number of years' service, and I was looking at these new staff thinking they're probably shitting themselves. It was quite scary.'

Aural reminders of the greater number and potential might of those imprisoned echoes Sykes' (1958) point about the contingent and negotiated nature of power:

> 'It means that, to me, that all prisoners are aware of their perceived injustice, they all agree that something bad has happened, and they're all on the same page. And that's not good. Rightfully or wrongfully, that's not good. Yeah, I've not heard it often though, thank god.' (Tone, officer)

Banging was a reminder that unofficial contracts of cooperation could always be redrawn or withdrawn altogether. When banging gathered momentum in numbers and volume, it emphasized the potential power of the collective. In this sense banging can be understood as a ritualistic expression of mechanical solidarity (Durkheim, 1893). This could be particularly powerful in HMP Midtown where the small space meant there was little opportunity to diffuse, dissipate or contain frustrations. The effect on collective mood could be profound.

Arrhythmic: Bangbang ... bang. Bang ... bang

Arrhythmic banging encompasses a range of expressions of emotion from extreme frustration to distress and despair. Disordered banging is often the sound accompanying 'smashing up' or the colloquial 'flat packing', the sustained destruction of cell and property. The person inside might be experiencing acute distress and/or wishing to go off the wing, whether to Seg or transfer, either because they are finding it hard behind the door or wish to avoid other issues. If this occurred close to canteen day, it usually indicated the incumbent was in debt they were unable to pay. Often people want to force a move, though of course motivations vary: "nine times out of ten, when prisoners are violent on the wing, it's 'cause they want to be taken off the wing. They want to be transferred. They want to be segregated" (No. 1, governor).

Rapid: moving location around the wing

Always celebratory, like a sonic Mexican wave, and normally heard during sporting events. I stayed behind one evening to listen to the men listening to a Midtown football match on home turf. I was able to monitor the game by men's response to goals, near misses, unpopular referee decisions and the other team scoring. I had been advised by staff, as well as one or two prisoners, to make sure I caught this: "when the football's on, or the tennis, the atmosphere's brilliant ... you hear the cheers, you hear the chants, and I can remember feeling really buzzing after that. And like the guys. It was so powerful" (Joanne). The emotional climate of the prison sounded markedly different. This was an evening match, and despite it being an important Midtown game the volume declined as the evening wore on, seemingly in keeping with a collective code to limit noise levels and disturbance after certain hours (the match concluded after ten).

Banging communicated a complex range of information and emotion. It could also function as a means of redressing unequal power relations by imposing an effect on others through noise. As sound can impact cognitive function and concentration, as well as being a nuisance, causing distress and adversely affecting health, this effect could be keenly felt (for example, Klatte et al, 2013; Basner et al, 2014).

Power, the institution

Sound is used to impose cultural and spatial dominance in a range of settings from warfare to shopping malls (DeNora, 2000; Cusick, 2008; Walsh, 2008). Noise – unwanted or unrestricted sound – was implicated in unequal power relations and their contestation at Midtown. Schafer (1994) asserts that power is embodied in the freedom to make noise without censure. Who defines what is noise, as well as who enjoys respite from it, are means of enforcing social relations and the disparities of power which characterize them (Keizer, 2012). In prison people have little control over their exposure to noise (Wener, 2012). Banging was a means of redressing the balance, however fleetingly. An answering call to prolonged exposure to 'banging doors … keys jangling, shouting and screaming' (Owens, 2012: 32) which could result in sonically induced feelings of fear and dread (Goodman, 2012).

There was a decline in the use of alarms during my time at Midtown, which illustrated an awareness of how crucial sound could be in altering the balance of power in unforeseen ways. I neglected to ask directly what the reason behind this was but noted that such was the size of the wing, staff could make themselves heard quite easily in the event they required support, without sounding it. Diane suggested the decline in use of alarms was a direct and systematic result of a change in operational leadership. She was a relatively new member of staff at Midtown, a resettlement worker who had been subject to the impact of Grayling's probation 'reforms'[1] ('transforming rehabilitation') and had migrated into the prison. While Diane had only been there for three years, and considered herself relatively 'new', she had been around long enough to perceive a change in the soundscape which she attributed to a more settled prison: "all the time you felt there was general alarms going off which has changed quite dramatically actually … there's been quite a dramatic reduction in general alarms".

Listening to a conversation among senior management while attending a meeting before beginning fieldwork, there was agreement about the potential for alarms to escalate rather than pacify. They heightened a sense of disruption as well as being painful and agitating. Associated with trouble and disorder, alarms heightened both the awareness of and response to this unsettled state rather than de-escalating disturbance. Signalling danger and threat to safety, alarms offered a hard delineation of role within the prison, sharpening the particular social arrangements of the prison habitus (Bordieu, 1992). At the same time, alarms were a feature of the soundscape over which only those sounding them had immediate control, painful to hear and disruptive to daily rhythms. This shift in policy illustrated how change in governance and flows of power could manifest in the prison soundscape.

Sound allows for a wider-ranging consideration of how power 'reaches into the very grain of individuals, touches their bodies and inserts itself into their actions and attitudes … learning processes and everyday lives' (Foucault, 1980: 39). Restricting treatments of power to the immediately relational narrows the ways that the impact of punishment and power on the incarcerated body can be understood. Sound extends the field of enquiry beyond the peripheries of vision and through physical boundaries. Flows of power are more diffuse and variegated than can be captured without acknowledging and accounting for the significance of its sensory dimensions. Sound evokes physiological, affective and cognitive responses comprising an experiential pathway to memory (Stansfeld, 1992; Barrett et al, 2010; Klatte et al, 2013). The potency of the symbolic violence in locking keys and slamming doors lay in flows of power laden with meaning that transcended the immediate parameters of daily interactions.

Flows of power were discernible in the movement of the community through its spaces (Moran et al, 2013). Goffman talks about the centrality of admissions procedures to processes of acclimation to the institutional environment, rituals which signify a 'leaving off and a taking on' – a 'trimming' – of the former self to replace it with the institutionalized identity (Goffman, 1961: 27). These processes were more visible among staff on the way out, signified by the importance of shedding rituals. Joanne indicated the importance of these: "If you've got stuff on your mind, don't hand them keys back until you've talked it through."

Prisoners underwent perhaps the most significant process of 'taking on' of identity on the way in. Reception processes constituted rhythmic rituals of admission:

> Rituals of immersion, step by step. Van. Wait. 'Permission to unload?' Decant. Wait. Cell. Come forward. What you can have, what you aren't allowed. Don't beg, steal or borrow. Don't tamper with the electrics and follow the prison rules. Are you rattling?[2] Paperwork. Process. Paper, split, staple, shuffle, signatures. Picture taking. Card. Whirring of the card machine, has its own song: di dooorrrr ... diiii di dooorrr. Sounds flat and jolted if jammed or empty. Fingerprint. Search. Strip. Prison outfit. Sort kit. Keep your socks and boxers. 'Next.' Wait. Nurse. Wait. Escort to First-Night Centre. Ship in. Ship out. Prop. Papers. Mountains of paper and property documenting history, 'risk', what they came in with, what they're leaving with; bagged, tagged, boxed and accounted for. (Fieldnotes)

Reception at Midtown, friendlier, more intimate and less frenetic than others I had been in, had particular rhythms which reinforced its particular purpose in processes of 'prisonization'; absorption into prison life (Clemmer, 1940). Both staff and prisoners battled to redefine borders of the self in opposition to the intrusive soundscape of the prison. The prison echoed wider mechanics of politics and coercion, acting upon the body to rearrange, coerce and to institutionalize (Foucault, 1977). Sound was heavily implicated in embodied processes of 'institutionalization': "All these noises, getting us used to things we shouldn't be getting used to" (Marlon). Marlon was referring to the way in which the prisoner is conditioned to accept the prison environment through continual exposure to the institutional soundscape. Kevin underscored the significance of sound in processes of institutionalization by drawing attention to the similar processes of various institutions of control:

> 'I thought of you on a visit. My little 'un heard the bell and said: "It must be dinner time" cos he hears the bell at school. "Daddy has to go and have his dinner now".'

Kevin's son placed the prison firmly within the matrices of agencies of social control, echoing Foucault: 'Is it surprising that prisons resemble factories, schools, barracks, hospitals, which all resemble prisons?' (Foucault, 1977: 228). The prison soundscape was inextricably bound up with processes accustoming those who lived and worked there to the social life of HMP Midtown.

17

Singing Frogs, Looping the Slam

Those who had passed through the doors of Midtown – and, almost invariably – other institutions repeatedly, were sometimes more dismissive of my line of enquiry. The phrase 'singing frogs' came from a conversation with David, a governor visiting from Bermuda. He was somewhat resistant to the idea prisons were noisy, but tacitly understood the role acclimation played in this. He was too deeply embedded within the rhythms of the institution to consciously discern them.

Sound was heavily implicated in processes of institutionalization. Prompting people to reflect on their shifting interpretations of the soundscape provided a means of assessing both their degree of familiarity with the environment and feelings about the place and people within it. For some, familiarity with the prison soundscape reflected sustained contact with a broader range of institutions with which its clangs and bangs reverberated. For others, the soundscape was a particularly harsh aspect of the environment, compounding and exacerbating other conditions, including ASD[1] and PTSD.[2]

While waiting for staff to assemble for a security meeting, I sat with David. He enquired about what I was doing and expressed incredulity that I held keys and seemed to move around with freedom. When I explained my purpose, he responded:

> 'I've never thought of prisons as noisy places. I still don't but it reminds me of friends we have who visit from Canada. They can't sleep at night for the singing frogs, they go all through the night and make a racket. We're so accustomed to it we don't hear it.'

The exchange between David and I raised a central point: does sound matter if it is not perceived as significant by those you speak with? And if so, why and how? When I asked how he relaxed, he said: "I like to unwind, no talking. Sometimes I like to just drive around. If I go straight back home, I'm a different person." His dismissal of the significance of prison noise was contradicted by his use of sound (and space) as part of his shedding ritual. Manipulating his sonic environment was crucial for David, in guarding against 'spillover' of his work life into his private life. Curating his soundscape allowed him to leave the prison behind, to 'shed' it (Crawley, 2004). David was using sound to impose clear distance between work and private spheres of his life. This period of silence comprised a solid sound border, protecting against the permeation of the prison into time at home. His efforts to avoid 'spillover' by imposing demarcations between these parts of himself were efforts not to take the "different person" he presented within the prison social system into his family life. Keenly aware of the potential for blurring between places and identities, David used sound to guard against *distanciation* between work and home life.

Looping

There was a process of acclimation to the sound environment, after which specific aspects, or 'discordant notes', assumed greater importance as a focus for concern. Kathleen referred to this when she spoke of her move to Midtown many years before:

> 'Midtown is more compact and squashed in ... and I sat there, and it was just noisy you know? Like there was the clattering of this and keys, gates, doors banging, and I sat there, and I thought, ooh, I don't know if I like this or not ... I'll give it six months (laughs). Yeah, been a long six months!'

Diane expressed awareness of undergoing a process of acclimation to the environment, and used our interview as a means of reflecting on her current position:

> 'I think it's quite good to be reasonably new because you do get institutionalized and probably slightly immune to it and I can see that happening to me and has happened to me, so if I think about my initial impressions, might be useful to recall, to be honest.'

Processes of institutionalization had audible components which were both a source of fear and uncertainty. Sound provided a frame for cultural reference, evoking auditory memories of other institutional settings. Quiet, or an absence of notable sounds, had its own particular significance within Midtown. In encouraging members of the community to reflect on the soundscape of the prison it became clear that sensitivities and emotional responses shifted over time, as people became acclimated to the environment. Officer Tone made this clear when he explained that:

'the fear came from them assuming that I'm an officer and wanting something and just not knowing what to do ... and then after a while when we as a group went on the wing and I got to see people and so forth, that dissipated quite quickly.'

Initial fear and discomfort arising from the prison soundscape became quickly replaced by an understanding of what it signified, but sound was interwoven with processes of institutionalization; acclimation to the institutional environment as Gee illustrated:

'Well, it makes you act stupid, see. I hear that bell all the time, so I made up a song: "ding, ding that's the sound of the bell". I'd never do that outside. I'm normal me.'

In the case of alarms and clanging, sound altered both communication (forcing people to raise their voices to be heard above the din) and movement (hard metallic sounds vibrated through the body, while loud alarms abruptly, if temporarily, stopped people in their tracks). In these ways sound was implicated in processes of accustoming prisoners to their role. The prison landscape is characterized by a lack of softness and elaborate locking/unlocking rituals of doors and gates which act as symbolic reinforcements of the carceral environment (Jewkes and Johnston, 2007). Various responses to the aural environment worked to further impose prisoner identity upon the individual. Efforts to enact resistance could be subverted in the service of institutional processes. Goffman refers to this process as 'looping', a defensive response – in this instance to avoid or anticipate unpleasant sensory experience – is then targeted, reducing the ability of the 'inmate' to defend themselves against processes of mortification (Goffman, 1961: 41). Sound was integral to the process of looping, as responses to the sonic environment whether protective or immersive mire the individual further within the soundscape, and thereby within the prison environment. Shutting oneself in cell – which a number of those I spoke with did habitually – to deprive an officer of the opportunity to bang the cell door are examples of this.

The soundscape imposed a particular feeling of discomfort for some. Their responses served to remake the form and function of the institution and the social relationships within it. Officer Tone described his unease when he began working at Midtown:

'And I remember walking down the rotunda and I was by myself, and I needed to get somewhere. And they were all out. And I got to the door that leads you on to the wing. And I was afraid, really afraid. God, I don't want to go in there ... I don't want to go ... and I turned back, and I went another way.'

When I asked him: "What was it that made you feel like that?", he responded: "There's so many people." Being familiar with the environment I knew full well that the outer door offered little view of the wing beyond, requiring unbroken sight through two small, grubby windows. I said so: "But you weren't on there?" He answered:

> 'No, the sheer, yeah, I suppose the noise. Which wasn't noise it was just the volume of conversation that let me know that everybody's out. And I think that the fear came from them assuming that I'm an officer and wanting something and just not knowing what to do. So I found another way to get to where I wanted to go.'

The soundscape of the main wing reminded him of his rookie status and his concern about being found inadequate. His avoidance of the soundscape reinforced his sense of the expectations of his uniform as well as the uncertainty and potential vulnerability of dealing with a prison population who vastly outnumbered him. His response to what he heard further institutionalized him by invoking his expectations of his role, reinforcing his officer identity.

"Now I think he's alright"

In HMP Midtown, enquiring about the soundscape emphasized the subjective and changeable nature of noise. Tonk explained there was one officer who was very loud. He acknowledged this could be irritating to some, but his noise was welcome because he now regarded their relationship in positive terms:

> 'When I first come here though, it used to annoy because I think I was singled out because I'm an IPP ... they wouldn't give me nothing ... so I never used to like all of them, the screws ... Can you hear him echoing the wing off? But now I think he's alright cos he gave me a cleaning job. You know what I mean? So, when he's shouting an' that, I know it pisses other people off but I'm like "Yeah go on Mr Tawny, you ain't pissing me off anymore, you're alright, I like you!"'

His relationship with the people and place determined how he interpreted others' behaviour and consequently how positively he responded to Officer Tawny's shouting (he shouted quite a lot). In talking about his changing relationship with the staff, and this aspect of the community, Tonk also indicated that his interaction with the soundscape was influenced by how he felt. In turn, this influenced how he responded to the soundscape in a looping effect which further reinforced his acculturation to the environment:

'Cos I'm strong I don't mind being in the environment I'm in. So if like, I get on well with everyone I don't mind hearing them on the wing, but if I'm making enemies or I'm angry or down and I keep hearing someone I'm like "Fucking hell, is he gonna shut up or what?" You know what I mean? And I'll probably tell him to shut up. But because I get on with everyone, I don't mind everyone making noise. You know what I mean?'

Tonk suggests that if he was "angry or down" he might regard intrusive sound negatively. In a delicate mental state, sound, certainly made by people he was irritated with, would be regarded as agitating. The feelings evoked by the soundscape for Tonk, were coloured, possibly determined by, how he was experiencing the power of the prison rules. In this sense, getting work and so forth, the practical pains of attempting to progress (particularly as an indeterminate sentence for public protection (IPP) prisoner in a local prison) were both associated with the way staff exercised their discretionary power, and how he faired as a subject of it. Being held within a prison whose regime was designed for those passing through or near release, on a sentence without a definite end point heightened Tonk's sense of vertigo. It was how he faired in navigating these processes which determined how he responded to the soundscape. His response, whether agitated or amused, reinforced and sustained his relationship and role within the prison. Tonk's interpretation of the sounds he was subject to was bound with his personal feelings about their source. This was regardless of whether the interaction was directly between him and the person in question. Sound mediated these institutional relationships and served to intensify his emotional response to them, a destructive relationship echoed by Lamar, who was not a local and wished to move out so he could progress with his sentence plan:

'Within two minutes of your door open it sounds like it's a youth club out there. Do you know? Years ago, you woke up, and it'd be quiet. People'd be more calm. It's difficult to explain, do you know? But from the minute I wake up in the morning, and sometimes it's them and all their noise that wakes me up, or someone playing some hardcore, or some rock like headbanging music. Like straightaway you're up, you're in a different mindset. They've not got no respect. Why they just blasting out their music when the door's just opened? Then next minute, "Oh have you got a sugar, have you got this?" You know, you're in bed. They can see you're physically in bed and they're coming in your cell, "You got this, and you got that?" Then five minutes later the officer's like bang up so straight away when you wake up in the morning, you're in a bad mood.'

Lamar's adaptive response of hostility to deter people from intruding in his space then shaped subsequent interactions with staff. In Tonk's account, his changing relationship with sound indicated his emotional state. His feeling about the soundscape was also linked with his experience of the institution and the people within it. Tonk felt he was doing okay at that point and was quite buoyant about the soundscape as a result, though he was aware his feelings were not necessarily shared by others ("You'll find people who're not comfortable. Shy. And the noise to them is like, it's angry noise, but it ain't, like, to us it's fun, messing about, but to shy people it's intimidating"). In this sense his adjustment to the prison environment represented routinized behaviours which corresponded to the order of the prison. Tonk spoke about his familiarity with the prison environment and his adaptation to it: "I adjust to this type of environment because that's been me all my life." He attributed his comfort in the prison to his familiarity with its routines. For Tonk sound acted as a means of conveying both his current relationship with the prison and his identity within it. His expression of acculturation to the carceral environment – shouting and being "boisterous" – was, by his own account, sometimes interpreted as disruptive which in turn encouraged staff to place further restrictions on his movement. This process further embedded him within the rituals of the prison, and the perpetual tension between resistance to being banged up behind the door, and the imperative to bang prisoners up as a means of maintaining order.

Damage

How Tonk felt about the staff and the place were bound up with how he was experiencing his sentence. These relationships were mediated through sound. He knew his own contributions to the soundscape were open to negative interpretation: "Because I'm loud and a bit boisterous, they were banging me up behind my door like, the whole time." Tonk presented his boisterousness as a facet of identity with such regularity he appeared to take comfort in it as a means of reasserting his sense of self against the institution. Another example of looping in that his loudness, often a response to the conditions of imprisonment, provoked punitive responses. Restricted by the prison space and rules as well as his reply, Tonk found himself repeating these behaviours, which in turn reinforced his place within the prison. In contrast, Cameron was considerably more reticent, and separated from the general population as he found the environment too challenging. He also referred to his relationship with the sound environment as a source of potential for trouble: "I got mental health issues, so the best place for me is down here. I got PTSD[3] and I don't like crowds and it's too noisy out there, too much going on and it makes me crazy, and I fight." Cameron was happier protected from the bustle and temptation of the main wing, but his consensual removal from it mired him further in the depths of the institution.

Tonk's account indicates that sound operated as a means of gauging wellbeing and the mutually reinforcing effects of ongoing communications between prisoner, staff and prison. The extent to which an individual was getting on and getting by was correspondingly indicated by how they expressed their interpretation of the soundscape. Talking about sound was a way of exploring how people experienced the effects of the prison environment. Sound simultaneously indicated how individuals were navigating the complex configurations of power in the prison and how they were feeling. While I was talking with people in the First-Night Centre, a prisoner, briefly staying there, responded to my conversation with another. He remained in his cell, and I had been careful not to talk to him through the doorway to preserve his peace. I knew he identified on the autistic spectrum and was distressed, but he overheard our conversation and responded from within his cell:

'Sound, you say sound? Only the keys and banging, they're difficult to cope with. They draw, they draw ... hang heavy on my shoulders. When I hear the keys coming it makes me anxious. It makes me really anxious. If they could put me somewhere quiet, away from the noises?' (Prisoner, fieldnotes)

While he did not refer directly to his condition, associations between autism and sound sensitivity are well documented (for example, Stiegler and Davis, 2010). It is difficult to obtain accurate figures but there is broad acceptance that people with a host of neurodivergent challenges are significantly over-represented in the prison population, and reflections such as this were not uncommon: "I'm not diagnosed but I've been told I've got Asperger's. It's bad for that innit, cos all the cells are on top of each other. It's like sensory overload sometimes, and the way they talk to you" (Matt, fieldnotes) (CJJI, 2021). Goffman makes the point that mortifications upon the sense of self are distinct from psychological distress, though this can enhance the mortification process (Goffman, 1961). It was clear, though, that for these prisoners, the impossibility of escaping from a soundscape they experienced bodily, added to their difficulty coping and intruded upon their sense of self. The more attempts were made to retreat from the soundscape, the more engaging with the prison community was likely to become problematic. The soundscape was an inextricable element of the prison environment, both mediating and amplifying discomfort. While prisoners more frequently expressed difficulty with the sound environment (citing a diverse range of issues: PTSD, insomnia, depression, ASD, all of which are significantly over-represented among the prison population – Allely and Allely, 2020;

CJJI, 2021), this did extend to some members of staff: "It is noisy. It is too much. Will they give us compensation for the damage?" (Officer Rafferty). "Are you going to do something about this din then? Affects our mental health" (Officer Smith). The soundscape permeated the inner world of these individuals, provoking protective responses which served to further sensitize and heighten awareness to the institutional environment. Some consistently made significant contributions to the soundscape themselves, but at no point indicated an awareness that this might be similarly negatively experienced by others.

Prisoners and staff recounted relationships with the soundscape that elicited behaviour which consolidated their position within the institution. Both prisoners and staff felt the soundscape encroaching upon their senses of self, evoking fear, agitation and anxiety. For Tonk and Cameron, relationships with the soundscape increased the likelihood of being subject to additional punishment, while evasive action mired others further within the institution. Sound also worked as a proxy for wellbeing. How people interacted with and interpreted the soundscape indicated how well they were coping, and how able they felt to reassert a sense of self against the overwhelming wall of institutional sound.

18

'The Auld Triangle'

The soundscape was intimately bound with the process of becoming acclimated to the rhythms and routines of Midtown. Long-term exposure could desensitize to its effects, but this did nothing to reduce its impact on their orientation to the institution. Auditory aspects of routines worked to anchor people further within its rhythms, reverberating with expectation and experience. These sounds also echoed with broader, cultural representations of the prison. Film, television and music are littered with examples of dramatic renditions of life behind the wall. Representations of the prison in folk music have long been an interest of mine. Growing up in a part of London with a large Irish community, I cannot remember a time I was unfamiliar with rebel and folk music. 'The Auld Triangle' is one such song, variously attributed to Brendan Behan and the Dubliners.[1] It appears in Behan's play *The Quare fellow* (1954) but is credited to his friend Dick Shannon. The song itself refers to the 'triangle' at the gate of Mountjoy prison. It was hit with a hammer to signal various points of the routine and could be heard far and wide 'all along the banks of the Royal Canal'. The auld triangle reverberated with the meanings it signified, of place and punishment. Its song rang a sense of cultural ownership of Mountjoy, and a belonging signalled by sharing in its meanings, reinforced with every repetition. Midtown's tune similarly echoed with expressions of belonging and ownership.

There was no triangle at Midtown, but its bell was rung at key points of the regime, engraved with the year the prison opened nearly 200 years ago. The bell was firmly entrenched within the daily rituals and routines of the prison, signifying the history of the place, its position in the local community and its meaning for those currently living and working within it. The bell's position at the centre of the prison meant it could not be heard from beyond the walls. As Kevin's son demonstrated, it was audible to those coming to visit friends and loved ones, reaffirming Midtown's purpose in the consciousness of those who passed over the threshold. There were other aspects of the prison soundscape that did transcend the walls, reaffirming connections to the prison in their hearing. Sounds of the prison evoked memory and a sense of belonging, anchoring the prison in people's sense of self, and identities within and beyond the prison walls. Much of the power of the place derived not from those within it, but from the meaning of countless cultural representations saturated in its walls and reverberating in the triangles and bells, their memory lingering in the imagination long after leaving the prison:

> 'I've walked by this jail, and I've heard the aggro bell go and I've gone like that to my Missus: "There's an incident happening in there." She's gone: "No you ain't." I've gone: "Here you are, see them three staff, watch them run straight in the jail." She went: "How do you know?" I says: "It's my manor, I know."' (Stretch)

Feelings of loss and exclusion were amplified by the soundscape. Tensions between various modes of time and space in the now of prison and the then of home were sharpened by sounds evoking memory of other times, people and places. The absence of children's voices among the din of the men, bittersweet memories elicited by songs played or hummed by neighbours, the rumble of traffic, all enhanced feelings of loneliness, separation and the yearning for intimacy. Auditory imaginations evoked soundscapes of hopes for future freedoms, and revisitation of happier times, heightening the sense of dislocation associated with the carceral present. Inner worlds hummed with connections beyond the walls, lengthening the corridor and shrinking the cell. As in a Piranesi[2] picture, the dizzying effects of disconnection were enhanced by distortions of space, as well as time (Gallo and Ruggiero, 1991).

Accounts of temporal experience, elicited by sound, highlighted the wider implications of routinization. Memories of former prison life resonated with sound-elicited memory. As Cam recounted: "I've been in jail ever since I was 15, so all I hear, every day, is keys. Even when I get out, if I've been out on the road, all I hear is keys and I think I'm in jail." Cam also provided an illustration of how sound, and its links with memory, lent an elasticity to time which challenged singular and narrow conceptions of space. I asked him if there were "sounds in here that remind you of outside?" He answered: "Nah, what I hear outside reminds me of inside." The soundscape of prison had, for Cam, become privileged in his sense of place, and had therefore come to dominate his memory, overwriting other aspects of identity. This may well have been a temporary reflection of his circumstances at the time. He was on a pre-sentence hold at Midtown and eager to move on to a prison offering opportunities to fulfil his sentence plan, as well as better conditions.

Enquiring what prisoners and staff were hearing and what that meant to them, disrupted linear notions of time. This reinforced the sense of time and space as intrinsically connected and mutually constituted (Parkes and Thrift, 1980; Moran, 2012). When participants reflected on the soundscape, their elaboration on shifting senses of time and space emphasized the multiplicities these were simultaneously experienced in. Sound both mediated and reconstituted time and space by eliciting recollections and evoking social meaning, as Joanne illustrated:

> 'I might hear people shouting or there's like a fight, you just automatically turn round, and it places you right back in the world of where you work. I can remember, I was out on a Saturday night and a fight was kicking off and you just know the sounds, you know the voices, the shouting, and you can hear running around and things, and in that split second it can put you straight back in.'

In this instance the potency of the prison and the social life within it operated independently of individual agency. Joanne expressed a sense of mechanical solidarity being evoked involuntarily by sounds which reasserted her identity as a member of the Midtown community, concerned for its stability. Both staff and prisoners shared similar reflections about being transported back inside and this has been a feature of conversations with people in various prisons. While visiting a Category C prison and sitting with officers while they had their lunch, one asked "Tell us why we wake in the middle of the night to the sound of alarms?" to murmurs of recognition from colleagues. Sound converged with social, temporal and spatial aspects of prison experience.

Triangles and bells

Behan's evocation of the triangle of Mountjoy as a means of characterizing prison life emphasizes the role of sound in reinforcing prison's cultural potency. The song is a staple favourite, cementing associations between sounds of the prison (and song), identity and belonging. There are, of course, many other folk and rebel songs about the prison, often juxtaposing its deprivations with ideas of nation and belonging, but 'The Auld Triangle' explicitly marries the rhythms and routines inside the prison with its cultural signification of place and identity. The lyrics echo the rhythmic time of the triangle, jingle jangling through cultural consciousness. 'The Auld Triangle' demonstrates the role of sound in mutually reinforcing processes of culture, place and identity and the role of the prison within them (Hudson, 2006). In singing about the sounds of the prison and its position in prison life, particular expectations of sensory experience are interwoven in cultural depictions of places of punishment. The prison soundscape correspondingly reverberates with its cultural significance. The jingle jangle resonates with rhythms of the regime, and the weight of the keys, conjuring sonic signifiers of the prison, cementing its occupation in cultural consciousness, and reinforcing its potency.

Ideas and expectations, forged in cultural representations of the prison, inform our understanding of the soundscape, of what it means and how it feels. Rhythms and routines of daily life echo and resonate with culturally informed expectations, enhancing the impact of sound upon the bodies of those inhabiting prison spaces. Everyday comings and goings remake these spaces in the auditory image formed by exposure to its cultural representations. Clangs and jangles vibrate through the body with the additional force of broader memories and meanings. Incarcerated bodies feel the sounds not only in their own hearing but also with the force of their former experience and that of all who have passed through these places, reconstituting time and space for those entangled in the ebb and flow of daily prison life.

> A hungry feeling came o'er me stealing
> And the mice were squealing in my prison cell
> And the old triangle went jingle jangle
> All along the banks of the Royal Canal
> To begin the morning a screw was bawling
> 'Get up you bowsie and clean up your cell'
> And the old triangle went jingle jangle
> All along the banks of the Royal Canal
> On a fine spring evening the lag lay dreaming
> The seagulls wheeling high over the wall
> And the old triangle went jingle jangle
> All along the banks of the Royal Canal
>
> (Behan, 1954)

Behan evokes the signification of the triangle at Mountjoy to draw on its broader resonance with the cultural imagination. The potency of these significations is reinforced at every singing, every playing of the song. The lyrics associate the mundane everyday activities of prison life ('clean up your cell' and 'a screw was bawling') with the broader cultural resonance of prison sounds (the 'jingle jangle' of the 'old triangle'). In this way the song both depicts and is itself a part of processes of remaking the potency of the soundscape's signification. The retelling of these sensory recollections informs a collective knowledge, a social history which both resonates with and reinforces the power of the prison through the jingle jangle of the old triangle.

The prison soundscape reverberated with the power of its cultural meaning, but this power could be adapted, and harnessed by different actors. While processes of institutionalization were sounded and reinforced in rhythms and routines these could also be inverted in narratives of cultural ownership and belonging which prisoners used with regularity. These statements of territorial pride inverted the sense of power over place and belonging, as well as signifying the wider relationship between prison and community. Midtown had an unusually high local population. The "biggest house in Midtown" belonged to them. The reverse was also true – they belonged to Midtown, and so narratives of local identity were anchored in associations with the prison and its broader community.

"The biggest house in Midtown"

Stretch had been in and out of Midtown for most of his life and considered Midtown "home". He was keen to demonstrate familiarity with his territory, as well as to claim it and routinely referred to Midtown as his "manor". Declarations of ownership worked to subvert the totemic power of the place, to harness it in service to defiant expressions of identity. Stretch repeatedly expressed an understanding of the place and its operations that surpassed many of those charged with its running. Staff might falter, unsure where trouble was coming from or be slow to respond to a colleague in need. Stretch exhibited no such hesitation. He and his fellow prisoners were adept at reading the climate of spaces they spent considerably more time in than staff, and in many cases had been visiting for much longer than staff had worked there. Stretch was at pains to point out that officers were admitted to the building on the accommodation and understanding of the prisoners: "We allow them to come into work. If we didn't want them in this building, they would not be in this building and that's the truth. Seriously. They don't understand." Expressions of cultural ownership were bound up both with exertions of agency and identity work. Prisoners these men might be but imprisoned within *their* prison.

A number of those I spoke to likened Midtown to a local council estate (for example, Tommy, Officer Rose). Tonk was one of a number who regularly referred to the prison as "the biggest house in Midtown". When challenged for nosiness by an officer, he reported retorting: "We're here more than you, this is our home." This emphasized not only a shared understanding that there was power in knowledge, but also an assumption of a right to know as a Midtown local. Declaring cultural ownership was an act of resistance to the stigma of the prison. Rather than internalizing the stain of consignment to geographies of exclusion (Sibley, 1995), the men worked to weave the prison into their stories of identity and belonging. Midtown featured in narratives of sound, space and identity in which the local had undisputed supremacy (Cohen, 2012). Interviews were peppered with references to regional areas and how they related to the prison, alongside an insistence that I get to grips with local geography. They had no patience for my dyspraxia. A significant portion of my interview with Stevie was taken up with his insistence I recognize the specific chicken shop he lived next to. Explaining I was a Londoner did nothing to alleviate frustration with my local ignorance, but I was often inclined to interpret this as an eagerness to bring me into their stories in a gesture of community. Stretch was more focused on internal geographies of the prison and was at pains to let me know he watched over me. He viewed the prison as his domain, asserting his dominance in terms of knowledge and influence:

> 'I've ruled the roost in here for like 25 years. What I said in here went. You know what I mean? My manor. You hit staff without us knowing about it you got weighed in ... You beat someone or robbed somebody without anybody knowing about it you got ... we'd pass through a little council first, you got done in.'

Lugs illustrated the way Midtown identity was carried more widely between prisons as well as within Midtown: "We all stick together if you noticed, us Midtown lads ... Anywhere if we go out the country, not out the country if we go ... Stafford ... that's the first thing we'd be looking for. If we went Dovegate, or Lincoln." In this way sound was interwoven with expressions of identity and social order, subverting the stigma represented by the social and spatial boundaries of the prison walls. Midtown was "home", "our manor" (Stretch, Tonk). Influxes of prisoners from other local communities were often met with battles to assert supremacy despite mutual recognition of respective territories: "You'll find every community prison like this ... they always come here and try to disrupt this place, but we won't allow it" (Stretch). Tales of the latest triumphant assertion of dominance rattled with collective social histories spanning decades: "When Strangeways went up 25 years ago, they brought 'em all here. They were like "Yeah, in the morning, soon as unlock we're on it, we'll smash it up." [But] we won't allow it" (Stretch). Personal relationships with people and place were interwoven with broader social histories spanning prisons over much of the country, with Midtown always at their centre. It was poignant to note that there was often a greater degree of consistency in the relationships between the men – whether familial, quasi-familial or friendly – than between loved ones left behind in that faraway place of home, minutes down the road.

Prison, sound and the cultural imagination

These songs and stories echo and amplify the cultural potency of the prison, a totem of the nation state regardless of how particular configurations of society shift conceptions of punishment (Brown, 2009; Kaufman and Bosworth, 2013). The imposing presence of the prison on the historical and cultural landscape mirrors its physical form, looming large in local geographies (Grovier, 2008). Songs, literature, film and art draw on this significance to paint recognizable frames of cultural reference. Prison buildings and their soundscapes resonate with the symbolic power reaffirmed by these broader cultural touchstones which layer cultural, social and political meaning on personal experience. Sound amplifies the imaginative as well as the physical components of prison, uniting them with mundane aspects of daily lived experience. Daily life inside is partially shaped by the deeper symbolic meaning of the jingle jangles which keep the rhythm of the routine.

New prisons are built ever further from the city skyline in favour of secluded spaces beyond the peripheries of public view (Johnson, 2005). While this signifies shifts in penal culture it will do little to dislodge the significance of the prison as it features in the cultural imagination where it forms a continual focus as metaphor for mental anguish. From Elizabeth Barrett Browning to 'Prisoner: Cell Block H', the potency of the prison draws endless fascination. The buildings and their gory histories have similarly perpetual, voyeuristic allure as the phenomenon of 'dark tourism' and popularity of prison museums attest (Welch, 2015). The prison as representation of social isolation and exclusion is an endlessly recurring motif in literature and art, from Dickinson to Dickens (Dickinson, 1862; Dickens, 1936; Smith, 2011). Every clang, clank and creak reverberates with the force of endless evocations of the prison in broader cultural consciousness.

Evocative representations of the jingle jangles of the prison layer the complex interplay between memory and experience, imagination and expectation in navigations of everyday life inside. Clanks and bangs of daily coming and going in the prison correspondingly filter outwards. The sounds of idleness, the search for industry amid the hustle and bustle on the landings similarly echo with wider meaning. Searches for a sense of purpose, in the meaninglessness of acres of time in which nothing much happened, was experienced as an additional dimension of punishment and one which transcended the walls. Learning how to navigate the endless corridors of idle time was a perpetual preoccupation for many at Midtown.

19

The Hustle and Bustle

The polyrhythmia of a good day buzzed and hummed with toing and froing, comings and goings of a community getting on with everyday business. Wings thrummed with calls for gym and shop, preparation for visits and the endless search for irons and deodorant to make themselves as presentable as possible for all-too-brief and emotionally laden reunions, staff offering one another a brew and the purposeful scuffing of rubber on lino. Various strains of the soundscape crackled with daily life in ways which seemed to echo with activity and occupation. As rhythms became increasingly discernible, the partial truth of this became more apparent.

> In prison, time accumulates a new dimension. You try to eat it away rather than enjoy it. If a prisoner is having difficulty with his station the days become hopelessly long, he is doing 'hard time'... and a frequent answer when one tells of his troubles is 'you're on your own time' or 'don't press my time.' (Cohen and Taylor, 1981: 100)

As Cohen and Taylor assert, the passing of time took on new challenges and complications in the context of life inside. The constraints of the prison presented a continual challenge to the common pursuit of keeping busy. As Ket pointed out, both prisoners and staff were engaged in doing "what they've got to do to live, and to earn, to hustle, to get by" – the collective soundscape this engendered comprised an array of practices, which parcelled and passed time. In themselves quite meaningless, idle "bitting and bobbing", as Officer Rose referred to it, was both dictated by the necessity of endless attempts to meet the most mundane of needs, and a means of relieving the mundanity of boredom. There were parallels between the hustle on the wings, and on the streets in town, where considerable numbers seemed caught in a perpetual waiting. There were opportunities too, to make a little money or repay outstanding debts in the knowledge their paths would cross with those they owed, inside or out. Tommy referred to this:

'You've got people coming in here to make money, cos they earn a hell of a lot more in here than they do out there, which I don't see how that works but there you go. S'pose a tenner a day's better than nothing, innit? Not like you're going up Oxford Street.'

When asked what a good prison sounds like, Derek responded: "A calming sound, it's a settled sound. It's like the sound you get when you're going on a busy high street. It's hustle and bustle but there's no sounds of aggravation, there's no threatening noises." 'Hubbub' is a useful means of describing, if somewhat underplaying, the sensory experience of prison life; and the frenetic sensation of standing amid the seemingly chaotic din of a busy environment. Emily Cockayne (2008) uses this as a focal point for exploring social life, though the hard-to-reach environment she seeks to understand is the past, rather than hidden corners of the present. The rhythmic regime was intertwined with order and its fluctuations. Attentive listening revealed the strands of occupation in nothing much. As the cacophonous din greeting me when I walked on to the wing gradually revealed its secrets, it became increasingly clear that much of the ebb and flow was comprised of empty activity. These pointless efforts to pass the time were meaningful in the doing of them rather than their content, sounding continuities between the task of getting on and getting by between inside and outside.

"You've got to keep busy, else your head will pop"

Difficulty accessing all manner of services and opportunities were reflected in the constant stream of enquiries from those I had yet to speak to: "Miss, are you education/probation/resettlement/OMU?" Men frequently whiled away precious association queuing outside an office for someone who never showed, in defiance of the vague schedule posted on the door. Obtaining basics was characterized with frustration and inefficiency as well as a broader dearth of resources. New arrivals would be on the hunt for receptacles to hold food. Those wanting to paint their cells embarked on herculean missions of obstinate determination. Cleaning materials remained bizarrely elusive in a place where infection could spread at a staggering rate. Perceptions of shirking, though, were met with vocal disapproval: "I'd sack you if I was cleaning officer." "Why?" "You're lazy, look at all the shit you've missed." Duke complained: "You can't do nothing in here", and despite efforts to introduce more education and additional work, demand vastly outstripped supply. Failing to engage in meaningful activity risked being interpreted as lack of engagement with the regime and its 'rehabilitative' ideals; being identified as risky could restrict access to purposeful labour. At the same time, there was a dearth of things with which to meaningfully occupy one's time, and so the means of doing so necessitated creativity and ingenuity.

A pair of plastic gloves, pointedly displayed in the back pocket and gestured to while rushing by – a key tactic of Lugs – indicated vital industriousness that was not always apparent. Obtaining equipment and posing it somewhere prominently (sometimes asking me to "watch" over it) lent the appearance of a man fleetingly interrupted in his diligent industry. Looking busy was key to *being* busy: "I don't hide nowhere; I just keep walking" (Ned). Lamar expressed his difficulty in finding purposeful ways to do his time:

> 'Education-wise there's nothing for me to do here. There's nothing for me to do at any prison. So they struggle to put anything on my sentence plan cos I've done everything, cos I'm on a nine-year sentence. I struggle to find out who my probation officer is. When I got my Mum and my sister to ring them, they didn't know who I was. Because the probation system has changed in the last couple of years, and because I haven't been in for so long, hadn't been in contact with them for so long, it seems like my file or whatever's just gone into the bin, so they didn't know about me.'

For Lamar the challenge of disposing of his time constructively echoed the value he perceived himself to have been assigned in the broader system. His stoical response to the endless impediments to getting on were quite typical. The way to comply with unseen and inconsistently applied rules and systems created a sense that there were neither: "So I'm just keeping doing what I'm doing and hoping that gets me through it" (Lamar).

The men frequently shared their quests for something meaningful and reported progress. Boyd was chuffed to get a spot in the Kitchen and wanted me to visit so I could see him at work, as well as hear the difference in a place where everyone was (relatively) happily occupied. I never did make it while the men were there, too concerned about disrupting the sacred mealtime routine. Nathan was keen to do a business course he had been talking to Education about. This may not have been entirely unrelated to his passion for growing weed but nevertheless demonstrated a willingness, a desperation, to do. Robert showed me drawings he had done, as did Dermot who drew for his partner's brother with learning difficulties. Richey displayed some of the most impressive photo-realistic art anyone had ever seen. Others showed me furniture made from cardboard, expressing pride in ingenious DIY[1] solutions for decoration, functionality or increased privacy. These involved all manner of salvaged, repurposed and sometimes unlikely items. An HMP toothbrush had an astounding array of purposes but – a profoundly apt metaphor for various aspects of prison life, and the prison itself – was notoriously bad for brushing teeth. I never felt able to take Tommy up on offers of coffee in his cell, much as I wanted to. Aside from enjoying his company and wanting to participate in commensality, I was most keen to see his home decorations. He had managed to cover his cell in rugs, the provenance of which remained unclear but made his determination to "just go with the flow" a little easier.

Random means of keeping busy were audible in the barking, spitting rhyme, singing, whooping, occasional good-humoured calls to "bring out your dead" in response to the bell-sounding association. Enforced idleness was experienced as an additional dimension of punishment which the men often complained about and considered a major source of "trouble". The sometimes-stultifying boredom of the institution gave rise to a range of behavioural responses which did little to alleviate it longer term but could serve to amuse and kill some time. 'Weird ideas' could be harmless in origin and/or outcome, but in combination with 'doing nothing' could also be a recipe for trouble of varying degrees (Corrigan, 1979). Toad excitedly stopped by one day to tell me about a practical joke in progress. "Everyone knows about it but him." He had concealed laxative in coffee and orange juice before sharing it with his unsuspecting pad mate. "He's going to be squitting all night ... he's drunk it all!" he told me with a near-infectious glee. I ruined this hilarity when I confirmed this was *his* pad mate. Toad had not considered the implications of inducing chronic diarrhoea in the person with whom he shared an uncovered lavatory, situated inches from where they both slept.[2]

Camouflage

There was a new contract from the Ministry of Defence offering the men the means of knotting camouflage netting. Those on standard and enhanced[3] would get priority and it offered slightly better pay.[4] Officers, charged with fulfilling quotas for stints in the workshop, often found themselves unable to locate willing participants. The limited potential for stimulation offered by making the netting was not perceived as meaningful or desirable for most, though others found it impossible to ingratiate themselves sufficiently to obtain work. This added to perceptions of time and its disposal as a source of punishment in content as well as form:

> 'So then if you want to put money on your phone credit you've got to work. But you want to keep me banged up 22, 23 hours a day yeah? Seven days a week yeah? Four weeks a month. And then expect me to have pristine behaviour. Like me, the energy I've got inside me I'll never be perfect, obviously if you keep me in my pad for that long I'm gonna misbehave, cos there's nothing else for me to do and I get super bored. There's nothing else for me to do but be mischievous and misbehave and do fucking shit cos it's all about trying to get that energy out of me. And then they go from that to saying that alright,

we're not going to give you a job cos your behaviour's not perfect, but my behaviour would be more perfect if you gave me a job and I'm not sat in my pad, bored out my nut for 24 hours a day.' (Duke)

Duke had previously spoken about his ADHD and difficulty keeping himself occupied. For him, being denied the opportunity to spend time more constructively was a threat both to his sense of self and mental health. In contrast, Stevie was often accommodated with work and additional trips to the gym in recognition of his vulnerability. In his case, keeping him occupied in attempts to stabilize him was sometimes a threat to others' rhythms of industry, requiring a delicate balancing act with others' needs to work effectively rather than chaotically.

Painting always seems to be underway but despite the apparent industry of the gentlemen it was not always entirely clear what had been painted or to what effect. 'Wet paint' signs abounded, but these were less than reliable indicators of its location or existence. Consequently, every round of painting was accompanied by handprints, which both ruined the job and necessitated re-painting of other areas. Thus, much like the anecdote of the Forth Bridge, the job was a perpetual one. Its meaning at Midtown was subverted. The comfort and accomplishment lay in the doing of it rather than in doing it well, or in its completion. My fieldnotes reflected on this unoccupied occupation of time:

> Lots of people shipping and they got all the stuff so ... Shout, shout. Organization. 'Keep 'em moving.' 'Fucks given??' 'Miss, Oi, Miss, you going for a poo?' 'You got to time it right.' Smell of liver and onions for dinner. Bleurgh. 'Sounds purposeful now, doesn't it?' 'Better than this morning', I reply. Estates wait to fix a ladder to ladderless bunks. 'WORKSHOP'. Crying off education, going to library. Loitering, avoiding, hiding to avoid lock-up. Constant battle, herding cats. Grown men crouching under stairwells and squeezing in corners. Masters at avoiding eye contact and looking like they might be doing something. Leaving me looking after abandoned paint pots, or functionally positioned chairs while they wander off to conduct business/see a friend/God knows what really.

There was no more purpose in finishing the painting than hope its commencement would prove efficacious in improving the environment. The uncertain state of surfaces comprised an additional dimension to the regular roulette of leaning or touching anything. The unwritten rules of interpersonal interaction extended to the walls and railings. I would often spend long days, mostly standing, listening, observing, writing and chatting to people. If I sought to lean against surfaces I would be warned; "Oh,

I wouldn't touch that Miss." Industry and occupation were the elusive goal, but the pursuit of purposeful time-passing was set against perceptions of a worsening system:

> 'It seems like the system's on its lowest point ever. It seems like there's no money, there's no staff. There's no time out to facilitate anything. You know cleaning products, just to clean out your cell is a problem. Everything seems like it's on its ... the prison system's broken ... it's unsafe. Mamba's changed everything.' (Lamar)

Metronome and machine

An absence of meaningful activity could shape prisoners' perception of how deeply they were embroiled within the system and how keenly punishment was felt. Cohen and Taylor's description of E-wing, the high-security deep-end of HMP Durham,[5] emphasizes how the absence of hustle and bustle reflected deeper submersion within the penal system. They emphasized the lack of sensory indicators of industry as signalling the meaning and purpose of the wing. Occupying time was explicitly connected to the challenges of psychological survival but also the extent to which busyness, and its absence, signalled closer proximity to the surface, to life on the out.

> The atmosphere in Durham maximum security wing differs from that in other parts of the prison. There are no long lines of prisoners moving in and out of the building, no such bursts of sound, no crowded rooms, no clanking machinery. This building is designed for no other purpose than success – fully to contain its inmates. Its success is measured exclusively by its impregnability. (Cohen and Taylor, 1981: 70)

While lifers, those with long sentences looming and suffering the uncertainty of an indeterminate sentence for public protection (IPP) passed through Midtown, it was a local prison and as such a place where most were rapidly on the move. The vast majority hailed from the area, and so the sensescape hummed with markers of the broader community from which most of these people were drawn. Shouts of "Midtown" were not unusual, particularly during football season. Locally flattened vowels were detectable in shouting and conversation around the wing. Other habits and familiar rhythms also found their way inside. As time went on, seeing familiar faces from inside the walls was a part of my own everyday life outside. I could often identify those I had spent some time talking with from the rhythms of their gait, idly ambling around town or speedily rushing by while arguing with a partner. Continuities between outside and in became more discernible as I trod familiar paths around the city.

Patterns between inside and out increasingly revealed themselves alongside my ability to identify them (Lefebvre, 2004). Forms and functions of the regime echoed in its soundscape, exposing the granularity of how power and agency were exercised both by and through the Midtown community. Cristoph Neidhart (2002) uses depictions of sensory experience to explain transitions and transformations of a post-Soviet Union Russia. Sound played a central role in imposing order (for example, using fixed radio signals and public address systems). Shifting social conditions were discernible in the sensescape. Rusche and Kircheimer (1939) argue that the changing demands of the labour market shape prevailing forms of punishment. Marshalling time in prison is a crucial mechanism for harnessing the labour of the prison population to the service of industrial demands. The bell, the count, shouting for court, the crackle of radios and sounding alarms, similarly formed the rhythms of an orderly day inside. Portioning the day into dulling, standardized chunks echoed the repetitive labours of the factory; 'the regular tolling of the gong, calling to toil or to meals, accentuates the enervating routine' (Berkman, 1912: 117). Likewise, strains of empty occupation within the polyrhythmia of the day echoed the enforced idleness many experienced on the out.

The draining effects of interminable boredom mimicked the absurdity of spending endless amounts of time loitering outside the job centre or hanging around outside the hostels skirting the prison. Much of the prison day consisted of waiting. A stone's throw from the prison, those consigned to appointments at the job centre milled about outside. Similarly caught in the cycle of hanging around without much prospect of anything in particular, their numbers outstripping the capacity of staff and the building to meet demand. Like many mid-sized cities up and down the country, Midtown suffered the consequences of a decline in traditional industries and the changing requirements of the labour market. Unemployment was close to twice that of the UK average, in most urbanized areas (ONS, 2022).[6] Many of the men at Midtown were left behind, prompting consideration of what becomes of the relationship between the prison and the factory (Melossi and Pavarini, 1981) when the factories cease production, and the prison is so starved of resources it is unable to furnish many of those in its care with any meaningful means of occupying themselves. Lamar reflected on the relationship between inside and out: "It's not even just prison, in society it's hard. Especially in this day and age, it's so hard to be successful or to get anywhere you wanna go."

On the way into town, I sometimes spoke with those asking for money or a Maccy D's[7] who told me of their difficulty in becoming unstuck. Hostels were filled with the habits they sought to escape, trapping them in between street, unemployment, prison and hostel. Homeless people coming into Midtown were immediately recognizable. They often shared details of their circumstances but were easily spotted by their enthusiasm for the daily menu (in marked contrast to everyone else) and the rapidity with which their skin improved. I should just note that the food at Midtown was often remarked upon by prisoners as "banging". It was prepared by a dedicated team and had less distance to travel. Effectively creating conditions favourable for fuelling the labour market in the prison relies on equitable living standards, however spartan (Melossi and Pavarini, 1981). This symbiotic relationship is disrupted by the increasingly complex matrices of socio-economic deprivations intertwined with imprisonment. For some, the prison offered respite from perpetually chaotic and desperate conditions on the street (Schneider, 2023). Those seeking an escape from the street and hostel found material as well as psychological comfort in the rhythms of Midtown. The reassurance offered by the familiarities of the prison environment did nothing to offset the effects of succumbing to its rhythms and their attendant imposition of a debilitating time signature (Gallo and Ruggiero, 1991). Dave makes this connection explicit when he draws parallels between his time at Midtown and past work experience outside:

> 'On the outside you get a lot of people, homeless for instance … and I've been involved in a bit of homeless help on the outside. And when you see homeless people, they've got nowhere to go, no food, they've got nothing, They come to prison, they get put in to prison. They think, this is it, I've got somewhere to sleep, I've got food, smoke, all my stuff, and to them it's great. They're not outside, sat on the street, begging. They're not freezing cold, they're getting medical attention. They're getting looked after, they're getting clothing, you know, it's like, brill. But they're being locked up. But they're not, they're not worried about that.'

Justin was one for whom this story was all too familiar. I chatted to him as he came through for dinner from the First-Night Centre and he explained: "Who burgles businesses without gloves? I do cos I want to get caught. I can't be homeless, it's getting worse. They tell me I've no connections when my Dad's side are here!" Justin explained he needed a break from the hectic chaos of associations with other substance users on the streets, but also spoke of the difficulty finding accommodation in areas where connections with home and/or family were unrecognized by those working in 'the system', and thus not supported.

Examining the rhythms of daily life at Midtown replaced conceptions of legitimacy in the broader meaning and purpose of the regime with absurdity. Individuals sought to enact agency by navigating the complex and conflicting channels of power emanating from people and place. Rules were arbitrary and life was hard and violent. Doing time and dispensing with it were preoccupations requiring both diligence and ingenuity. Efforts to drive and maintain the rhythms of the day were correspondingly demanding given enervating boredom and required the cooperation and participation of broad sections of the community in a multiplicity of ways to keep it ticking over. There were audible components to the practices concerned with maintaining the rhythms of the day. While these were motivated by a range of personal interests from peace to survival to reliably sourcing biscuits, they were central to the maintenance of order.

20

Phasing

There was a comforting respite from the enervating boredom of prison life in working cooperatively to get by and get on. This was indicated by the number of different behaviours from all sections of the community which worked to reinstate regular rhythms in the wake of their disruption. Audible components of these efforts were instructive for what they revealed about the nature of order and its maintenance. Processes concerned with reinstating stability were complex and multifarious, co-produced by various members of the community – prisoners and staff – rather than imposed from above.

Phasing is a phrasing in music which denotes separate parts playing the same piece but at different tempos, moving further apart before coming back into unison. I use this to collectively refer to the set of practices concerned with reintroducing polyrhythmia whether in the wake of an arrhythmic episode or a period of staccato unease. These took various forms, some organized and systematic, such as controlled unlock or putting everyone away for ten minutes so the staff could reset. There were also informal and individual efforts from various quarters. While these endeavours were spontaneous and separate rather than concerted, the resulting stability was co-produced, the outcome of various actors and actions. Focusing on daily rhythms revealed the multiplicities of behaviours, and agents, affecting the sound environment to restore order and to lighten the emotional climate of the wing.

One of many questions I puzzled over as I worked to understand the environment was what distinguished an ongoing series of events, or prolonged 'spikiness', from an isolated incident. I am not convinced I have an adequate answer, or whether I was imposing post-hoc understanding. Perhaps its complexity resists easy or formulaic explanations. What did become apparent as I listened to the environment was the range of people and approaches concerned with smoothing over, relieving tension, getting the routine back into gear, as if recovering a normal heart rate after a palpitation. The prison environment was likened to a 'pressure cooker'. When disorder occurred, it might be fleeting or part of an ongoing spate of raised levels of violence and disruption to the routine. Where residual disruption took some time to dissipate, resuming a steady rhythm was a process, a series of steps which reset the rhythms of the day (Sparks et al, 1996). This movement 'from tension to peace' has received considerably less attention than might be predicted given its relation to order (Liebling et al, 2010: 8). Examining this process is central to understanding the basis for a stable environment. Phasing is a useful term for capturing the diversity and complexity of the forms this process could take. There are examples of this in a variety of musical genres, but one of the most widely known and accessible is 'A Day in the Life' by The Beatles (1967) (on the 'Sgt. Pepper's Lonely Hearts Club Band' album). Harmonic pendula provide a more kinaesthetic metaphor. Like a Newton's cradle, these move back and forth rather than from side to side, falling out of sequence, seemingly chaotically before resuming syncopation.[1]

There is little uniform about this process, nor the events that precede it. More serious, prolonged events may take longer to recover from, whereas minor incidents might be sufficient to alleviate the tension surrounding their occurrence. In this sense, unlike within a piece of music, there was nothing predetermined once set in motion. Getting things back to 'normal' – the "everyday tune that's normal for here" – could be initiated by staff, by prisoners or a combination of both, but it did have an aural quality, as did the restoration of a 'good' day. Phasing is a useful way of describing the aural qualities of shifts between disruption and regulation in the emotional climate. The fluctuation between greater and lesser degrees of order in the prison environment could be interpreted as a necessary tension, reaffirming cohesion and restoring the dialectic which maintains equilibrium (Durkheim, 1893). An entry in my fieldnotes includes several examples, both of a sense of impending trouble and individuals – both staff and prisoners – working to relieve it:

> There'll be another incident today. A bad one. Not just Midtown lads. Nottingham, Birmingham, and now Coventry. Something's got to go ... "Any more for exercise, it's a lovely day, get out there" shouts officer. "Bring out your dead" shouts a prisoner to laughter.

Going right back into it

'Sometimes in the morning, when we unlock, you can hear how boisterous it is, when they all come out of the cells and they're running round doing their dodgy deals and they're all getting off and doing whatever they need to do ... then some mornings they'll come out and its subdued, and you just know. Something's gonna go. Don't know what it is, it'll probably be somebody's gonna come out and batter somebody else, something like that. But you can sense it's gonna happen, but you just don't know what it is. And then it happens. You deal with it and then everything goes back to normal ... racket and noise and banging. Just the way it is.' (Officer Rose)

Officer Rose was explaining a phasing process. Tension was palpable, the incident occurred and then "everything goes back to normal". The skill deployed in restoring the regime could be likened to the methods used to address a biorhythmic dysfunction – such as a panic attack, or a palpitation – kicking the normal rhythms back into place by lowering blood pressure or slowing breath to restore normal rhythms. Lefebvre terms this 'eurhythmia': healthy interaction between two or more rhythms (Lefebvre, 2004). While not explained in those terms by staff, the necessity of getting things back to routine was repeatedly referred to as a core requirement for those in charge of the wing (for example, Officer Rose, Derek, Officer McKie).

The second 'potting' that occurred during my time at HMP Midtown was Kayleigh's. It was a meticulously planned and therefore particularly unpleasant incident. She was pelted with faecal and urinary contributions, collected from an undisclosed number of prisoners over a bank holiday weekend, with bleach tablets thrown in. She returned to the wing almost immediately, despite having suffered profound unpleasantness which earned her much respect. When I arrived on the wing, learning of what had just transpired, I was struck by the level-mood. The wing sounded in good humour and staff appeared relaxed. I couldn't work out why this should be, particularly given this was the second such incident in a relatively short space of time. What I was hearing was in fact audible relief. No one had been hurt and it 'felt' like the tension had cleared. Richey described the sound of tension: "I keep on thinking it's kicked off cos the sound keeps dropping." In the case of an isolated incident, once it had happened the sense of relieved tension was palpable/audible. On a side note I would argue potting, however unpleasant, was about assaulting the dignity rather than the person; a warning which served to rebalance a sense of respect. It had a specific, instrumental purpose and was part of a wider code of penalties to deliver a message in response to perceptions of injustice, albeit with a brutal method of delivery.

More concerted and extended periods of disruption might require staff action. These varied depending on severity and range of options available to the officer in charge, as well as their distinct styles. One such technique was to stagger unlock, like preventing curdling by adding eggs slowly when making a cake:

'People are feeling tense. Prisoners are frustrated cos they've been locked up so much. But we need to get them out ... what we would do then would be a controlled unlock, so instead of half the landing you might do eight or ten cells ... and try to keep it under control, and then just gradually get back to normal.' (Officer McKie)

The reverse also offers a means of recalibrating the rhythms of the day, locking everyone up to reset the daily rhythm:

'I've shut the wing down just to deal with it. Cos I think sometimes the staff need a break when things are a bit hairy. And I'll shut the wing down I will, I'll put everybody, give the staff ten minutes just to get themselves back together again, and we just start again. Go right back into it.' (Officer Rose)

Officer Rose suspended the day to allow the staff a moment to regain composure without the additional pressure of a wing full of men. This represented a temporary disruption to the day and more time behind the door, neither of which was ideal nor greeted with enthusiasm. Having been present in the case of delays to unlock, and unscheduled but short periods of time behind the door, both were considerably easier to tolerate for the men than the prolonged, additional time behind the door that could result from leaving the tone unchecked. This 'movement from tension to peace' (Liebling et al, 2010), described by the officers, echoes the assertion that order must be 'worked at' (Sparks et al, 1996). This aspect of prison officers' work is largely unexamined which has the effect of framing processes of restoring order as something mysterious and unknowable, as if they comprise a secret set of skills resting in arcane jail craft.

Phasing emotion

A good day was characterized by the atmosphere of the prison (Liebling et al, 2010: 8), bound with expression and interpretation of emotions; feelings. Emotions could be rapidly transferred in prison spaces; emotions are social things (Franks and Doyle McCarthy, 1989). If the sonic environment conveys moods and emotions, affecting and inducing emotional responses, this raises the possibility that sound is intrinsically bound up with the social relations which allow for the maintenance of order (Leibling, 2004). Emotions and their construction are central to long-standing conceptions of social solidarity in general, and criminal justice specifically (Fisher and Koo Chon, 1989; Loader, 2011). Part of 'a continuum of affectivity that links human bodies to their physical and social environment' (Fox, 2015: 301). Sound was a vital means of mediating emotion at HMP Midtown as well as assessing and affecting the emotional climate. Emotion has a central social purpose in binding the collective and reaffirming social bonds

(Durkheim, 1893, 1915). Ket emphasized the importance of a sense of solidarity among staff as well as what he perceived to have been lost: "It really has totally changed ... They don't move as one now. They do, but not how they used to. They try to but you'll never get that again. Never." While there are various points of divergence between different groups and actors, prison can be understood as a collective society, bound by shared beliefs and feelings (Durkheim, 1893). Emotion reasserted a sense of the collective, dissipating tension by asserting the mechanical solidarity which bound Midtown's social world.

This could also work in the opposite direction. Ship-ins of large numbers of prisoners could disrupt the equilibrium. Distrust and animosity between prisoners from neighbouring towns, often led to disorder and/or violence. Resulting tensions could be felt and heard. Earlier on in fieldwork, a number of prisoners were moved from London. The stark contrast in rhythms, both in movement and speech, were immediately recognizable as was the disruption to the general sound ecology. I recognized these as rhythms of home but discerned a discordant effect which was commented upon by staff and prisoners. While this did not receive sufficient or comprehensive press coverage, this had been a particularly volatile period in recent history, there were various incidents of disorder and unrest in prisons resulting in groups being decanted to Midtown. The arrival of clusters of prisoners overnight, following disruption at other places, caused corresponding upset which both staff and local prisoners worked to contain. This altered the delicate emotional balance and could result in a variety of problems which the newcomers would be blamed for. At one point "It's them new Birmingham lads" was a repeated response to a query about why the day felt spiky.

Contributing to the soundscape was a means of uniting the community. Making sounds of rituals and routines of daily prison life engendered a sense of belonging, which created a corresponding harmony in the feeling of shared purpose (Durkheim, 1915). In prison society, where people cannot escape one another for the duration of their sentence or shift, this sense of coming together was central to knitting tensions in the social fabric. As Tone reflected when talking about banging, assertions of group identity could be a potent and sobering force for the community. While I was at Midtown the staff began staggering men back in from exercise, after 60 or so had failed to move back to cell as instructed on a previous day. Staff found this "scary", as "they just stood there" (Lena, officer). Standing still and quietly would usually be regarded as a mundane and benign act, but in prison this confronted staff with the sudden, unscheduled force of a group whose collective strength far exceeded their own. This incident was both a powerful reminder that staff were outnumbered, and a broader illustration of the contingent and fragile nature of order.

"It keeps us all going"

There was no subsequent explanation for this episode, but its significance was signalled both by immediate adaptations of the regime and the staff response to it. While group behaviour was powerful, individuals could also act in ways which had a significant effect on the community. There were staff who consistently acted as rhythmic pacesetters alleviating tension with laughter, singing and joking. Mitzy was a long-serving officer who was very well regarded by prisoners. She was a strong communicator, and equally expressive when displeased. Often, she would sing around the wings and made a point of greeting people by name. Others, more usually junior, female members of staff would often join in with the singing which would travel with them around the wing as they went about their working day. This lightened the mood and contributed to a sense of stability which was reflected in the positive way she was spoken of by prisoners:

> 'She always tells me stories. She's really, really good to tell you the truth. Since I've been here, she's been really, really good with me. Even when I was going through things with all different officers she was really encouraging.' (Lamar)

Ket, a long-serving officer who had begun in CARATS[2] had a particularly pronounced role in steadying the day's tone. He retained a sense of separateness, partially because of historical mutual antipathy between those aligned with this new initiative and the traditional "black and whites", which made him more approachable for prisoners. He was unfailingly good-humoured, and his laughter was treasured by a variety of people who identified it as a source of morale-boosting around the prison. Trina, another officer, spoke of how the staff could "hear his laugh over the comms, it keeps us all going". When I asked what would happen if he went quiet, she told me "we'd all worry". These members of staff infected the emotional climate, phasing the mood back in to a settled, rhythmic thrum.

Phasing, then, was often (though not exclusively) affected by deliberate actions which served to shift and lighten tensions as well as to restore order; processes which could be discerned aurally. In this way sound signified operations of power which worked to restore order and equilibrium. While phasing occurred on a larger scale as part of formal prison procedures, these also constituted frequent micro-acts which worked to dissipate tension before it erupted, or to assist in the restoration of peace in its wake. Ket explained how he used his mood to influence others:

> 'When I first started, I was on a mission. There was this lady, and she was just miserable. Miserable as sin. I thought you know what? I'll put

a smile on her face; "Good morning love, how are you?" Everyday. Slowly but surely, a smile! Got ya!'

Davey shared an appreciation of Ket's upbeat temperament: "It's a good laugh is that. Yeah, he always is like that, Ket." When interviewed Ket spoke of generally positive and cooperative interactions with prisoners; I made an automatic association between that and his manner. This may have reflected my appreciation of his friendliness as much as the effect I observed, but his account, during interview, of occasions he had felt profoundly "let down" by the actions of individuals reinforced this impression. His tone was consistently warm and upbeat. There were also examples of prisoners deliberately working to evoke collective sentiment to alleviate tension and restore stability:

'Laughter's good in here, isn't it? You need it. It diffuses a lot of situations … there was a situation in here a couple of months ago, just before Christmas, and it was getting out of hand. So, I just stripped off and ran down the landing. It just diffused it.' (Stretch)

Humour was a consistent source of camaraderie and diffusion of tension. Repeatedly identified as crucial to positive relationships with staff; "you'll have some officers that are more than happy to have a laugh and a joke and treat you like a normal person" (Duke). Stevie said similar: "Some officers I can just have banter with. Just have a laugh with them you know what I mean? Not gonna cross the line though … just talk to them innit." He also identified this as being pivotal to maintaining good terms with those he lived with: "I make mates quick though innit, I just get on … everyone says I'm funny an' that … making them laugh and that."

Accounting for the association between sound, emotion and order enriches understanding of the activities and interactions occurring at the peripheries of stability. The maintenance of order and the 'work' this entails can be understood as encompassing a far broader scope of social life than might otherwise be apparent. At HMP Midtown, 'order' comprised both officially sanctioned and formal staff practice, alongside micro-interactions which could have profound, rippling effects on the wider emotional climate. These processes worked to reaffirm social cohesion, as well as to disrupt it. Phasing allows for an appreciation of the ambiguity and complexity of the fluid continuum of degrees of order. Rather than echoing the degree to which power is exercised, or made manifest in the regime, order is a complex symphony of interactions, activities and emotions. Phasing more usefully described the process of movement between levels of stability. It was less clear what contributed to discrete instances of disorder and more concerted episodes of instability, perhaps because these relied on complex and shifting recipes of community and individual behaviour.

Time on the wing created space to listen and learn the array of activities and expressions geared towards easing tension. Both staff and prisoners worked to keep the rhythms of the day ticking over. In the event of disruption to the everyday tune, staff and prisoners worked to co-produce rhythms for its restoration and maintenance. Sustaining order, and the emotional climate that denoted and underpinned it, was a community effort. Rather than being imposed by an abstract recognition of authority, it was spurred on by numerous formal and informal contributions from those engaged in daily life at Midtown. These efforts might be independent from one another, and frequently unacknowledged, but the resulting order was a co-produced effort.

21

Polyrhythmia Revisited

Discerning the rhythms of everyday life at Midtown revealed the polyrhythmic nature of a stable, orderly day. Further distinguishing between the comings and goings in prison spaces illuminated the ways people experienced and remade them in everyday activity. Phasing was part of this broader spectrum of activities in which the polyrhythmia of daily activity was implicated in the maintenance and re-affirmation of order. These multiplicities of daily rhythms comprised the substance of order and it is the instructive potential of this I return to.

The everyday tune was the benchmark. Motivation for compliance was cooperation rather than acceptance of authority. It was about the comfort of community and the ontological security offered by rhythms and routines rather than acceptance of legitimacy of the regime which provided the spur for going along with the hustle and bustle. There were many reasons individuals identified for seeking a 'good day', but these motivations were not obviously related to conditions for the breakdown of stability. Listening to the Midtown soundscape presented further disruption to the idea of a direct antonymic relationship between order and disorder (Carrabine, 2004).

Humming along to the everyday tune

The polyrhythmic tune of everyday life at Midtown was used as a means of gauging an orderly day, as well as being a signifier of disruption and instability. Bell rings and shouts took a while to decipher. As I made sense of the sonic environment, these pace-setting markers, reassuring in their consistency, served to punctuate more fluctuating and disparate aspects of the soundscape. Nevertheless, it was the broader soundscape which provided vital information about the climate on the wing and its state of order.

> 'How can I put it ... You can always tell how a prison's gonna be when you come in in the morning, if you can hear ... Say you come in this prison at quarter past, half past seven in the morning. It's nice

and quiet, you know everybody's calm and seckled ... but you know if you come in in the morning and you can hear music playing early, and banter, you know there's trouble in the place ... seriously.' (Stretch)

The stuff of daily existence and social interactions which comprised it were captured and reflected in the soundscape. Listening provided me with a means of decoding rituals and routines, familiarizing myself with the rhythms of prison life as far as was possible. Cues for developments and disruptions were audible, and signalled where current preoccupations of much of the community were likely to be focused. The ear of the community was attuned to the rhythms of the day, a means of gauging the temperature and whether all was well: "The tune's playing, it's the perfect tune, everything's great, yeah? ... Why?" (Derek, officer).

The Pavlovian bell at Midtown punctuated the day, signalling points in the routine. The significance of sound to prison daily rituals is underscored by a number of prisoner accounts (for example, Berkman, 1912; Solzhenitsyn, 1962; Irwin and Owen, 2005). Tom Rice explores how the hospital soundscape – specifically 'repetitive electronic noise' – served to remind patients of their illness by reiterating their status as patient (Rice, 2013: 8). The soundscape developed and reinforced a collective identity, reminding patients and medical staff of their roles within the hospital setting. At Midtown, few sounds were more rhythmically regular than the bell which sounded set points every day, occupying both symbolic and practical importance within the prison community. As with other bells, its ringing reinforced roles and relations, reverberating with its historical significance and signifying the stability of order and structure (Corbin, 1998).

'I like ringing the bell. See ideally the bell, the bell situation is ... everybody should all be, you should ring the bell, at their given time, and prisoners and staff should all know what that means.' (Officer Rose)

Aside from the odd, cheeky (and muted) clang, the prisoners did not sound it though the bell was easily accessible to all (and nearer to my standing point than ideal). Kitchen staff did not ring it. Neither did OSGs.[1] The bell might be rung by staff not in charge of the duty, but only if they were performing certain functions (such as overseeing association). Of those sanctioned to ring the bell, only certain of those staff would do so and only at specific points of the day. Some staff expressed reluctance to use it – one older officer expressing refusal to ever do so. I wish I had taken the opportunity to ask him more, but it was often difficult to catch staff. The officer in charge would ring it for collection of lunch and tea. This was the lynchpin of the day. A crucial point of the regime on which timeliness and smoothness for the rest of the day depended. The bell was an aspect of the soundscape which reinforced awareness of status, role and identity, both an inescapable imposition of the prison's constraints on autonomy and a rhythmic source of reassurance.

A good day was bound with the extent to which these rhythms maintained a predictable tempo. Everyday polyrhythmia was the marker deviations and departures from the regime were measured against. Much of prisons literature uses disorder as the instructive state for establishing what has gone wrong. It is the breakdown of order, major disturbance and rioting which form the focal point for working towards prevention of recurrence. For the Midtown community, "the everyday tune that's normal for here" was the point of reference and means of gauging the emotional climate. Motivations for contributing to cooperative efforts to maintain it varied, but the reasons people gave for doing so were explicitly connected to the comfort and security of a day going well.

Rhythms and routines

The ebb and flow of movement and routine throughout the prison day were marked by the bell, which regulated and ordered the day, signifying phases of the regime. The prison bell was a symbol of social and practical order, indicating what was happening next and where people were expected to be – a means of organizing both prisoners and staff. Complying with the regulation of the bell ostensibly signalled assent, but individual motivations were more self-directed than it might appear. Will, awaiting a substantial sentence, far from his first, indicated his conformity to the rhythms of the day allowed him to utilize these signals in service to his own daily rituals. For him, this practice was a means of ameliorating the constraints imposed by the prison and navigating his own way through its spaces:

> 'That bell's pretty bad. But I think, the bell, when you hear the bell it's like an action noise. It's like you're coming out in the morning, and you've heard the bell, ding, so you're like "oh, bell"; coming out. So, I don't know if you're pleased to hear it, more, but that's when my day begins you know what I mean? Ding. Then I'm like, out the door, routine starts ... Seven o'clock every morning I get up out of bed, I'll have a coffee, I'll have my breakfast, I get my gym kit ready. Brush my teeth. Sit there and watch telly til' the bell goes. Door opens, straight to the phone, ring the missus, then go to gym. Come back at 9.'

For Will, the significance of the bell was not what it meant, but that "it means something though, doesn't it? ... it's more an action noise. Like, what's happening?" Will had carved out his own routine within that of the prison – one which suited him and reflected his stoical attitude that "you have to work your ticket, don't you?" Rather than adapting his consciousness in line with the bell, he had adapted the meaning of the bell for his consciousness. Will used the bell to mark the days of his sentence and routine – one which allowed him to get by, echoing Gidden's assertion that "the maintaining of habits and routines is a crucial bulwark against threatening anxieties" (Giddens, 1991: 39).

The regime produced routinized rather than docile bodies. Seeming compliance was motivated by different factors, but dull acceptance was not always among these. In Will's case he had chosen the path of least resistance – a kind of obedient dissent. He went along with the routine, carving out his own place within it as an everyday tactic for moving through prison spaces. This allowed him to get through the prison day as comfortably and pleasantly as he could. He was practically conscious of the routine, its legitimacy or otherwise was of limited concern or relevance in so far as it did not impinge on his day (Giddens, 1984). Will had adopted a set of tactics for navigating daily prison life (de Certeau, 2011; Jewkes, 2012). Social interactions with potent aural signifiers, such as the bell, allowed for a more nuanced understanding of how these formal aspects of prison life were navigated by individual agents. Will exercised his autonomy in subverting the mechanics of order, moving in the spaces between and deriving comfort from the reassurance offered by the hustle and bustle of the everyday.

Dave, an older man surprised to find himself in prison for the first time, indicated how central order was to prison life:

> 'It's just what the system is, you know, the bangs and the dings and the dongs. The rattle of the keys. I think you get used to it after a bit … your life revolves around the clock and the bells and the whistles.'

Dave's assessment of his relationship with the soundscape indicated that for him, too, adjusting to prison life was a matter of routinization rather than docility. Tommy's assessment of the role and significance of order similarly implicated a recognition of the security that lay in a predictable (and preferably full) regime. "It would be better if there was more order. More things to do … if there was more of a structure. There has to be more order or else nothing's gonna get solved." I was attempting to probe his reasons for wanting more structure, and belief in the importance of "order" which he clearly and explicitly equates to "structure" rather than authority. Like most I spoke with, he referred to declining experience and skills among an increasingly young and transient pool of officers. He felt many were uninvested and/or palpably frightened. Strict divisions between old and new (more experienced and younger) staff were a feature of conversations about relationships. When I explored this a little further with him his desire for order was rooted in a belief in the importance of structure, as he had said, rather than a more abstract notion of broader legitimacy either of the regime or those charged with imposing it. "Respect doesn't come into it cos you're in jail and you're there as punishment so a lot of it's gone already, so what it is, you just have to do." Respect, for Tommy, was a matter of mutual regard, rendered impossible by the circumstances of incarceration. A desire for order, for a good, predictable 'everyday' was bound with the comfort and reassurance of routine and motivated by a human instinct to cooperate. There was ontological security in the familiar hustle and bustle, and with that a greater likelihood of safety and survival in an environment which could prove continually perilous.

Strangeways and the false dichotomy

The Strangeways prison riot of 1990 was the longest prison riot in the history of England and Wales. This was part of a broader spate of disturbances at various establishments including Glen Parva, Dartmoor, Cardiff, Bristol and Pucklechurch among others. Strangeways was the most concerted of these, so it is perhaps inevitable these events are cemented in our consciousness in this way. It does also serve to obscure the extent of foment about the state of our prisons at the time, as well as the nature and forms disturbances take when our prisons reach boiling point. It was in the wake of these disruptions – and their fatalities – that the Woolf report was produced.[2]. The point of the inquiry was to understand the reasons for the breakdown in order, with the aim of preventing recurrence (Woolf, 1991). Priorities of the time – staving off another Strangeways – shaped the foci of investigation. Identifying the conditions for disorder were seen as paramount for shoring up its opposite. As Eamonn Carrabine (2004) points out, the percipience of using disorder as a starting point for understanding its avoidance has gone largely unquestioned. Assumptions arising from this practice have shaped much of prison studies in the 30-odd years since.

Focusing on disorder as a means for understanding the nature of social stability in prison environments has shaped an implicit assumption that conditions for order are directly antithetical to disorder. Eager to avoid a repeat, the report sought to assess the conditions in which these disruptions had occurred as a means of identifying the basis for maintaining peace on the wings. Focusing on prisons at the points of greatest tension within a system creaking at the seams was a rational place to seek clarity about what had gone wrong. The understanding generated from this approach, without a comprehensive review of the state of the estate, painted a partial picture, and one which has shaped approaches to the problem of order in its wake (Sparks et al, 1996; Carrabine, 2004). Taking disorder as the focus of research, and as the pressing research question, reinforces the implicit assumption that order acts as a proxy for diagnosing its absence. Those at Midtown clearly indicated that their reasons for contributing to the stability of the regime were different from those motivating a withdrawal of cooperation. An absence of perceptions of legitimacy in treatment and conditions as an impetus for disorder should not be taken as affirmation that the opposite is true. It was difficult to form an inference that cooperation indicated acceptance of the fairness of authority from the Midtown community. These distinctions become clearer when exploring these ideas from within the prison community, its disruptions and its everyday rhythms, rather than adopting a top-down reading of the environment.

Sparks et al's *Prisons and the Problem of Order* (1996) spoke to Woolf's findings. It was here that 'legitimacy' was identified as an explanatory device for understanding the necessary conditions in which men would recognize the authority of the institution as just and valid. As a means of assessing the quality of both staff–prisoner relationships and between these and broader operations within institutions, legitimacy provides an instructive marker. It is a useful means of explicating some of the social processes bound up with order. Members of the Midtown community suggested it was less instructive as a means of assessing motivations for complying and cooperating with the regime. Tommy echoed Carrabine's assertion that prison is fundamentally comprised of a legitimacy deficit, which prompts the question why riots do not occur with far greater frequency (Colvin, 1992; Carrabine, 2004, 2005). Shifting the frame for understanding order in this way is more helpful for illuminating the conditions for its breakdown. Pressing deprivations, boredom and injustice are aspects of daily experience inside, as those I spoke with at Midtown made clear. This does not result in perpetual unrest, though does contribute to an understanding of the complex sets of circumstances in which major incidents of disorder do arise (Carrabine, 2005: 903).

People at Midtown got on and got by as a means of shoring up their sense of security and lessening concerns with safety and survival. The daily hustle and bustle was not characterized by endless assessments of the justification for individual predicaments but by cooperative impetus to keep it going. There was an ontological security derived from the rhythms and routines of the everyday tune and it was this that provided the marker for assessing the stability of the environment. Attending more closely to the ebb and flow of life from within the community made motivations for compliance more audible, disrupting notions of a simplistic antonymic relationship between order and its breakdown. While the hope that drawing attention to the parlous state of the prison system would result in substantial reform proved short-lived (Jameson and Allison, 1995), the legacy of Strangeways has nevertheless proved profound.

In contrast to the point of departure for much academic work on prisons, a good day was the starting point for discerning how stable the wing was for those living and working on it. While my research was restricted to one prison, those I spoke to had considerable experience of the broader estate and they frequently drew on this broader bank of knowledge when talking with me. Listening revealed the complexity and diversity of social actors, activities and the processes which comprised order and the polyrhythmia that characterized it. When listening within the Midtown community, it became evident that order relied on a far wider range of actors than might be supposed if an assumption of the sanctity of authority for its operations were relied upon. Rather, order was co-produced by many in the prison community as a means of getting on and getting by. Maintaining polyrhythmic activity relied not only on goodwill and cooperation but also the broad desire for industry which formed the everyday tune that was normal for there.

22

Bells, Whistles, Ships and Prisons

Sound is particularly pertinent in a place where fields of vision are often heavily restricted. Prisons are strange spaces and require a careful, slow ear to discern the routines and rhythms that comprise the 'everyday tune'. Once the ear adjusts, audible aspects of social emotion become more discernible, as does its role in safety and survival. Focusing on the everyday is closer to more traditional ethnographies though differs from a substantial strain of prison studies more concerned with the extraordinary. Exploring the community's relationships with the soundscape, working from within, challenged assumptions about the basis for order. Sound marks out time, conveys power and is implicit in processes which both reinforce and disrupt stability. Familiarity with polyrhythmic and arrhythmic daily tempos revealed the co-produced, cooperative work stability depended upon. This challenges the wisdom of viewing prison life primarily through the prism of security and enhances understanding of the lasting effects of imprisonment for all who spend time in these environments.

Using sound as both method and focus shifted my frame of understanding considerably. My proximity to those I worked with was brought closer. My sensitivity to their broader temporal and spatial experience within, through and outside the prison was simultaneously heightened. This prompted greater scrutiny of how to portray Midtown and its people. Faithfully representing something of those who gave so generously of themselves is, rightly, an endless concern. So too, though, is the way we depict the stories bound up in ideas we co-opt in our own accounts. The tales we tell, and how we tell them, matter. In writing about Midtown, I hope I have gone some way to capturing the perilous rip tides lurking in the shallower waters of a local prison, as well as the endless warmth and accommodation extended to me while I loitered, hopefully.

It was only when Bear, Midtown's writer in residence, pointed it out, that I realized how closely the innards of the prison resembled a ship. Vulnerable and segregated prisoners languished in the sun-starved, close, subterranean hold, the twos – the ground floor – could be likened to the deck, the netting resembled rigging and so on. The otherness of prison spaces rebounded in the soundscape, evoking the broader social memory of strange, other places. Outlets for our imagination and a means of grounding ourselves in social life, heterotopias – strange places which serve to upset and shore up those of the wider, social world – have a profoundly important function for the rest of us, that resists efforts to demystify them (Foucault and Miskowiec, 1986).

English linguistic quirks heighten the sense of heterotopia the prison represents – one 'lands' as if travelling by plane, is 'on' a wing or landing, as if sailing through a separate dimension from the world beyond the walls, and 'ships out' when leaving. This was echoed in the enduring impact of the prison soundscape, a force which traversed direct spatial and temporal experience of the place: "The minute I hear keys I'm back inside." Both direct immersion within the prison community and memories evoked by it resonated in the soundscape. The prison derives some of its power by imposing a sense of other. It permeates memory, experience and expectation, and enhances a longing for, as well as a distancing from, home through the imposition of a sense of somewhere else.

Listening

Initially, foregrounding sound was somewhat disorientating. There was a disconcerting freedom to pursue research, prompted by the day and by those I spent time with. While this approach was ideal for the unpredictability of prison life, it also made enquiry less bounded. Practice was fluid and responsive to events and issues as they emerged. Posters, consent, debrief and information forms were, of course, distributed in text format. At Midtown though, whether because directives and bad information always appeared in printed form, or because of literacy issues[1] – an accurate gauge of which is far more complicated than regurgitated and problematic statistics would have you believe – receipt of the message broadly depended on its verbal delivery. As time went on this became second nature. If I perused a spare copy of *Insidetime*[2] I would read it to anyone displaying interest. I was sometimes thanked for the sensitivity this reflected, because the individual was not a confident reader. In truth I had merely learned to be a little better at not making assumptions.

Midtown was teaching me lessons in inclusivity, albeit ones I was slower to learn than ideal. This process amplified the potential of this approach for disrupting hierarchies of power, and correspondingly, upsetting systems of authoritative knowledge. I was speaking with the experts and seeking to learn from their insight. My relative ignorance was emphasized by the unfamiliarity of the soundscape, and many of those I spoke with were warm and facilitative in recognition of my genuine desire to learn. Attempts to understand Midtown were collaborative affairs, in which feelings, memories and experiences held instructive potential. A greater democracy of the senses as sources of knowledge combatted the idea of the mind as a higher and separate root of understanding. Our joint enquiries had little time for that long-standing Cartesian mind-body dualism which has shaped the ocular-centric lens of Western culture. We strove to understand beyond the peripheries of vision.

Time and space

Much of this book explores how our understanding of space and time is reconfigured when the social significance of the soundscape is accounted for. The pursuit of this research, and the freedom I was extended to do it, were also reliant on time and space. I was able to conduct slow research, to immerse myself in the field and lent sufficient latitude to develop meaningful relationships with both the people and place of Midtown. As pressures mount, and academics are increasingly obliged to account for every contribution in ways that risk stripping its meaning, the freedom to conduct open-ended research requiring time and investment is under ever-greater threat. This project would not have been possible were it not for the unusual and extensive privilege of my studentship at Leicester University, nor the precious relationships with people at Midtown, who were generous beyond measure with their time, trust and insight.

Midtown, like all prisons, was a place of violence – an old and dirty building, no more fit for purpose than its purpose is fitting. Alongside the brutality of the place, and sometimes that of its people, was staggering warmth and kindness. Its closure has been scheduled and postponed several times now. I cannot mourn an end to the subjection of hundreds at a time to its knackered plumbing, cramped conditions and crumbling, grimy walls. One day soon I expect to see an article in the local paper pop up on my social media, detailing plans for an economy-enriching 'bouji' bar and boutique hotel, along the lines of Malmaison.[3] This will be a sad day. Personal sentimentality is certainly a factor, but so is what this development will signify. The closure of Midtown sounds another death knell for the small, local prison and with it a penal culture that, while deeply flawed, offered some continuity of community life. Staff and prisoners were mutually invested in one another, offering greetings to each other as they passed by outside or remarking on their children's development. I knew, too, of staff visiting one another in trying times. This was far from universal, but made possible by local proximity,[4] and with it a sense of community was fostered and sustained. There was antipathy too, but some relationships between and among both staff and prisoners (some of whom were related, whether through blood or quasi-familial ties spanning decades) signified enduring bonds.

The power of punishment shaped the experience of the soundscape. It was reinforced in vibrations through the walls, in the inescapable clangs, bangs, thunks and rattles. It was in radios, alarms, shouts and screams as well as cherished moments of hearty laughter and snatched commensality. Punishment was also conveyed in absence – in the imposition of a day and night subject to idleness if not stillness. There was no children's laughter in the bowels of the prison, or clatter of domestic mundanity. Nevertheless, humanity was smuggled in, snatched in moments of staggering kindness and accommodation. There was no love in the concrete, but it hosted plenty.

Representations

My impressions were necessarily partial. I frequently saw, and heard, only what I was permitted to. There are ethical limitations to how far one's gaze should extend, too. In this sense I end as I began, by noting how much of prison life takes place behind the door. In that sense the distinctions between this particular social world and social life more generally are perhaps more polarized in our portrayals of them than reality. In attempting to present simplified, accessible stories we risk flattening those they belong to. We are all in the business of stories, but the responsibility to try to do them justice is immense. As we all do, I would end interviews by asking if there was anything else they wanted to add, any glaring omission my ignorance had deafened me to? Duke had held off our interview, whether because of his ADHD-led energy surges around the wing or because his sentencing was pending. We sat down after he had received a substantial sentence and was struggling to adjust. Much of our interview had been spent reflecting on what this meant, how unsupported he felt and his determination to fix on the future, so I was surprised when he answered:

> 'It's a good job there's people like you who do come in, and they do care what people have got to say, cos without people like you that whole feeling of being alone is just there, and nothing to change it. But it's good just to have a say. It's good to have a talk to somebody about what jail's really like because people don't really care about jail. They don't really care about prisoners, they don't really care about nothing, they just live their life, unaware of the monstrosities that occur.'

I spent some time finishing up with the men and saying goodbyes. In truth this was more a dawdling technique. I did not want to go. I did not want to miss their updates. I had not learned enough. If I ever do catch up with him, I hope Duke recognizes something of himself and his social world in these pages.

Representations of the community were interdependent. Stories people told about others, frequently served to express aspects of the tellers' identity rather than the subject. I often found they were not repeated by those who had featured in them. Often the men wanted to alert me to perceptions of injustice. What was most notable about this was how frequently they were drawing attention to others rather than themselves. Presiding over a lively focus group while working as a research assistant at another prison, the men waited until we had reached a certain point of the conversation to alert us to Karl who was serving an indeterminate sentence for public protection (IPP). Doing time alongside those subject to such injustice was a profound impediment to achieving the quality of relationships necessary for successful drug treatment, the men argued. The respect and support demonstrated by carving out space for Karl to be heard was typical. This illustrated the need for deeper immersion, to better create space for capturing the complexities of social life and social experience inside. The Midtown community was characterized by care, kindness and understanding as much as it was chaotic upheaval and relentless noisiness. These impressions went further to honouring the humanity of those I encountered, counteracting the frequently flattening representations of those in prison as individualistic, instrumentally driven, selfish and brutalized. These one-dimensional accounts do those inside a profound injustice, and correspondingly hamper our attempts to understand the basis for cooperation and community.

Prisoners may suffer a civic death in relation to connections with the outside, but there was a bustling civic life within. In some respects, divisions between staff and prisoners' experience were more demarcated in expectation than reality. While staff got to go home, for the duration of their working day or night, they coexisted with those they oversaw. On their days off they frequented the same supermarkets, walked the same streets and bumped into one another in the same corner shops. Coexistence dictated a necessity of civility. Listening to daily life rendered this more audible, and in so doing revealed a continual process of negotiated, if informal, co-governance. Discretion and pragmatism were evident in officers' practice too, but this was a social world in which people not only navigated the mundanity of daily activities, but also shared in monumental, seismic moments of life and death.

There are stories, too, in the work we draw from and the ideas we stitch into our own tapestries of meaning. It is all too easy to misrepresent texts we come to assume we all know backwards in their retelling. But do we? Did Goffman intend his conception of a 'total' institution to mean the walls were impermeable, or that mortifications were focused on the point of reception into these places? To what extent is our reading of 'backstage' and 'front-stage' social life dependent on class-ridden notions of privacy and personal space? Do we accurately reflect Sykes' complex accounts of the contingent and partial practices of power and its translation to everyday on the wing? Have we become so accustomed to drawing on Sparks, Bottoms and Hay for their treatment of order and control that we overlook their reflections on the socio-political context they were working in? Do their broader accounts of how power operates in prisons over time and space become lost in our compression of their contributions? We are all products of the times and places we occupy and of the distances we navigate, and bridge – if we are lucky.

Rip tide

Midtown was a local-local prison. I am not a local, but while I used my southern accent and attitude – as well as my trainers, never underestimate the value of a pair of 110s – to initiate conversation,[5] I was living close enough that I could establish some broader familiarity with points of local cultural reference. I had not had a plan to focus on any one prison, local or otherwise. I had not, in truth, expected to be accommodated at all. The nature of my research made direct comparison less important and, given the breadth and depth of collective experience, in some respects I really could have been in any part of the estate. The stars, and some insightful, adventurous personalities aligned to make Midtown my focus, and I shall be forever grateful.

Local prisons are often overlooked in longer-term contemporary research projects. High security is portrayed as occupying the deep end of both research and system. Again, though, this contrasts with the way demands of working in different parts of the prison estate are viewed by those who do so. A focus on this part of the system underplays the complex and multifaceted ways in which various prisons are experienced as well as by whom. Local prisons are less often the subject of longer-term studies nowadays, dismissed as too unstable, trifling, unrepresentative. This flattens representations of what is a profoundly frenetic environment with a population of diverse needs and experience. Senses of submersion in the system may be more uniformly deeper in high security, but it is often in the shallower waters that unpredictable rip tides threaten to drown.

As I have said, much of this book is about time. It would be remiss not to acknowledge how fortuitously timed my project was. I caught Midtown in a purple patch. I watched with dismay as factors beyond the prison's control threatened the tenuous, but palpable, peace it had enjoyed at the beginning of my time there. The system was stretched beyond breaking point, held together with ad hoc concoctions of prison-issue toothpaste, fear and goodwill. Midtown, a small decrepit Tardis-like dinghy of a prison, was cast adrift on oceans of complacency, neglect and political expedience. It was just about staying above water. As was the case with many individuals, the buoyant sense of identity the Midtown community enjoyed was chronically eroded by relentless waves of challenges it could not hope to meet. Midtown was captured in the rip tides of a system beset by crippling staff attrition, parlous resources, an endlessly swelling population and the lack of a matrices of systems of support and welfare needed to effectively support those being cast back out to sea.

Coda

'Coda' denotes the concluding passage in a piece of music. Just as in music, many of these motifs appear again, and again. Prison compounds challenges of those with already fragile physical and mental wellbeing, neurodiversity, PTSD – from an array of traumatic events, experience of abuse, violence or time in the services – and further attenuates links with home and the means of sustaining or making one. At Midtown, despite some valiant efforts, it was impossible to adequately address the issues their population presented with. Homelessness, mental and physical illness, unemployment, substance use, debt and problematic relationships with family and children all threatened to drag many of those at Midtown under. Staff bemoaned a breakdown in order they lacked the means to reinstate, while the men perceived a lack of investment, skill and care from many of the staff. And yet, there were profound distinctions in the way relationships with individuals and perceptions of the broader estate were spoken of. Those at Midtown indicated how we might more accurately think of the prison social world, the composition of order, those who participate in its maintenance and how they do so. They had much to say about what a healthy prison might look (and sound) like as well as better accounting for the multifarious harms imposed on those who linger in these spaces, whether through work or through contact with the sharp end of the criminal justice system. We know bigger is not better,[6] just as we know what happens when injustice and neglect are piled too high for too long. The long-term impact of COVID[7] regulations remain unclear, but they will not have done anything to alleviate the needs of a system and a population under ever-greater strain. Violence and self-harm remain at staggering levels. As I spent longer at Midtown, it became increasingly striking that while both staff and prisoners consistently used the soundscape as a barometer for safety, it was passed on through folk memory and learned experience rather than training or induction.

This book is not intended to valorize punishment or particular ways of delivering it. I was prompted to conduct research in prison, and hope to continue to do so, out of a desire to understand how these places of violence have come to inhabit such an unassailable potency and unquestioned legitimacy in our cultural consciousness. This is a study of a small, local prison at a point where these penal environments are being replaced by ever-larger builds, and ever-greater populations. For all the privations of the Midtown environment, there were aspects of community life which were a source of great support and comfort to many moving through their spaces. If we must have prisons at all, both Midtown and the broader estate are in dire need of an overhaul – resources, facilities, better staff conditions and incomparably heightened levels of training. Better food, regimes, relationships, and education, improved prospects for work and pay, advanced health and mental health care, advanced substance use counselling and treatment. Genuinely joined-up, comprehensive support getting into work, with secure housing at the point of leaving, and all the possibilities created by that, are the most basic requirements for meaningful improvement. Timely access to an optician's and dentist's would be a start. It is hardly conducive to ensuring the best outcomes when people are released with failing vision and diminishing numbers of teeth. Effective response to these challenges must, at the very least, involve a holistic assessment of the impact of a shattered system of social care and support. Prisons are not equipped to compensate for this absence. The requirements of punishment or 'rehabilitation' cannot possibly be met by a place beset by such vast and conflicting demands. Complacency has led us to this point – its remedy lies way beyond the prison walls. This is a book about sound in prison, which is about neither prison nor sound.

23

Shipping Out

Rhythms in movement and daily activity through prison spaces reveal much about the nature of life inside and I had anticipated moving around as I familiarized myself with the daily ebb and flow considerably more than happened in practice. Prisoners, of course, were not free to come and go through the gates, and I was in no position to escort them. Staff were busy and I was conscious of the need to minimize the nuisance I represented. As I have stated elsewhere, much of my time was spent standing in the same spot on the main wing. People could find me if they chose, avoid me if they did not want to engage and staff knew where I was. Adapting to the conditions of the prison environment offered many lessons in research practice. Once the ear attuned and sufficient time had been spent standing still, these strategies amplified the significance of leaving, arriving and waiting. So much waiting.

Shipping out is a term which captures the otherness of prison spaces and the cultural roles that ships and prisons play. They are 'other' places against which we measure our relative belonging. Our here-ness assumes definition when contrasted with the there-ness behind the wall. Boats and ships are spurs to the imagination of the great and mysterious beyond: 'In civilizations without boats, dreams dry up, espionage takes the place of adventure, and the police take the place of pirates' (Foucault and Miskowiec, 1986). Prisons similarly shore up our sense of social belonging. Setting sail and disembarking signify the arrival and departure from watery mysterious realms. In prison, leaving and arriving take on potent, ritualistic meaning. Being a constant point of reference as the tides of movement ebbed and flowed around me taught much about the nature of the prison and its relationship with the outside. Like an awkward pebble in the tide of hustle and bustle, I was sensitized to the comings and goings of others. Adopting this strategy heightened my awareness of spatial and temporal experience in relation to inside and out, and other times and places. This became more poignant as I prepared to leave Midtown myself.

So much of Midtown life seemed to revolve around arriving, leaving or waiting to do one or the other. Prisoners, staff and those visiting for personal or professional reasons came and went with rhythmic irregularity. I noted in my fieldnotes that when I had attended visits there were always crying children on the point of leaving. It was not always clear whether it was distress at leaving a loved one behind or the fraught nature of visits. One evening, I escorted a student through the visits area. Her guide dog became uncharacteristically uncooperative and visibly disturbed. The officers overseeing security remarked that the dog must be able to "smell the emotion" lingering in the corridor. Had the dog not provided a benign proxy for exploring the emotionally laden environment, I imagined, perhaps unfairly, the staff would have been more resistant to acknowledging the palpable distress of many moving through these spaces. Reflecting on these states of waiting, departure and arrival emphasized the significance they represented in relation to connections to people and place. The prospect of movement was a frequent topic of conversation and the thrum of a good day on the wing often contained a substantial element of sounds of greeting old friends, new arrivals and embracing those leaving. "I'm off to Stocken tomorrow." "Good news, Grendon have accepted me" (fieldnotes). My inclusion in these conversations reflected an assumption I would understand and share in the significance of their meaning. There was no place for expressions of misgivings or sadness in these celebratory conversations, so I kept them to myself.

Leaving, on a jet plane

> When a prisoner leaves, his kit is carried to reception, often by a few others who wish him well on his onward journey – or better still, on the out. Everyone shares in these moments. They break up the day and offer the prospect of hope, if by proxy. The excitement of movement, somewhere, anywhere. 'My friend's leaving today, off to Ranby' one of the men calls out to me in explanation. (Fieldnotes)

Leaving had specific rituals. Those chosen (pad mates, friends, relations) would gather as the ostensible subject of the ritual prepared and packed their belongings in clear plastic bags. Rounds of hugs, back-slapping and well-wishing were followed by a procession of those seeing him off, each carrying something, presumably by way of justifying their inclusion in the ceremony. These were happy occasions, and much of the community would share in the vicarious excitement of seeing someone popular depart. Not everyone had these relationships to ground the significance of their departure. I noted an exchange heard from the wing: "You speak English?" "No." "You're going back to Romania. Pack your kit. You're leaving on a jet plane." The officer, who I generally thought of quite fondly, began to sing this enduring John Denver (1966) classic to a rather bemused gentleman who I was confident spoke very little English. Not for this individual the 'leaving off' ritual.

Staff also recognized the significance of these comings and goings from Midtown, though my experience at other prisons suggested this was far from universal, and I do not assume it was universally applied at Midtown either. One day, while I was at reception, there was an increasingly heated dispute:

> 'Prop'[1] bartering with Geoamey over what they would take, what 'head office' would allow and what the receiving prison would accept. This takes extraordinary turn when an hour of debate and increasingly heated arguing, accompanied by several phone calls to prisons, governors, receptions and head offices takes place. There is heightening resistance to taking a lifer's gear, to which he's entitled, from the Geoamey[2] guy. As officer later points out, this is his life, here, in a series of tagged, clear plastic bags. I ask what will happen if they refuse. The prison will pay to have it delivered they tell me. The calm is viciously punctured by this ongoing argument. The reception orderly is agitated; one member of staff completely (though understandably) loses her temper. Eventually they go. With stuff. Victory. (Fieldnotes)

As Officer Slater explained, gesturing at the bags holding the sum of this man's worldly possessions: "See this here, this is his house." Affirmations of identity and dignity formed part of these leaving rituals, even in their confirmation of impermanence.

Frequently, this also worked the other way around:

> Fella walks in with bag of belongings. 'Back again?!' he's greeted. 'Yeah, just landed' he confirms. Comings and goings are both greeted with happiness and enthusiasm. Only now I've been here a long while I realize just how many come and go from around and about. Always see them on the streets. Frequently not recognized either because we didn't speak, or because they are off their faces. (Fieldnotes)

Coming and going was a permanent feature of life at Midtown. This included greetings of genuine warmth between some prisoners and staff, such was their mutual affection and familiarity. The rapid 'churn' worked in multi-directions, prison-to-prison, occasionally interspersed or preceded by stays at other institutions, and traversed well-worn lines between inside and outside. Lamar explained what this looked like from the perspective of someone who wanted to ship out:

> 'What I couldn't believe is that how you can have people having mamba attacks every single day, do you know, on mamba every single day, but

you do nothing to help them. And when they get out, they're chucked out without no homes, without no jobs, on a hostel which is full of the people they was on the wing with six months ago. Do you get what I'm saying? And then it's hard for a normal person to get a job or some accommodation out there. It's a hard world out there right now, never mind for prisoners, who are so far behind, a lot of them. So far behind. Do you know what I mean? They haven't got the erm, the motivation, self-esteem, they haven't got nothing. So when they get out they feel it's too hard for them to do anything, and I think they feel like it's more comfortable for them to be inside prison. Do you know? Which is very dangerous.'

Lamar's account of the continuities of disadvantage and vulnerability between here and there reflected his experience of a deteriorating prison system. In doing so he made a compelling point about the impossibility of looking to a resource-strapped prison to compensate for social, political and economic failings. Conditions on the streets of Midtown were not conducive to avoiding time at HMP, but time in HMP Midtown did little to prepare those in its care for more successfully navigating its streets.

Leaving rituals of the kind previously referred to were reserved for moves which were long awaited or sought after. There were many other instances of 'shipping out' which were greeted with considerably less enthusiasm. Forced or threatened moves are an under-represented form of power in prison, though Sparks et al (1996) consider their function as a powerful means of compelling compliance in those otherwise disinclined. Their potency lies in the potential for imposing greater distance and difficulty maintaining connections between people and place. Being moved to an unknown destination against one's will was also a forceful means of instilling a sense of loss of agency (Sykes, 1958; Warr, 2019). Opposition to moves, while centring on proximity to loved ones, 'home' and the potential for meeting sentence-plan stipulations, was also informed by formidable banks of collective knowledge, spanning much of the estate.

Catalyst and comparison

Portrayals of the spate of prison disturbances in the early nineties as a singular event – *Strangeways* – is not untypical of the atomized representation of our prison population. History is contingent, and the complexity of the prison difficult to capture. It is understandable, inevitable, perhaps, that we focus on specific institutions, issues affecting sub-sets of the population or themes adapted as lenses to make sense of our enquiries, as I have. These representations frequently obscure the extent and vibrancy of shared knowledge and culture between those who occupy these spaces. The collective knowledge and experience of those living and working in our prisons comprises a rich social history we often fail to take account of. Word travels with as much frequency and rapidity as people through the system (as well as with the speed and light of digital technology). Those inside were rarely unaware when trouble was coming, or speculation about the reasons it had sparked. Much of the immediate catalyst for disturbances at Winson Green,[3] for example, was said to stem from repeated failure to get prisoners to medical appointments or respond to requests for special purpose release.[4] My static position over much of the length of my time at Midtown brought this collective sense of movement and knowledge into stark relief. Experience of other places was a useful means of sharpening reflections on the particularities of Midtown. My failure to move was a standing joke, but by no means limited my learning to what was immediately perceptible to me.

I spoke to members of staff before I moved into the inner circles of the prison, and formed many of my first impressions from comparing their descriptions to what I could hear. As I became more familiar with the environment, I was often struck by the way they contrasted experiences as a way of defining their work identities in relation to their current place at Midtown. These comparisons related not only to different prisons but also, often, distinct parts of the estate. The No. 2's assertion that Midtown was "unique" was arrived at through time and visits at a host of other institutions. Derek's likening of Midtown's environment to the intensity of undiluted squash resulted from his range of experience in the women's and high-security estates. Kathleen identified her discomfort when arriving at Midtown as stemming from its contrast with her previous experience. She also credited the distinction between the environments at Midtown and Belmarsh as having enhanced her skill set: "I think the service in London, is like a different service. The prisoners are different, and it's just like yeah. It was just a really good grounding and I'm glad I started there." Officer Rose derived great comfort from predictable routine, both personally and professionally. An ex-serviceman, he had worked at an Immigration Removal Centre and referred to his time there as a means of emphasizing his profound discomfort with insufficient order:

> 'I hated it. I absolutely hated it. Because it wasn't a prison. It had no regime … Well it did have a regime. Unlock at 8 o'clock, lock em up at 8 o'clock, everything else in between was just a fudge. So I didn't like that. I'm probably disciplined in that respect as well cos I like routine and regime as well and there was nothing. Ah, I just didn't like it … just couldn't adapt to that way of running.'

Staff derived a sense of working identity and belonging from the institutions they spent time in, and much like prisoners, frequently enquired about where else I had been and what my impressions were, perhaps with a view to adding these reflections to the bank of intricate, accumulated knowledge.

Prisoners similarly drew from their wealth of experience of other prisons, other parts of the estate and other institutions. Their narratives often chimed with broader observations about the social characteristics of many of those in prison.[5] Stevie and Stretch had been looked after by the state; Red had residual issues from his time in the army. Ned had extensive experience of childhood incarceration having spent time in all three Secure Training Centres:[6]

Me: How many prisons you been to?
Ned: Medway and Rainsbrook, Oakhill … Cookham Wood, Feltham, Ashfield, Portland, Ashfield's a nonce jail now, I don't know why. They fucked up man, that was a good jail as well. Erm, Portland, erm, Lancaster Farms, erm, whereafter that? Erm, Littlehey, that's a nonce jail now as well. Erm, Bellmarsh, Thameside, Isis, Bullingdon, Lowdham Grange, where else? I think that's about it …

There was a pride in displaying knowledge of the system, though regret was often expressed about the loss of time this represented. Whether it was the gendered nature of our interactions, I did not detect bravado but a willingness to share and compare understanding in relation to my curiosity, and theirs. It often seemed to me that I could make it around the entire estate if I just stood there long enough. My London was coming out.

Inside/outside

In recent years increasing attention has been devoted to the potential of walking methods. Credited with heightened possibilities for enacting agency and foregrounding environmental experience as well as for eliciting different responses, this is part of a growing recognition of creative and imaginative approaches to research. I enjoyed considerably more freedom of movement when developing a pilot because I was less established, and I was escorted by officers. Somewhat counter-intuitively, carrying keys diminished my ability to go where I liked, or rather, to go where I wanted when I wanted to. Initially, working this into my method was a matter of making virtue out of necessity. Over time, this shifted the methodology. Staying still facilitated closer attendance to a soundscape I could not freely move within. This shaped my understanding of the place and its people. Providing a consistent point in the daily hubbub refined attunement to the soundscape and the rhythms within, around and between the prison and its broader community. Being a static point in a sea of bustle also shaped relationships between myself and others, as Elvis indicated when he said: "We like hanging around you, you're always calm." Staying put lent me a sense of rootedness which facilitated deeper interaction and a greater sensitivity to the movement of others but made it harder to leave. I had grown fond of many, and developed an affection for the place, as enduring as it was unexpected. I mourned the impending closure which, while postponed repeatedly was surely on the cards (Midtown is still open and accommodating ever-greater numbers). The No. 1 suggested I should have been included in the new staff photograph on proud display near the main entrance to the wing. When I told Kai I was on my way out, he responded: "Can you ask for a cardboard cut-out and put it in your place so we can stop and talk to you? Gonna miss you." It was time for me to go.

I set about leaving as I had arrived, by incremental degree. This revealed additional textures to the relationship between the place and its people. I could walk to Midtown from home and often liked to dawdle around the perimeter, getting a feel for the community that lay just beyond the wall. Nearby playing fields and public toilets hosted a shifting flow of humanity depending on the time of day. The general appearance of flats and shops declined the closer to the gate. The hostels immediately by and tower flats across the way housed some of those on the short-sentence merry-go-round during my time there. Weather, idleness and poor timekeeping sometimes prompted me to get a cab rather than plodding the drab walk into town. Questioning about my purpose would begin delicately if I was unknown to the driver, lest the nature of my visit was personal. Here, too, the mutual delicacy of navigating stigma and intimacy was thought-provoking. Rather than prolong their uncertainty I would tell them I was conducting research. If family or friends had been inside, their tone and conversation would reflect a closer acquaintance. If not, the familiar refrain was often repeated: they had read these places were like holiday camps, was this true? The imposing Midtown architecture was a fixed point on the skyline of their hustle and bustle around the city roads, but life beyond the walls remained a mysterious curiosity, on the edge of the community but just outside the periphery of its imagination.

I felt the shifting proximity between myself and members of the Midtown community most keenly in their leaving. Their excitement was infectious, but I also recognized the contingent nature of this hopefulness. Leaving rituals were about mutually buoying one another with the prospect of somewhere, something, else. Frequently, these faces would return, sometimes in a more haunted state than they had been when heading off with stuffed-to-bursting, clear-plastic bags over their shoulders and back slaps from their mates. I felt a surprisingly dense and complex set of emotions at their shipping out. Touched by their shared joy, for these were happy occasions. Hopeful for what this might mean for progressing through their sentence plan and placing sure feet one step closer to home. Sad at their parting because I had come to enjoy their company and insight. Deeply anxious about what might await them in more hostile, faster-paced, cut-throat environments, and how their fragile wellbeing might respond to these unforeseeable challenges. In a world characterized by the profound unpredictability of a debilitatingly predictable routine, how would they fare through those endless nights? It was hard to leave. There was no 'saturation' point, but an infinite number of songs still left to hear.

Notes

Chapter 1

1. The 'Independent Monitoring Board' formally 'prison visitors'. A body which, while reporting to and recruited by – albeit indirectly – the Ministry of Justice, 'independently' monitors the fairness of processes (primarily complaints) in prisons and immigration detention. During the COVID-19 pandemic, most monitoring has been conducted remotely. It remains to be seen how this has impacted their already questionable effectiveness.
2. 'Burn' is another name for tobacco. I began research at HMP Midtown prior to the tobacco ban which was introduced that August, rocketing the price of tobacco and, according to the men, increasing the number of incidents of 'mamba attacks' because the availability of tobacco with which to mix it was greatly reduced. Spice and mamba are names for synthetic cannabanoids.
3. There is, of course, no such prison. I call it this because regardless of how those participating felt at the time, we all deserve the option to move away from words and deeds of our past. It is not difficult to identify the place if you have some familiarity with the prisons of England and Wales, but equally, it adds little to do so.
4. 'Soundscape' refers to the aural components of a physical environment. The definition provided by the British Standards Institute includes dimensions of experience (expectation, memory, emotion) which do not reflect sound as it is heard, but rather as it is interpreted within particular spatial contexts (BSI, 2014).
5. See Herrity, K., Schmidt, B. and Warr, J. (eds) (2021) *Sensory Penalties: Explorations of the Sensory in Spaces of Punishment and Social Control* for additional reflections on this issue.
6. For the thesis: https://leicester.figshare.com/articles/thesis/Rhythms_and_Routines_sounding_order_in_a_local_men_s_prison_through_aural_ethnography/10310807
7. Population now stands at 'around 400' (www.gov.uk/ – last updated April 2022).
8. Prison term referring to the measure of how fast a prison population turns over.
9. These figures were checked against the latest HMIP inspection and IMB reports but have been excluded in order to conceal the identity of the prison, those who contributed to this research and are associated with it.
10. The prison governor – the person responsible for running the prison – is often referred to as 'the No. 1'.
11. When referring to the prison as it was during my fieldwork I have used the most up-to-date information relating to that period. This changes later in the book when I talk more broadly.
12. Indeterminate sentence for public protection. Introduced by the Criminal Justice Act 2003 and abolished in 2012.
13. Juvenile life sentence, also indeterminate works the same way as a discretionary life sentence in terms of parole.

NOTES

14. The deputy governor – junior only to the governor and acting up in their absence – is commonly referred to as 'the No. 2'.
15. All names, including that of the prison, have been changed to conceal identity. They are often riffs on nicknames or in-jokes between various members of the Midtown community, where I was let in on the joke. I made a conscious effort not to anglicize names when anonymizing them for what I hope are obvious reasons.

Chapter 2

1. A term for a makeshift filter for hand-rolled cigarettes, made of card or paper. This was prior to the smoking ban which was introduced at Midtown that August.
2. New admissions to the prison spent their first few nights here, where they received induction – various information about how to access services and navigate the complexities of prison life. In rare cases, such as those passing through who were particularly vulnerable, stays here might be longer.
3. I talk about this in more depth in Herrity, K. (2020) 'Hearing behind the door: the cell as a portal to prison life', in J. Turner and V. Knight (eds) *The Prison Cell: Embodied and Everyday Spaces of Incarceration*, London: Palgrave.
4. See here for a comprehensive thematic review on the experience of Black prisoners and prison staff: www.justiceinspectorates.gov.uk/hmiprisons/inspections/the-experiences-of-adult-black-male-prisoners-and-black-prison-staff/#:~:text=What%20did%20black%20staff%20say,accused%20of%20collusion%20or%20corruption
5. An English phrase meaning strongly and sturdily built.
6. Liebling et al make a similar point in *The Prison Officer*.
7. In theatre it is considered unlucky to refer to Shakespeare's Macbeth by name, and so it is alternatively known as 'The Scottish Play'.

Chapter 4

1. I did not enquire whether this relied on phones, a topic I found difficult to avoid given how prevalent they were (and are). Contrary to much populist misdirection, phones are a necessity in prisons where legitimately made phone calls are disproportionately expensive. This is particularly true where in-cell telephony is not installed, and, depending on regime, prisoners may have profound difficulties competing for access to a limited number of phones on the wing, with limited time out of cell.
2. Magnums are a kind of chocolate-coated ice cream.
3. The police sometimes wait to re-arrest someone at the gates at the point of release for other offences.
4. This was also a matter of practicality since some of these people were 'stuck' for longer and therefore around to develop interactions.
5. While in high-security parts of the estate he had encountered a number of friends and family of his victim which had placed him in considerable jeopardy.

Chapter 5

1. There were exceptions to this. Much to the amusement of those present, it was a prime spot for being captured by the odd individual who really wanted to talk, and sometimes at length. I was rather puzzled that this proved a popular location for sharing intimate details of health conditions or offence histories at considerable volume. There was but one exit, and I did not wish to be rude, which only made it funnier for onlookers.
2. Shouting out of windows is part of daily life in closed conditions among some parts of the estate. The term 'window warriors' specifically refers to unpleasant aspects of behaviour

conducted in this way – bullying, threatening and so on. The idea being that they are emboldened by the relative safety offered by being behind the door.

Chapter 6
1. The Independent Monitoring Board.
2. All key carriers are issued with a pouch which is attached to their belt, in which keys are held (also attached to the belt). In some security training the importance of not allowing prisoners to look upon your keys lest their photographic memories allow for reproduction is emphasized. Others restrict themselves to imploring you keep hold of them as loss of one key means considerable expense – as well as inconvenience and embarrassment – of replacement.
3. Pictures and names of each cell's occupants are usually displayed by its entrance.
4. Prisoners require officer escort, but this would have left two officers remaining on the wing. An impossibly small number to adequately deal with any additional development.
5. These fieldnotes originally appeared, though in a different form, as a guest blog for the comparative penology project, led by Prof Ben Crewe at the Prisons Research Centre in the Institute of Criminology, Cambridge University, available here: www.compen.crim.cam.ac.uk/Blog/blog-pages-full-versions/guest-blog-by-kate-herrity.
6. Shorthand for vulnerable prisoners. Both a location and a designation.
7. The Care and Segregation Unit, otherwise known as 'the block'.
8. Incomparably rare relative to self-harm and suicide, there are nevertheless instances of lethal violence meted out to snoring padmates; for example, *Irish Independent*: www.independent.ie/irish-news/prison-cellmate-stabbed-to-shut-up-his-snoring-26120728.html; *Wales Online*: www.walesonline.co.uk/news/wales-news/snoring-prison-inmate-beaten-kettle-21286015
9. In prison, reception is more commonly understood as the location where new prisoners are received and processed and is deeper within the prison. 'The gatehouse' is where external visitors are received, though usually there is a separate point of entry for those on prisoners' visitors lists. This may also be referred to as 'the gate' (but may or may not be situated where you might reasonably expect this to indicate).

Chapter 7
1. These fieldnotes were included, in different form, in a blog post for sensory criminology (https://sensorycriminology.com/2020/02/03/close-closer/).
2. Staff and prisoners spoke about police often being stationed at the gate on release day, to re-arrest people as they were tasting outside air. The perception was of deliberate cruelty. More likely it was born of convenience. Many of those at Midtown had unsettled living arrangements and a considerable number were on the streets. While in prison, everyone knew where they were.
3. For more on the concept of 'stain' as it refers to people convicted of sex offences, see the work of Alice Ievins (for example, 2023).

Chapter 8
1. These units were later rearranged to resume former locations in the prison. This recalled Tone's observations.
2. For a more extensive exploration of relationships between self and place in relation to cleanliness, see my chapter with Jason Warr (Herrity and Warr, 2023).

NOTES

Chapter 9
[1] See here for additional guidance on prison-related offences: www.cps.gov.uk/legal-guidance/prison-related-offences-0#:~:text=The%20maximum%20penalty%20on%20conviction,will%20normally%20require%20a%20prosecution. Zanco phones and various other designs more or less associated with HMP, but designed to be as functional but as small as possible, sometimes without metal to aid detection avoidance, have been around since at least 2007.

[2] Otherwise referred to as 'shitting up', the unfortunate recipient has a mixture of collected urine and faeces deposited over their person (or squirted from a suitable receptacle – such as a plastic bottle).

Chapter 10
[1] A number of prisons in England and Wales count writers or artists among their peripheral staff. They come to be known as 'in residence' when they have been there for a prolonged period of time though may, as was the case with Bear, move from prison to prison (he had worked in 17 by his estimate).

Chapter 11
[1] The practice of smuggling contraband, usually inserted in the rectum. Some prisoners talked about others coming back to prison specifically to trade – particularly in spice or mamba because the price was so high – to make extra money or repay debts.

[2] Prison term for controlling and restraining someone, referring to the act of twisting arms painfully behind the back to secure compliance.

[3] 'Segregation' refers to the Care and Segregation Unit. Segregation is a process by which a prisoner is removed from association with other prisoners under rule 45 (good order and discipline – GOOD, or own interests). A prisoner can be segregated and placed under an amount of separation and protection without being removed to 'Seg' in some circumstances, but it usually – and in the case of Midtown, always – referred to the unit as well as the state.

[4] Netting is hung from landings to prevent harm/self-harm from falling, being thrown or jumping over the railings. Climbing over the handrail to walk on the netting was a disciplinary offence. In Midtown this was the area where dirty laundry, toilet roll and other items were thrown for sharing or collection. Orderlies would often walk across it as a short cut or to retrieve said items. This generally passed without comment or censure. Like many prison rules it was a bit more complicated and arbitrary than appeared.

Chapter 13
[1] This frequently took the form of Control and Restraint (or C&R), a series of practices for forcibly, physically subduing prisoners.

Chapter 16
[1] Termed 'transforming rehabilitation' – the name given to the white paper, delivered in 2013, by Chris Grayling, then Secretary of State for Justice – the aim was to 'revolutionize' the way rehabilitation services were delivered in order to 'drive down' reoffending rates. The main feature of the plan was to split probation services between one, main, National Probation Service (NPS) and private-sector 'Commercial Rehabilitation Companies' (CRCs). CRCs became responsible for offenders in custody.

[2] 'Rattling' is a prison term for those suffering drugs withdrawal. Part of the reception process involves triaging those with substance use, and various other physical and mental health needs.

Chapter 17

1. Autism spectrum disorder.
2. Post-traumatic stress disorder (both ASD and PTSD are more prevalent in prison populations, as are learning differences and disabilities, and a host of neurodivergence – PRT, 2022).
3. There is a significantly inflated exposure to traumatic events within incarcerated populations, as well as a marked elevation in prevalence among these groups (Allely and Allely, 2020).

Chapter 18

1. A famous Irish folk band, generally known for their renditions of 'rebel songs'.
2. Giovanni Battista Piranesi (1720–78) painted imaginary prisons (among other things) and is reminiscent of Escher.

Chapter 19

1. DIY stands for 'do it yourself' and often refers to home improvement
2. There was no way to be sufficiently far from the toilet, but many I spoke with opted to sleep with their heads to the far end of the bed as a means of earning additional seconds in the event someone barged in after unlock. A number, such as Will, also ensured they woke well ahead of time so they were alert by this point of the day.
3. The incentives and earned privileges (IEP) scheme, introduced in 1995, was revised during Grayling's stint as justice secretary in 2013/14. The idea being to incentivize 'good behaviour' and impose levels: entry, basic, standard and enhanced levels depending on degree length of cooperation with the regime. It proved controversial, partially because of the resulting book and – to a lesser extent – guitar-string bans: https://commonslibrary.parliament.uk/research-briefings/sn06942/. Prisoners experienced its deployment as arbitrary and unfair, and often complained there was limited ability to obtain enhanced privilege and its perks, and all too easy to have them removed if subject to a series of 'nickings' which could themselves be experienced as arbitrary and unfair.
4. Rules relating to pay and spending are convoluted, slow to change and impose tight restrictions. Earning is very limited and spending generally set at around £15 a week. I include the Prison Service Order relating to pay: www.gov.uk/government/publications/paying-prisoners-for-work-and-other-activities-pso-4460. This blog post from the always-informative Russell Webster sets out broader explanation of spending and earning restrictions, as well as the lack of reform to these rules in recent years (the rate of pay not increased since 2002): www.russellwebster.com/earning-spending-money-prison/
5. Different prisons sound different for a range of reasons, not only because of their architecture but also because of their designated role.
6. I have included a link to the Office of National Statistics dataset for broader comparisons and national figures: www.ons.gov.uk/employmentandlabourmarket/peoplenotinwork/unemployment/datalist?filter=datasets
7. McDonald's fast food. Their milkshakes are often particularly popular with people on the streets.

Chapter 20

1. This depends somewhat on the weight of the separate pieces. I use it here as a metaphor but they do not always behave this way.
2. CARAT stands for counselling, assessment, referral, advice and through-care.

NOTES

Chapter 21
1. Operational support grade staff. Uniformed, key-carrying staff of relatively junior status.
2. The Prison Reform Trust helpfully host a summary: https://prisonreformtrust.org.uk/publication/the-woolf-report-a-summary-of-the-main-findings-and-recommendations-of-the-inquiry-into-prison-disturbances/

Chapter 22
1. Paper from Inspector of Ofsted assessing education in prison. 57 per cent of prisoners assessed were found to have reading level below expected levels for 11-year-olds: www.gov.uk/government/publications/prison-education-a-review-of-reading-education-in-prisons/prison-education-a-review-of-reading-education-in-prisons but this is not comprehensive
2. A paper widely distributed around prisons in England and Wales and focused on matters concerning those held in prison. See here: https://insidetime.org/
3. A hotel in Oxford, described by booking.com, as: a 'converted Victorian prison is now a stunning boutique hotel offering unique luxury accommodation in historic Oxford. Limited parking is available for a surcharge.'
4. See research from Borah Kant on staff cultures of prison and place.
5. My accent was also the subject of frequent mimicking, but this was preferable to making jokes about the size of my bum or perpetually messy hair, so I was happy to take it.
6. Woolf makes this explicit in his report (1991).
7. For more on the impact of COVID on prisons, see: https://covidandsociety.com/impact-covid-19-prisons/

Chapter 23
1. Prop = property. It is stored, swapped and distributed from reception.
2. Geoamey is a private company that transports prisoners and (sometimes) their property around the estate, and to and from court. In the company's own words it provides 'transportation and custody suite services for prisoners and young people in custody across the UK, England and Wales' (www.geoamey.co.uk).
3. HMP Birmingham.
4. Arrangement of special release on compassionate grounds, such as for attending funerals, which is usually restricted to the time of the event.
5. See Prison Reform Trust's Bromley briefings for comprehensive details about who is in our prisons: https://prisonreformtrust.org.uk/publication/bromley-briefings-prison-factfile-winter-2022/
6. Secure Training Centres are for children aged 12–17/18 who are deemed too vulnerable or young for young offender institutions. There are three of these, Medway, Oakhill and Rainsbrook. Systems for caring and imprisoning children in England and Wales are somewhat complicated. See here for more information: https://explore-education-statistics.service.gov.uk/find-statistics/children-accommodated-in-secure-childrens-homes or for an account of lived experience at the intersections between vulnerable children and the criminal justice system, see Gemma's account: https://sensorycriminology.com/2021/03/29/revealing-sensory-scars/

References

Allely, C.S. and Allely, B. (2020) 'Post traumatic stress disorder in incarcerated populations: current clinical considerations and recommendations', *Journal of Criminal Psychology*, 10(1): 30–42.
Armstrong, S. (2018) 'The cell and the corridor: imprisonment as waiting, and waiting as mobile', *Time & Society*, 27(2): 133–54.
Arnold, H. (2016) 'The prison officer', in Y. Jewkes, J. Bennet and B. Crewe (eds) *Handbook on Prisons* (2nd edn), London: Routledge, pp 265–83.
Attali, J. (1977) *Noise: Political Economy of Music (Theory and History of Literature)*, Minnesota: University of Minnesota Press.
Back, L. (2007) *The Art of Listening*, Oxford: Berg.
Barrett, F.S., Grimm, K.J., Robins, R.W., Wildschut, T., Sedikides, C. and Janata, P. (2010) 'Music-evoked nostalgia: affect, memory and personality', *Emotion*, 10(3): 390–403.
Barsade, S.G. (2002) 'The ripple effect: emotional contagion and its effect on group behaviour', *Administrative Science Quarterly*, 47(4): 644–75.
Basner, M., Babisch, W., Davis, A., Brink, M., Clark, C., Janssen, S. et al (2014) 'Auditory and non-auditory effects of noise on health', *Lancet*, 383(9925): 1325–32.
Beatles, The (1967) 'A Day in the Life', *Sgt. Pepper's Lonely Hearts Club Band*, UK: Parlophone.
Beetham, D. (1991) *The Legitimation of Power*, London: Macmillan Press.
Behan, B. (1954 [1978]) 'The Quare Fellow', in *Behan, the Complete Plays*, London: Bloomsbury.
Bentham, J. (1767 [1995]) *The Panopticon Writings*, in M. Bozovic (ed), London: Verso.
Berkman, A. (1912 [1999]) *Prison Memoirs of an Anarchist*, Introduction by J.W. Ward, New York: New York Review of Books.
Blesser, B. and Salter, L. (2009) *Spaces Speak, Are You Listening? Experiencing Aural Architecture*, London: MIT Press.
Bourdieu, P. (1992) *The Logic of Practice*, Cambridge: Polity Press.
Bourgois, P. (2002) *In Search of Respect: Selling Crack in El Barrio* (2nd edn), Cambridge: Cambridge University Press.

British Standards Institute (2014) BS ISO 12913–1:2014 *Acoustics – Soundscape Part 1: A Definition and Conceptual Framework*, London: BSI.

Brown, M. (2009) *The Culture of Punishment: Prison, Society and Spectacle*, London: New York University Press.

Canning, V. (2021) 'Sensing and unease in immigration confinement: an abolitionist perspective', in K. Herrity, B. Schmidt and J. Warr (eds) *Sensory Penalities: Explorations of the Sensory in Spaces of Punishment and Social Control*, Bingley: Emerald.

Carceral, K.C. and Flaherty, M.G. (2021) *The Cage of Days? Time and Temporal Experience in Prison*, New York: Columbia University Press.

Carpenter, E. and McLuhan, M. (1960) 'Acoustic space', in E. Carpenter and M. McLuhan (eds) *Explorations in Communication: An Anthology*, Boston, MA: Beacon Press, pp 65–70.

Carrabine, E. (2004) *Power, Discourse and Resistance: A Geneaology of the Strangeways Riot*, Aldershot: Ashgate.

Carrabine, E. (2005) 'Prison riots, social order and the problem of legitimacy', *British Journal of Criminology*, 45(6): 896–913.

Chee, F. (2002) 'Different strokes: moving to the beat of just one drummer. The acoustic dimensions of the sport of dragonboating', *Soundscape: The Journal of Acoustic Ecology*, 4(1): 10–13.

Chion, M. (2010) *Sound: An Acoustological Treatise*, J.A. Steintrager (tr), London: Duke University Press.

Clemmer, D. (1940) *The Prison Community*, Boston, MA: Christopher Publishing House.

Cockayne, E. (2008) *Hubbub: Filth, Noise, and Stench in England 1600–1770*, Connecticut: Yale University Press.

Cohen, E. (2010) 'Anthropology of knowledge', *Journal of the Royal Anthropological Institute*, 16 (Special Issue on Making Knowledge): S193–202.

Cohen, S. (2012) 'Bubbles, tracks, borders and lines: mapping music and urban landscape', *Journal of the Royal Music Association*, 137(1).

Cohen, S. and Taylor, L. (1981) *Psychological Survival: The Experience of Longer-Term Imprisonment* (2nd edn), Middlesex: Penguin.

Colvin, M. (1992) *The Penitentiary in Crisis: From Accommodation to Riot in New Mexico*, New York: State University of New York Press.

Conway, C.M. and Limayem, M. (2010) 'Adrift in the sands of time: a theory of temporal dissonance in the individual', *Proceedings of the Academy of Management Annual Meeting 2010*, Montréal, QC, 6–10 August.

Corbin, A. (1998) *Village Bells: Sound and Meaning in the 19th Century French Countryside*, Columbia: Columbia University Press.

Corrigan, P. (1979) *Schooling the Smash Street Kids*, London: Macmillan.

Cowell, H. (1996) *New Musical Resources*, Cambridge: Cambridge University Press.

Crawley, E. (2004) *Doing Prison Work: The Public and Private Lives of Prison Officers*, Devon: Willan.

Crewe, B. (2007) 'Power, adaptation and resistance in a late-modern men's prison', *British Journal of Criminology*, 47(2): 256–75.

Crewe, B. (2009) *The Prisoner Society: Power, Adaptation and Social Life in an English Prison*, Oxford: Oxford University Press.

Crewe, B., Warr, J., Bennett, P. and Smith, A. (2014) 'The emotional geography of prison life', *Theoretical Criminology*, 18(1): 56–74.

Criminal Justice Joint Inspectorate (2021) 'Neurodiversity in the criminal justice system: a review of evidence' [online], available from: www.justiceinspectorates.gov.uk/hmicfrs/publications/neurodiversity-in-the-criminal-justice-system/

Cusick, S.G. (2008) '"You are in a place that is out of this world": music in the detention camps of the global war on terror', *Journal of the Society for American Music*, 2(1): 1–26.

de Certeau, M. (2011) *The Practice of Everyday Life* (3rd edn), California: University of California Press.

DeNora, T. (2000) *Music in Everyday Life*, Cambridge: Cambridge University Press.

Denver, J. (1966) 'Leaving on a Jet Plane', *John Denver Sings*, available from: www.youtube.com/watch?v=SneCkM0bJq0

Desmond, M. (2016) *Evicted: Poverty and Profit in the American City*, New York: Crown Publishing.

Dickens, C. (1836) 'A visit to Newgate', *Sketches by Boz* [online], British Library, available from: www.bl.uk/collection-items/a-visit-to-newgate-from-charles-dickenss-sketches-by-boz

Dickinson, E. (1862) 'A Prison Gets to Be a Friend', in C. Miller (ed) *Emily Dickinson's Poems: As She Preserved Them*, Cambridge, MA: Harvard University Press, p 229.

Douglas, M. (1966 [2002]) *Purity and Danger: An Analysis of Concepts of Pollution and Taboo*, London: Routledge.

Durkheim, E. (1893 [1984]) *The Division of Labour in Society*, W.D. Halls (tr), London: Macmillan.

Durkheim, E. (1915 [2008]) *The Elementary Forms of Religious Life*, C. Cosman (tr), Oxford: Oxford University Press.

Edensor, T. (2010) 'Introduction: thinking about rhythm and space', in T. Edensor (ed) *Geographies of Rhythm: Nature, Place, Mobilities and Bodies*, London: Routledge.

Eliot, T.S. (1933) *The Use of Poetry and the Use of Criticism*, London: Faber and Faber.

Feld, S. (1984) 'Sound structure as social structure', *Ethnomusicology*, 28(3): 383–409.

Fernback, J. (2012) 'Sousveillance: communities of resistance to the surveillance movement', *Telematics and Informatics*, 30(1): 11–21.

Fisher, G. and Koo Chon, K. (1989) 'Durkheim and the social construction of emotions', *Social Psychology Quarterly*, 52(1): 1–9.

Foucault, M. (1977) *Discipline and Punish: The Birth of the Modern Prison*, A. Sheridan (tr), New York: Second Vintage Books.

Foucault, M. (1980) *Power/Knowledge: Selected Interviews and Other Writings*, London: Pantheon books.

Foucault, M. and Miskowiec, J. (1986) 'Of other spaces', *Diacritics*, 16: 22–7.

Fox, N. (2015) 'Emotions, affects and the production of social life', *British Journal of Sociology*, 66(2): 301–18.

Franks, D.D. and Doyle McCarthy, E. (1989) *The Sociology of Emotions: Original Essays and Research Papers*, Connecticut: Jai Press.

Gallo, E. and Ruggiero, V. (1991) 'Immaterial prison: custody as a factory for the manufacture of handicaps', *International Journal of the Sociology of Law*, 19(3): 273–91.

Garrihy, J. (2022) '"That doesn't leave you": psychological dirt and taint in prison officers' cultures and identities', *British Journal of Criminology*, 62: 982–99.

Giddens, A. (1984) *The Constitution of Society: Outline of the Theory of Structuration*, Berkeley, CA: University of California Press.

Giddens, A. (1991) *Modernity and Self-Identity: Self and Society in the Modern Age*, Stanford, CA: Stanford University Press.

Goffman, E. (1959) *The Presentation of Self in Everyday Life*, London: Penguin.

Goffman, E. (1961) *Asylums: Essays on the Social Situation of Mental Patients and Other Inmates*, St Ives: Penguin.

Goodman, S. (2012) *Sonic Warfare: Sound, Affect and the Ecology of Fear*, Cambridge, MA: MIT Press.

Grovier, K. (2008) *The Gaol: The Story of Newgate, London's Most Notorious Prison*, London: John Murray.

Harkin, D. (2015) 'Police legitimacy, ideology and qualitative methods: a critique of procedural justice theory', *Criminology and Criminal Justice*, 15(5): 594–612.

Hassine, V. (1996) *Life Without Parole: Living in Prison Today*, T.J. Bernard and R. McCleary (eds), Foreword (J. Irwin), Afterword (R.A. Wright), Los Angeles, CA: Roxbury Publishing.

Hatfield, E., Cacioppo, J.T. and Rapson, R.L. (1994) *Emotional Contagion*, Cambridge: Cambridge University Press.

Hearn, J.S. (2012) *Theorizing Power*, London: Palgrave Macmillan.

Hemsworth, K. (2016) '"Feeling the range": emotional geographies of sound in prisons', *Emotion, Space, Society*, 20(2): 90–7.

Hendy, D. (2013) *Noise: A Human History of Sound and Listening*, London: Profile Books.

Herrity, K. (2015) 'Prison sound ecology: a research design', unpublished MSc dissertation, Oxford: University of Oxford.

Herrity, K. (2021) 'Hearing order in flesh and blood: sensemaking and attunement in the pub and the prison', in K. Herrity, B. Schmidt and J. Warr (eds) *Sensory Penalities: Explorations of the Sensory in Spaces of Punishment and Social Control*, Bingley: Emerald.

Herrity, K. and Warr, J. (2023) '"This is my home": the prison as a site of domicide-through-displacement', in P. Davies and M. Rowe (eds) *A Criminology of the Domestic*, London: Routledge.

Herrity, K., Schmidt, B. and Warr, J. (eds) (2021) *Sensory Penalities: Explorations of the Sensory in Spaces of Punishment and Social Control*, Bingley: Emerald.

Herrman, B. (1968) 'Twisted Nerve', (theme and variations), original motion picture soundtrack, UK: Stylotone.

Hindes, B. (1996) *Discourses of Power: From Hobbes to Foucault*, Oxford: Blackwell.

Hudson, R. (2006) 'Regions and place: music, identity and place', *Progress in Human Geography*, 30(5): 626–34.

Ievins, A. (2023) *The Stains of Imprisonment: Moral Communication and Men Convicted of Sex Offences*, California: University of California Press.

Ignatieff, M. (1977) *A Just Measure of Pain: The Penitentiary in the Industrial Revolution 1750–1850*, New York: Pantheon.

Ihde, D. (2007) *Listening and Voice: Phenomenologies of Sound* (2nd edn), Albany, NY: State University of New York.

Irwin, J. and Owen, B. (2005) 'Harm and the contemporary prison', in A. Liebling and S. Maruna (eds) *The Effects of Imprisonment*, London: Routledge, pp 94–117.

Jackson, K. (2021) '"What should I do now?": navigating relational ethics in practice as an early career researcher as illustrated by a qualitative interview study about women's drinking practices', *International Journal of Qualitative Methods*, 20, [online], available from: https://journals-sagepub-com.ezp.lib.cam.ac.uk/doi/epub/10.1177/1609406920986044

Jameson, N. and Allison, E. (1995) *Strangeways 1990: A Serious Disturbance (The Inside Story of the Biggest Protest in the History of British Prisons*, London: Larkin Publications.

Jewkes, Y. (2012) 'On carceral space and agency', in D. Moran, N. Gill and D. Conlon (eds) *Carceral Spaces: Mobility and Agency in Imprisonment and Migrant Detention*, Farnham: Ashgate, pp 127–31.

Jewkes, Y. and Johnston, H. (2007) 'The evolution of prison architecture', in Y. Jewkes and H. Johnston (eds) *Handbook on Prisons*, Devon: Willan, pp 174–96.

Jewkes, Y. and Johnston, H. (2009) 'Cavemen in an era of speed and light technology: historical and contemporary perspectives on communication within prisons', *Howard Journal of Criminal Justice*, 48(2): 132–43.

Johnson, R. (2005) 'Brave new prisons: the growing social isolation of modern penal institutions', in A. Liebling and S. Maruna (eds) The *Effects of Imprisonment*, London: Routledge, pp 255–84.

Kaufman, E. and Bosworth, M. (2013) 'The prison and national identity: citizenship, punishment and the nation state', in D. Scott (ed) *Why Prison?*, Cambridge: Cambridge University Press, pp 170–88.

Keizer, G. (2012) *The Unwanted Sound of Everything We Want: A Book About Noise*, New York: Perseus Books.

Kerner, S., Chou, S. and Warmind, M. (eds) (2015) *Commensality from Everyday Food to Feast*, London: Bloomsbury.

Kilty, J.M. and Fayter, R. (2023) 'Trigger warnings, feeling rules and other lessons from the inside: the emotional labour of qualitative prisons research', in R. Faria and M. Dodge (eds) *Qualitative Research Methods in Criminology: Cutting Edge Methods*, Switzerland: Wiley.

Kitchen, J. (1991) 'Auditory imagination: the sense of sound', *The Georgia Review*, 43(1): 154–69.

Klatte, M., Bergstrom, K. and Lachmann, T. (2013) 'Does noise affect learning: a short review on noise effects on cognitive performance', *Frontiers in Psychology*, 4, available from: www.ncbi.nlm.nih.gov/pmc/articles/PMC3757288/

Kotova, A. (2019) 'Time ... lost time: exploring how partners of long-term prisoners experience the temporal pains of imprisonment', *Time & Society*, 28(2): 478–98.

Krebs, H. (1999) *Fantasy Pieces: Metrical Dissonance in the Music of Robert Schuman*, New York: Oxford University Press.

Labelle, B. (2018) *Sonic Agency: Sound and Emergent Forms of Resistance*, London: Goldsmiths Press.

Lefebvre, H. (1991) *The Production of Space*, D. Nicholson-Smith (tr), Oxford: Blackwell.

Lefebvre, H. (2004) *Rhythmanalysis: Space, Time and Everyday Life*, London: Continuum.

Lenc, T., Merchant, H., Keller, P.E., Honing, H., Varlet, M. and Nozaradan, S. (2021) 'Mapping between sound, brain and behaviour: four-level framework for understanding rhythm processing in humans and non-human primates', *Philosophical Transactions of the Royal Society B: Biological Sciences*, 376(1835): 1–15.

Liebling, A. (2000) 'Prison officers, policing and the use of discretion', *Theoretical Criminology*, 4(3): 333–457.

Liebling, A. and Arnold, H. (2004) *Prisons and Their Moral Performance: A Study of Values, Quality, and Prison Life*, Oxford: Oxford University Press.

Liebling, A., Price, D. and Shefer, G. (2010) *The Prison Officer*, London: Routledge.

Loader, I. (2011) 'Playing with fire? Democracy and the emotions of crime and punishment', in S. Karstedt, I. Loader and H. Strang (eds) *Emotions, Crime and Justice*, Oxford: Hart Publishing, pp 347–62.

Lyon, D. and Back, L. (2012) 'Fishmongers in a global economy: craft and social relations on a London market', *Sociological Research Online*, 17(2): 1–11.

Maguire, D. (2016) 'Troubled spaces', *The Royal Society for Arts, Manufactures and Commerce (RSA)*, 162(5566): 30–3.

Maguire, D. (2021) *Male, Failed, Jailed: Masculinities and Revolving Door Imprisonment in the UK*, London: Palgrave.

March, E. (2021) 'Proximity and distance: orality and aurality in prisoner writing', *Sensory Criminology*, [online] 18 January, available from: https://sensorycriminology.com/2021/01/18/proximity-and-distance-orality-and-aurality-in-prisoner-writing/

Mathieson, T. (1965) *The Defences of the Weak (Routledge Revivals): A Sociological Study of a Norwegian Correctional Institution*, London: Routledge.

Mathieson, T. (1997) 'The viewer society. Michel Foucault's "panopticon" revisited', *Theoretical Criminology*, 1(2): 215–34.

Mathieson, T. (2005) *Silently Silenced: Essays on the Creation of Acquiescence in Modern Society*, Winchester: Waterside Press.

McKee, E. (2000) 'Reviewed work(s): Fantasy Pieces: Metrical Dissonance in the Music of Robert Schumann. By Harold Krebs', *Notes*, 57,(1): 97–9.

Melossi, D. and Pavarini. M. (1981) *The Prison and the Factory: Origins of the Penitentiary System*, London: Palgrave Macmillan.

Moran, D. (2012) 'Doing time in carceral space: timespace and carceral geography', *Geografiska Annaler Series B, Progress in Human Geography*, 94(4): 305–16.

Moran, D. (2013) 'Between outside and inside? Prison visiting rooms as liminal carceral spaces', *Geojournal*, 78(2): 339–51.

Moran, D., Gill, N. and Conlon, D. (eds) (2013) *Carceral Spaces: Mobility and Agency in Imprisonment and Migrant Detention*, London: Routledge.

Ministry of Justice, The (MoJ) (2018) 'Offender management statistics quarterly October–December 2017 and annual 2017', available from: https://www.gov.uk/government/statistics/offender-management-statistics-quarterly-october-to-december-2017

Morin, K. and Moran, D. (2015) *Historical Geographies of Prisons: Unlocking the Useable Carceral Past*, London: Routledge.

Nakahashi, W. and Ohtsuki, H. (2015) 'When is emotional contagion adaptive?', *Journal of Theoretical Biology*, 380: 480–8.

Neidhart, C. (2002) *Russia's Carnival: The Smells, Sights, and Sounds of Transition*, Oxford: Rowman and Littlefield.

O'Donnell, I. (2014) *Prisoners, Solitude and Time*, Oxford: Clarendon Studies in Criminology.

O'Donnell, I. (2018) 'Reflections on solitary confinement'. Paper given at the Prisons Research Centre Conference, Institute of Criminology, University of Cambridge, 18–19 October.

Office of National Statistics, The (ONS) (2022) 'Labour market in the regions of the UK', available from: www.ons.gov.uk/employmentandlabourmarket/peoplenotinwork/unemployment/datalist?filter=datasets

Owens, F. (2012) *The Little Book of Prison: A Beginners Guide*, Hampshire: Waterside Press.

Parkes, D.N. and Thrift, N. (1980) *Times, Spaces and Places: A Chronogeographic Perspective*, New York: John Wiley and Sons.

Pickering, H. and Rice, T. (2017) '"Noise" as sound out of place: investigating the links between Mary Douglas' work on dirt and sound studies research', *Journal of Sonic Studies*, 14 [online], available from: www.researchcatalogue.net/view/374514/374515/0/0

Prison Reform Trust, The (PRT) (2018) 'Prison: the facts', Bromley Briefings, summer, available from: https://prisonreformtrust.org.uk/publication/prison-the-facts-summer-2018/

Rice, T. (2010) 'Learning to listen: auscultation and the transmission of auditory knowledge', *Journal of the Royal Anthropological Institute*, 16 (Special Issue on Making Knowledge): S41–61.

Rice, T. (2013) *Hearing and the Hospital: Sound, Listening, Knowledge and Experience*, Herefordshire: Sean Kingston Publishing.

Rusche, G. and Kirchheimer, O. (1939) *Punishment and Social Structure*, New York: Columbia University Press.

Russell, E.K. and Carlton, B. (2018) 'Counter-cultural acoustemologies: sound, permeability and feminist protest at the prison boundary', *Theoretical Criminology*, 24(2): 296–313.

Schafer, R.M. (1994) *Soundscape: Our Sonic Environment and the Tuning of the World*, Vermont: Destiny Books.

Schneider, L. (2023) 'Let me take a vacation in prison before the streets kill me! Rough sleepers' longing for prison and the reversal of less eligibility in neoliberal carceral continuums', *Punishment & Society*, 25(1): 60–79.

Serres, M. (2008) *The Five Senses: A Philosophy of Mingled Bodies*, M. Sankley and P. Cowley (tr), London: Continuum.

Shwartz, B. (1972) 'Deprivation of privacy as a functional prerequisite: the case of the prison', *Journal of Criminal Law and Criminology*, 63(2): 229–39.

Sibley, D. (1995) *Geographies of Exclusion*, Oxford: Routledge.

Simmel, G. (1903) 'The metropolis and mental life', in D.N. Levine (ed) *Georg Simmel on Individuality and Social Forms*, London: University of Chicago Press.

Simmel, G. (1907) 'The sociology of the senses', in D. Frisby and M. Featherstone (eds) *Simmel on Culture: Selected Writings*, London: Sage.

Sloboda, J. (2005) *Exploring the Musical Mind: Cognition, Emotion, Ability, Function*, Oxford: Oxford University Press.

Smith, C. (2011) *The Prison and the American Imagination*, New York: Yale University Press.

Solzhenitsyn, A. (1962) *One Day in the Life of Ivan Denisovich*, London: Penguin.

Sparks, R. and Bottoms, A. (1995) 'Legitimacy and order in prisons', *British Journal of Sociology*, 46(1): 45–62.

Sparks, R., Bottoms, T. and Hay, W. (1996) *Prisons and the Problem of Order*, Oxford: Clarendon.

Spencer, H. (1895) *Principles of Sociology, Vol. 1*, New York: Appleton and Co.

Stansfeld, S. (1992) 'Noise, noise sensitivity and psychiatric disorder: epidemiological and psychophysiological studies', *Psychological Medicine Monograph Supplement*, 22: 1–44.

Stickney, J., Budd, C. and Mark (2023) '"180 prisoners and the noise … it hits you, BANG!!": sensory systems, incarceration and resettlement', in J. Shingler and J. Stickney (eds) *The Journey from Prison to Community: Developing Identity, Meaning and Belonging with Men in the UK*, London: Routledge.

Stiegler, L.N. and Davis, R. (2010) 'Understanding sound sensitivity in individuals with autism spectrum disorders', *Focus on Autism and Other Developmental Disabilities*, 25(2): 67–75.

Stoever, J.L. (2016) *The Sonic Color Line: Race and the Cultural Politics of Listening*, New York: New York University Press.

Sykes, G. (1958 [2007]) *The Society of Captives: A Study of a Maximum Security Prison*, Oxford: Princeton University Press.

Tait, S. (2011) 'A typology of prison officer approaches to care', *European Journal of Criminology*, 8(6): 440–54.

Thomas, M.E. (1996) 'Conlon Nancarrow's "Temporal Dissonance": rhythmic and textural stratification in the studies for player piano' (dissertation).

Toch, H. (1992) *Living in Prison: The Ecology of Survival*, Washington, DC: American Psychological Association.

Toch, H. (1997) 'Hypermasculinity and prison violence', in L. Bowker (ed) *Masculinities and Violence*, London: Sage, pp 168–78.

Toop, D. (2010) *Sinister Resonance: The Mediumship of the Listener*, London: Continuum.

Vannini, P., Waksul, D. and Gottschalk, S. (2013) *The Senses in Self, Society and Culture: A Sociology of the Senses*, London: Taylor and Francis.

Walsh, C. (2008) 'The mosquito: a repellent response', *Youth Justice*, 8(2): 122–33.

Warr, J. (2019) 'Ghost in the sweatbox', *Sensory Criminology*, [online] 19 December, available from: https://sensorycriminology.com/2019/12/15/ghost-in-the-sweatbox/

Warr, J. (2020) 'Always got to be two mans: lifers, risk, rehabilitation and narrative labour', *Punishment and Society*, 22(1): 28–47.

Warr, J. (2022) 'Fire! Fire! – the prison cell and the thick sensuality of trappedness', in K. Herrity, B.E. Schmidt and J. Warr (eds) *Sensory Penalities: Exploring Punishment in Spaces of Punishment and Social Control*, Bingley: Emerald.

Weber, M. (1958 [1920]) *The Rational and Social Foundations of Music*, in D. Martindale, J. Riedel and G. Neuwirth (eds and tr), Carbondale, IL: Southern Illinois University Press.

Weber, M. (1904) *The Methodology of Social Science*, New York: Free Press.

Welch, M. (2015) *Escape to Prison: Penal Tourism and the Pull of Punishment*, California: University of California Press.

Wener, R. (2012) *The Environmental Psychology of Prisons and Jails: Creating Humane Spaces in Secure Settings*, Cambridge: Cambridge University Press.

Woolf, Lord Justice (1991) *Prison Disturbances*, April 1990, Cm. 1456, London: HMO.

Woolf, Lord Justice (1996) *Access to Justice: Final Report*, [online], available from: http://webarchive.nationalarchives.gov.uk/+/http:/www.dca.gov.uk/civil/final/contents.htm

Wright, S., Crewe, B. and Hulley, S. (2017) 'Suppression, denial, sublimation: defending against the initial pains of very long life sentences', *Theoretical Criminology*, 21(2): 225–46.

Index

A
absence, sounds of 24–5
accents 141
acclimation 105, 119, 121–2, 129
acclimatization 12–13
ADHD 87, 140, 163
admissions rituals 119
affairs 24
affection 113–14
agency 34, 38, 85, 94, 131, 142, 173
alarms 12, 43, 68, 92, 118, 123, 131
Allelly, C.S. 127
Allison, E. 158
anger 44, 50, 66, 70, 86, 125
anonymity 11
anxiety 51, 70, 72, 80, 90, 127, 156
Armstrong, S. 27
Arnold, H. 102, 106, 109, 114
arrhythmia 21, 74–80, 108, 117, 145
ASD (Autism Spectrum Disorder) 121, 127
association 72, 137, 154
Attali, J. 100
auditory imagination 16, 20, 130
auditory knowledge 4
'Auld Triangle, The' 129, 131–2
auscultation 3–5
authority 82, 97–9, 100–1, 108, 110, 111, 114, 153, 158
autonomy 15, 90, 155, 156
awake, being kept 43–4

B
'Baa baa black sheep' 35
Back, L. 4, 84
'backstage', lack of 48, 55, 164
bad day soundscape 73, 74–5, 77, 106, 115
  see also disorder; trouble
banging
  bang. bang. bang. (slow, rhythmic banging) 116
  bangbang . bang. Bang . bang 117
  bangbangbang (rapid, rhythmic banging) 115–16
  celebratory banging 117
  as emotional expression 72, 84, 104, 114–17
  group identity 149
  and the 'mood' of the day 71
  other prisoners' reactions to 44
  resonance beyond immediate hearing 96
  types of 114–17
  visiting times (lack of banging) 24
bang-up time 39, 43, 84
banter 151
Barrett, F.S. 119
Barsade, S.G. 71
Bear 160–1, 179n1
Beetham, D. 101
Behan, B. 90, 129, 131, 132
'behind the door' 114–15
bells 81, 82, 84, 120, 129–30, 142, 154–6
belonging, sense of 19, 129, 130, 131, 133, 149, 168, 172
Bentham, J. 94
Berkman, A. 142
'best sound you're gonna hear' 21–4
"big swinging dick" 36
Blesser, B. 32
blurred boundaries 56
boisterousness 87, 114, 126, 146
boredom 27, 139, 142, 145, 158
Bosworth, M. 134
bottom up power 98–9
Bottoms, A. 101, 110, 165
boundaries of the self 37
Bourdieu, P. 7, 118
Bourgois, P. 37
Boyd 20–1, 24, 32, 34, 53, 138
'breaking the pouch' 39
Brian 40, 44–5, 49
British Standards Institute (BSI) 16
Brown, M. 134
Brut/Old Spice 93–4
'bubbly' atmosphere 69–70, 71, 75, 77
bullying 14, 35
burn 68
busy, keeping 84–5, 136–44
  see also passing time

INDEX

C

'calm', complex meanings of 15
Cam 13–14, 34, 37, 60, 130
Cameron 126, 128
camouflage netting 139–41
Canning, V. 91
Carceral, K.C. 30
Care and Segregation ('Seg') 35, 43, 53, 77, 115
Carlton, B. 37
Carpenter, E. 32
Carrabine, E. 101, 106, 111, 153, 157, 158
Cedric 43
celebratory banging 117
cell alarms 43
cell fires 79–80
cell sharing 55
cells, avoiding going into 12
cells, conducting research in 50–1
"chaos" 5–6
chapel 13, 14, 33
Chee, F. 4
children
  children's voices missing from prison soundscape 130, 163, 169
  prisoners missing their 20–1, 24, 48
  visiting times 22–3, 24
Chion, M. 90, 114, 115
'churn' of people 5, 11
  see also release and return cycles
Claire 15
clangs 2, 81, 89, 92, 96, 97, 104, 123, 135
  see also bells
cleaning 84–5, 137, 141
cleanliness 54
Clemmer, D. 119
Cockayne, E. 137
cockroaches 40, 42, 43, 52
coercive force 92
Cohen, S. 4, 109, 133, 136, 141
Colvin, M. 158
commands 81
community, sense of 5–6, 110, 132–3, 149, 151–2, 164
compliance 107–8, 156, 158
concrete 40, 41, 93
conducting the noise 99–100
confinement to cells 72–3
consent 10
'contamination' 56
contraband 60
control over exposure to sound 16
Conway, C.M. 30
cooperation 82, 97–104, 107–8, 110–11, 114, 116, 158
coping strategies 6
Corbin, A. 154
Corrigan, P. 139

count, the 12, 42–3, 52, 142
counter-rhythms 87
COVID 166, 176n1
Cowell, H. 82
Crawley, E. 31, 69, 90, 122
Crewe, B. 10, 33, 43, 52, 91, 107
crowd noises 23
crying 23
cultural imagination 134–5
cultural representations of prison life 129, 130, 131, 132, 135

D

Dave 143, 156
Davey 36, 49, 54, 70, 79, 87, 92, 109, 151
David (visiting governor) 121–2
'Day in the Life' (Beatles) 146
de Certeau, M. 156
de-prisoning 31
Derek (officer) 31, 71, 75–6, 83, 99, 102, 105–6, 137, 147, 154, 172
Dermot 114, 138
description of HMP Midtown 5–6
desensitization 129
Desmond, M. 60
desynchronization 76
Diane (resettlement officer) 44, 115, 118, 122
dignity 24, 55, 61, 170
dimming of lights 41
dirt 54, 57, 93, 162
discordant noise 74, 76, 85, 122
disorder
  banging 117
  learning the 'everyday tune' 106, 107, 110, 111
  phasing 145–6
  polyrhythmia 155
  re-regulation after disorder 145–52
  riots 157–9
  as starting point in most research 157
  see also order
disputes 36
disruptive elements 69–70, 73, 77, 147–8
'doing time' 19, 26, 84
domesticity 24, 25
doors 104
Douglas, M. 57
Doyle McCarthy, E. 148
dreaming 93
'drowning out' some sounds 22
Drug Treatment Unit 41
drugs 14, 67, 68–9, 85
Duane 20
'dug'/pigeonhole 11
Duke 13, 68–9, 113, 137, 140, 151, 163
Durkheim, E. 4, 116, 146, 149
Dwane 61

193

E

earworms 70–1
eavesdropping, avoiding 40
ebb and flow 102, 132, 137, 155, 158, 168
'ecology of fear' 91
Edensor, T. 4
edgework 59
education department 33, 137
Eliot, T.S. 16
Elvis 16, 174
emotion
  emotional contagion 66–73
  emotional geography 32–8, 43, 52–5
  emotional phasing 148–9
  emotional transference 70
  'feeling' of the day 15, 69, 71, 75, 105–12
  'feeling the range' 69
  prison as emotional arena 29, 69–70
  'ripples' of emotion 71
  sound as audible emotion 66
  sound as modality of 33–4, 71
  visiting times 23
enforced idleness 27, 136–7
entitlements 84
entrance/exit rituals 32–3
escaping from soundscape, impossibility of 32, 37, 118, 125, 127
ethics 11, 12, 47–50, 59, 163
ethnography, sound rarely the focus of 4
etiquette 59
eurhythmia 147
'everyday tune' 105–12, 153–5, 160
  see also bad day soundscape; good day soundscape
exercise yard 63, 149
explaining research to prison community 15
expletives 79

F

face saving 36, 76
family visits 21–4
Fayter, R. 59
fear 91, 123
'feeling' of the day 15, 69, 71, 75, 105–12
'feeling the range' 69
Feld, S. 9
Fernback, J. 12
fieldnotes 10, 13
fights 36, 76, 131
fires 79
First-Night Centre 50, 53, 76, 114, 127
Flaherty, M.G. 30
'flat packing' 117
folk music 129, 131
food 58, 84, 86–8, 143
football sounds 20, 24, 46, 60, 117, 141
footsteps 40, 42, 76, 95
footwear 76

Foucault, M. 94, 100, 118, 119, 120, 161, 168
Fox, N. 148
Franks, D.D. 148
Fridays 68
friendships 24
frustration 23, 24, 27, 43, 69, 72, 104, 115

G

gait 40, 141
Gallo, E. 143
gangs 14
Garrihy, J. 57
gates 33, 53, 89, 96
gaze, aversion of 12, 25, 56
Gee 123
generators 42
Giddens, A. 85, 90, 103, 109, 156
gifts 60–1, 62
'give and take' 82
Goffman, E. 48, 55, 56, 57, 58, 114, 119, 123, 127, 164
'going on the netting' 78–9
good day soundscape
  arrhythmia 74
  harmony 73
  'hubbub' 28
  learning the 'everyday tune' 105, 106, 108, 110
  phasing 148
  polyrhythmia 81–3, 85, 87, 136, 137, 153–5
  as starting point 158
good prison soundscape 108, 109
Goodman, S. 91, 118
goodwill 98
Graham (officer) 84
'grassing' 63
Grovier, K. 135
gym 34, 140

H

habitus 118
hand dryers 57
hands in pants 22, 56
Harkin, D. 103
Harry 26, 85
Hassine, V. 93
Hatfield, E. 70
Hay, W. 165
headaches from noise levels 22
Hearn, J.S. 99, 100
Hemsworth, K. 33, 69, 71
Hendy, D. 32, 98
Herrity, K. 2, 3, 74, 94
heterotopia 161
hidden sonic world 34, 35
hierarchy within prison 53
Hindes, B. 100

INDEX

Hinduism 14
Hobbes, T. 91
home, sense of 19, 50, 133, 134
homelessness 142–3, 166
hospitality, importance of 23
'hubbub' 28, 52, 137
Hudson, R. 131
humour 79
hustling 84, 86, 136

I

identity
  attempts to retain 38
  belonging 132–3
  institutionalization 119, 123, 126
  leaving rituals 170
  masculinity 37, 38, 56
  prison overwrites other 130
  and racism 14
  staff 131, 172
idleness 27, 136–7
Ievins, A. 52, 178n3
Ignatieff, M. 100
Ihde, D. 16, 48
imagined futures 19
IMB (Independent Monitoring Board) 1, 11, 15
information as commodity 94–5
institutionalization 55–6, 119, 121, 122, 123, 126
'intelligence' 14
intelligence reports 64–5
interview, relegating the 10–12, 13
intimacy and ethics 47–50
intimacy and lack of privacy 55–6
IPP (indeterminate sentence for public protection) 29, 37, 110, 124, 125, 141, 164
ironwork 40

J

Jack 76, 77, 91
Jackson, K. 48
jail craft 72, 74, 99, 105, 148
Jameson, N. 158
jangling of keys 89, 90, 96, 131, 135
Jean 15
jeering 77
Jewkes, Y. 27, 82, 123, 156
Joanne (substance use worker) 66, 93, 95, 115, 117, 119, 131
Johnson, R. 135
Johnston, H. 27, 123
Justin 143

K

kackerlacka 52
Kai 174
Kant, B. 181n4
Kathleen (officer) 75, 122, 172
Kaufman, E. 134
Kayleigh 147
Keizer, G. 15, 118
Kerner, S. 87
Ket 30–1, 84, 87, 111, 136, 149, 150–1
kettles 60, 84
Kevin 119–20, 129
keys
  jangling of keys 89, 90, 96, 131, 135
  memory evocation 130, 161
  night-times 39, 41
  punctuation 84
  researcher holding 41
  in songs about prison 131–2
  in soundscape 89–96, 127
'killing time' 28
  see also passing time
Kilty, J.M. 59
King 72
Kircheimer, O. 142
Kitchen, J. 16
kitchens 32, 138
Klatte, M. 117, 119
knowledge, sound as source of 94–5
Kotova, A. 19, 29–30
Krebs, H. 30

L

Labelle, B. 32
Lamar 14, 20, 24, 108, 125, 126, 138, 141, 150, 170–1
laughter 11, 23, 24, 31, 98, 150, 151, 163
laundry 87
leaving rituals 32–3, 169–71
Lefebvre, H. 21, 74, 81, 82, 84, 102, 103, 105, 142, 147
legitimacy 100–1, 109–12, 143–4, 156–8
legitimation 101, 104, 110
Lena (officer) 95, 149
library 33, 61–2
Liebling, A. 102, 106, 109, 114, 146, 148, 177n6
Limayem, M. 30
liminal spaces 21, 30, 33
listening
  cell fires 80
  decoding rituals and routines 154
  to legitimacy 100–1
  as means to survive and thrive 12
  metrics of time passing 32
  to order 101–4
  as part of officer skill set 77
  for power 13–15
  to power 113–20
  power of 45, 49
  race and racism 13–14
  reading the soundscape 105–6
  researcher positionality 161–2

as a sociological art 4
watching versus listening 25
window-to-window communication 35
local geographies 133–4, 135
local nature of Midtown 5, 29, 65, 92, 114, 129–30, 133–4, 141, 162, 165
localism 14
loneliness 40, 43
looping 122–4, 126
'lost' time 30
loudness 2, 36–7, 40, 57, 70–1, 72, 75, 84, 123, 126
loved ones, memories of relationships with 20–1
lovers 24
lowering of volume 41
Lugs 27, 34, 36, 47, 49, 51, 54, 74, 79, 84, 85, 87, 92, 94, 111, 134, 138
Lyon, D. 84

M

Maguire, D. 38
mamba 44, 67–8, 69, 141
March, E. 91
Marcus 90
Mark, Officer 71
'markers' of time 21
see also bells; rituals; routines
Marlon 119
masculinity 37, 38, 56
Mathieson, T. 49, 95, 111
Matt 127
McCafferty, Officer 55
McKee, E. 30
McKie, Officer 69, 116, 147, 148
McLuhan, M. 32
mealtimes 9, 84, 86–8, 138
meaningful activity 137–9
meaning-making, sound for 15–16
medical issues, discussion of 55
Melossi, D. 142, 143
memory evocation 18, 19, 20–1, 92–4, 119, 122, 130, 131
mental health problems 37, 43, 78, 115, 126, 128, 166
metal 40, 41, 42, 93
metronomes 141–4
mice 42
Mitzy (officer) 150
Mo 28
modality of emotion, sound as 33–4, 71
Mondays 68, 69
Mooch 26, 27, 34, 64, 84, 85, 94, 111
'mood hoovers' 72–3
'mood' of prison 69, 75, 150–1
moral codes 77
Moran, D. 19, 21, 119, 131
Morin, K. 19
movement, as means to pass the time 27

'mugged off', being 36
multimodality 21, 25
music
at anti-social volume 47
certain songs 21
'everyday tune' 105
folk music representations of prison 129, 131
loud music 71
night-times 40, 42
phrasing 145
sociology of 100
songs about prison 129, 131
sound as modality of emotion 34
temporal dissonance 30
Muslims 14
mutual meaning-making 16
mutual support 38

N

Nakahashi, W. 70
Natty 37
Ned 138, 173
Neidhart, C. 142
netting 78–9
neurodivergence 13, 87, 121, 127, 166
Niall 67
night patrol 39, 42, 46, 53
night-times 21, 39–45, 53, 117
No. 1 (prison governor) 10, 12, 35, 39, 50, 64, 85, 117, 174
No. 2 (second-in-command) 10, 36, 70
'no good sound in prison' 21
noise as 'sound out of place' 57
noise exposure, lack of control over 32, 37, 118, 125, 127
'noisy', complex meanings of 15
non-linearity 19, 130–1
normality, resumption of 146–7
numbing out 6, 95
nurses 41

O

O'Donnell, I. 21
Ohtsuki, H. 70
ontological security 90, 95, 101, 103, 109
order
bells 154–5
'everyday tune' 105–12
learning the 'everyday tune' 105–12
legitimacy 111
listening to 101–4
and power 99–100
restoration of 145–52
routinization 156
social significance 16
see also disorder
otherness 14, 161, 168

INDEX

outside, being and hearing noises from within 19–20, 39, 129–30
outside noises coming into prison 20, 66
outsiders versus locals 29
Owens, F. 118

P

"pad rats" 37
pain of being in Midtown 19, 20
painting 140
panopticon 94
paper, pieces of 62
Parkes, D.N. 19, 131
passing time 26–31, 39, 84, 136–44
 see also busy, keeping
Pavarini, M. 142, 143
Penguin biscuits 60–1
performative masculinity 37, 56
personal hygiene 54
Pete 71
phasing 145–52
Pickering, H. 57
pipes, talking through 34, 78
planes, sound of 20
polyrhythmia 81–8, 98, 106, 108, 136, 145, 153–9
'pottings' 63, 77, 147
power
 authority 82, 97–9, 100–1, 108, 110, 111, 114, 153, 158
 bottom up power 98–9
 collective 116
 different places sound different 32–3
 and dignity 57
 disentangling power and order 97–104
 disruptive elements 73
 dominance over space 35
 entrance/exit rituals 33
 flows of power 12, 49, 51, 89, 97, 98, 113–14, 119
 focus on disorder 107
 keys 90, 96
 knowledge as 94–6
 legitimacy 100–1, 109–12, 143–4, 156–8
 listening 13–15, 28, 49, 113–20
 punishment 92
 rebalancing 57
 relational 49
 restoration of order 150–1
 sound and unequal power relations 32–3, 117–18
 'sousveillance' 12
 symbolic power 89, 135, 155
 visiting times 25
 window warriors 34
 window-to-window communication 35
powerlessness 28, 51, 92
predictability 8, 28, 82, 85, 87, 101–2, 109, 111, 155

'pressure cooker' 145
prison governor (No. 1) 10, 12, 35, 39, 50, 64, 85, 117, 174
prisonization 119
privacy 11, 24, 38, 40, 48, 55
PTSD 121, 126, 127, 166
punctuation 84
punishment 92, 114, 139, 163

Q

quiet
 complex meanings of 15
 good day soundscape 108
 library 33
 at night-times 21
 night-times 40, 42
 oppressive 40
 as precedence to violence 15, 76
quiet spaces 33

R

race and racism 13–14
radios 22, 44, 95, 96
Rafferty, Officer 128
raised voices *see* shouting
rapid changes in atmosphere 66
rats 43
Ray 72
reading the soundscape 18, 72, 74, 105, 106, 109, 133
Red 71, 173
regime of prison day 83–5, 154–6
relationships 11–12, 113–14, 134, 162
release and return cycles 5, 28, 29, 170
relief, audible 147
religion 14
repurposed items 138–9
re-regulation after disorder 145–52
researcher positionality 9, 12–13, 165
respect 14, 24, 36–7, 38, 42, 59, 64, 94, 125, 157
retreat from social spaces 37
rhythms
 arrhythmia 21, 74–80, 108, 117, 145
 conducting the noise 99–100
 counter-rhythms 87
 different kinds of banging 114–17
 disentangling power and order 97–104
 dislocation of time 28
 ebb and flow of life 28
 eurhythmia 147
 and human experience 4
 ontological arrhythmia 21
 of order/disorder 106–7
 polyrhythmia 81–8, 98, 106, 108, 136, 145, 153–9
 predictability 109
 resumption of steady 146
 time as marker of 19

of violence 76–8
and the writing of Midtown's story 7
see also bad day soundscape; good day soundscape
Rice, T. 4, 57, 154
Richey 51, 138, 147
riots 68, 107, 111, 157–9
'ripples' of emotion 71
risk minimization 64
rituals
  bells 129, 154
  decoding rituals and routines by listening 154
  entrance/exit rituals 32–3, 54, 169–71
  learning the 'everyday tune' 109–12
  listening to 154
  locking/unlocking 123
  rhythms 101
  shared meaning-making 107
  staff leaving rituals 54
Robert 20, 27, 61–2, 69, 115, 138
Ronald 66
Rose, Officer 33, 75, 82, 85, 99, 106–7, 108–9, 111, 133, 136, 146–7, 148, 154, 172
routines
  bells 129, 154
  daily regimes 83–5
  decoding rituals and routines by listening 154
  learning the 'everyday tune' 109–12
  listening to 154
  markers of 18, 129, 130, 154
  power and order 100–1, 102, 103
  routinized bodies 156
  security routines 39, 41
  temporal/spatial boundaries 19
Ruggiero, V. 130, 143
rules 62–3, 66, 125
Rusche, G. 142
Russell, E.K. 37

S

sadness 70
Salter, L. 32
sanctuary 37–8
Saturdays 22
saving face 36, 76
Schafer, R.M. 117–18
Schneider, L. 143
Schumann, Robert 30
screaming 2, 43, 44, 53, 106, 118, 163
Seamus 43
second-in-command (No. 2) 10, 36, 70
security routines 39, 41
'Seg' (Care and Segregation) 35, 43, 53, 77, 115
segregation 14
self-harm 42, 44, 46–7, 49, 166

sense-making processes 10
sensory overload 95, 127
Serres, M. 3
shady corners 41
sharp sounds 75
ship, similarity of prison to 160–1, 168
shouting 23, 34–5, 70, 71, 72, 94, 124, 131, 141
showering 38
Shwartz, B. 57
Si 37
Sibley, D. 133
Sid 28
silence 29, 62–3
Simmel, G. 4, 32
singing 71, 98, 150
'singing frogs' 121–8
Slater, Officer 170
sleep 27, 37, 43–4, 71
slow research 162
small size of Midtown 5
smells 56, 67, 93–4
smiling 11
Smith, Officer 128
snoring 42, 55
social exclusion 27
social history 132, 172
social purposes of spaces 32
social theory 100
sociology of the senses 4, 73
solidarity 110, 116, 131
solitude 33
Solzhenitsyn, A. 102, 154
sonic attacks 90–1
sonic spaces 34
sound as a complex phenomenon 15
sound as audible emotion 66
sound as modality of emotion 33–4, 71
sound sensitivity 126–8
soundscapes 16
'sousveillance' 12
Soviet Russia 142
spaces, finding for interviews 11
Sparks, R. 19, 101, 102, 107, 110, 114, 146, 148, 157, 158, 165, 171
spatiality 32–8, 81, 131
Spencer, H. 4
spice 69
'spikiness' 69, 145, 149
spillovers 31, 72, 122
staccato 23, 79, 145
staff
  assaults on 63, 75
  attention 96, 99
  attitudes to dirt 54
  attunement 105
  bell ringing 154
  blurred boundaries 56
  building research relationships with 64

INDEX

control of information 95
flows of power 98–9
footsteps 40, 42, 95
home-work delineation 30–1, 122
interpersonal power relations 92
jail craft 72, 74, 99, 105, 148
loudness of 124
marks of a good officer 111
mental health 128
outnumbering of 149
positive vibe 110
processes of 'mood' 70
'reading' the soundscape 74
recognition of gait 42, 95
relationships 113–14
rhythmic pacesetters 150
saving face 36
sense of community 111
sensory overload 128
staff leaving rituals 54
use of time 85
stain 52, 54, 57–8, 133
Stansfeld, S. 119
stethoscope-ing 3–5
Steve 67, 111
Stevie 46–8, 51, 87, 134, 140, 173
Stickney, J. 94
stigma 51, 52, 53, 55, 57–8, 133, 134, 174
Stillman, Officer 32
Stoever, J.L. 13
Strangeways riot 157–9, 171–2
Stretch 7, 12, 18, 34, 35, 37–8, 48, 69, 77–8, 82, 92, 93, 96, 113, 130, 133–4, 151, 154, 173
subterranean areas 53
Sundays 22
surveillance 12, 94
survival strategies 93, 103, 113, 158
Sykes, G. 48, 53–4, 114, 116, 164, 171
symbolic power 89, 135, 155
symbolic violence 7, 89

T

Tait, S. 109
Tawny, Officer 124
Taylor, L. 109, 136, 141
tea 60
temporal dissonance 28–30
temporal sense 18
temporal vertigo 21, 27–8, 30
tenseness 91
tension, sounds of 68, 70, 71, 75, 77–9, 85, 103–4, 130, 147, 151
Terry (Bulldog) 49
texture, sound adds 18
Thrift, N. 19, 131
time
  disruption of linear 130–1
  distortions of 26–31, 39

essence of sentencing and imprisonment 19
  'markers' of time 21
  occupying time 26–31
  passing time 26–31, 39, 84, 136–44
  relationship with sound 4, 18, 19, 21
  temporal dissonance 28–30
  temporal sense 18
  temporal vertigo 21, 27–8, 30
  time-space distanciation 85
Toad 139
tobacco ban 67, 68, 176n2
Toch, H. 37, 74
toilets 22, 36, 51, 55, 56
Tommy 34, 40, 90, 91, 109, 133, 136, 138, 157, 158
Tone, Officer 53, 77, 95, 115, 116, 122–3, 125, 149
tone of voice 70
Tonk 34, 36, 66, 110, 124–5, 126, 127, 128, 134
Toop, D. 4, 18
total institution 48, 164
touch 49
transparency 64
Travellers 29
Trina (officer) 150
trouble 67–9, 71
  see also bad day soundscape; disorder; tension
TVs 34, 41, 42, 71

U

under the breath, voices 23
unfairness 111
unrest 67
  see also disorder; tension
unwanted sound, inability to exclude 32, 37, 118, 125, 127
Urfan 14, 37, 60
'us and them' 77

V

Vannini, P. 4
vermin 43
vibrations 34, 123
violence
  assaults on staff 63, 75
  coercive force 92
  deficits of legitimacy 111
  and disorder 111–12
  functions of 35–6
  louder volume of 70
  in order to get taken off the wing 117
  preceded by quiet 15, 76–8
  'reading' the soundscape 74
  rhythms 76–8
  symbolic violence 7, 89
vision
  decentring 9, 12

lack of visual stimuli 54
remaining in staff's 12
restrictions on 114, 160
watching versus listening 25
visiting times 29–30, 136, 169
visits 21–5
volume of noise 71, 75
  see also loudness; quiet
volunteer staff 22, 23
Vulnerable Prisoner Unit (Veeps) 36, 43, 53, 86

W

waiting 27, 136, 142, 168–9
walking research methods 173–5
warfare 90–1
Warr, J. 13, 80, 94, 171
washing/keeping clean 54
watching versus listening 25
Weber, M. 100
weekends 22
Welch, M. 135
wellbeing, gauging 127, 128
Wener, R. 16, 90, 118
Wes 69
whispering 23, 95
whistles 72
Will 27, 78, 92, 155, 156
'window warriors' 34
window-to-window communication 35
wing rats 14
women's voices 22–3
Woolf report 110, 157, 158, 181n5
word arrow 61–2
Wright, S. 19, 27–8
wrongly accused 14

www.ingramcontent.com/pod-product-compliance
Lightning Source LLC
Chambersburg PA
CBHW051544020426
42333CB00016B/2095